STOP THE PRESSES!

—◾◼◻—

John Bohannon has broadcast buffs howling
over this wild and wacky collection of
America's silliest scenarios. Turn the page for
more rave reviews of

KICKERS

KICKERS:
All the News
That Didn't Fit

John Bohannon

BALLANTINE BOOKS • NEW YORK

For Barbara and Adam.
And Little Wee.

Library of Congress Catalog Card Number: 87-91657

ISBN 0-345-34623-8

Manufactured in the United States of America

First Edition: February 1988

Foreword

■ ■ ■

Most people keep up-to-date on current events by watching the evening news on TV. Tom Brokaw tells us everything we need to know. So does Dan Rather. And Peter Jennings. But, with time out for commercials, a network TV news broadcast has only twenty-two minutes to give us the major news. What about all the stories that Tom, Dan, and Peter just didn't have enough time for?

Here are the news stories that didn't get broadcast —on TV, at least—the equivalent of the movies' "face on the cutting room floor." These stories did, however, find a home on my broadcasts on the CBS and NBC Radio Networks. These are true stories about people being themselves, getting into trouble, doing silly things in public.

John Bohannon

Acknowledgments

Many of my friends and colleagues in radio and TV took the time to read KICKERS and offer their comments, and I appreciate their help. My thanks to Rita Sands and Don Swaim of WCBS; Gary Nunn and Andy Fisher of NBC; Don Rollins of UPI; Gene Klavan of WNEW; Marlene Sanders, formerly of CBS; and Willard Scott of "Today" on NBC-TV.

Many thanks, too, to David Black of Greenburger Associates for his guidance, and to Chris Cox and Christine Lazor of Ballantine for their assistance.

I'm particularly grateful to Kevin Gordon of NBC for his excellent illustrations. That guy really has drawing power, doesn't he?

The following stories, reported by the Associated Press, United Press International and Reuter, appeared, in a different form, on my network radio broadcasts. They are true stories about people being themselves. In this untidy world and these uncertain times, we must laugh at ourselves occasionally because we're all in this together. And we're all we've got.

Contents

1 Oops!

Somebody Will Notice It

SPRINGFIELD, ILLINOIS—A program to attract business and improve the state's economy got off to a bad start. Officials had to destroy a thousand green-and-white buttons with the slogan, "Build Illinois."

The buttons were made in Indiana.

A You-know-what-Compliment

BIRMINGHAM, ALABAMA—Members of the Southpaw International organization voted in favor of bestowing its Left-handers of the Year Award on author James A. Michener and actress Kate Jackson.

Both are right-handed.

Life Imitates Art

PORT ORCHARD, WASHINGTON—It looked like a scene from a popular TV show. Judge James Maddock was presiding in a crowded County Superior Court when two women wearing leotards burst through a door and jogged into the courtroom. Judge Maddock thought it was either a practical joke or a possible violent attack by sexy terrorists, but he recognized the women as they jogged past his bench and out a side door. They were Pat Ancich and Gayle Wakefield, two court reporters. And they were just as astonished as everyone else.

The judge informed the jurors that this was not a competition with *Night Court*, and called a recess. A moment later in his chambers the red-faced joggers explained that they usually wear leotards for their daily

3

exercise session in an empty jury room and had jogged through Judge Maddock's courtroom, expecting it to be vacant, too.

They also expected a severe reprimand, but the judge decided that their embarrassment was punishment enough.

Gotcha

DUBUQUE, IOWA—They had to scratch the ninth race at the Greyhound Park because the lead dog in the pack caught the motorized lure, a large fuzzy white bone.

But the Textbook Says...

CHELAN, WASHINGTON—A forest fire spread over 450 acres in the western region of the state before fire-fighters brought it under control. A spokesman for the U.S. Forestry Service said four hikers—who were not identified—accidentally started the fire because they had read that experienced campers always burn their toilet paper after using it. The spokesman also said that the hikers were recently graduated doctors from the Harvard School of Medicine, who found out the hard way that the Washington State wilderness is not like the East.

By the Book

FORT CARSON, COLORADO—A clerk at this U.S. Army base filled out a requisition order form for a headlight costing $6. Following procedure, he used the base's computer system and punched in an eleven-digit code number. One digit was incorrect, but the military supply clerk at the other end didn't know it, because the order carried no description, just the item number. So he sent back a seven-ton ship's anchor costing $28,560.

No one questioned why an Army base a thousand

miles from the nearest ocean would need an anchor. Army officials kept the anchor for a few weeks, hoping that some other branch of the service might need it. But there were no takers. Apparently the Navy had all the anchors it needed. So the Army shipped the anchor to the Pueblo Army Depot, about forty miles away, for storage.

An Honest Mistake, Honest

MOSCOW, RUSSIA—Some flight attendants from Pan American World Airways on a stay-over in Russia often play a game to keep themselves occupied. They search their hotel rooms for hidden microphones, which they say they always find.

On one recent trip they failed to find the bug, but they did discover a metal plate under the edge of the carpet. Using a screwdriver, they lifted the plate up and saw a strange device, which they loosened with a pair of pliers. Suddenly, from the floor below, they heard an enormous crash and shattering of glass. A moment later they were surrounded by hotel security officials and the KGB. The adventurers had sent a huge chandelier from the ceiling below to the floor, just missing several people in the lobby.

Their hotel bill included repairs that totaled twenty-six hundred dollars.

Who Needs an Area Code?

NEW YORK CITY—When Nicholas Daniloff, a reporter for *U.S. News & World Report*, was being held in Soviet custody in Moscow on spy charges, Mr. and Mrs. James Marra of Wantagh, Long Island, began getting phone calls from irate Americans all over the metropolitan area. The callers were demanding that Daniloff be released immediately. The Marras were astounded by the deluge of calls and finally learned that it was because the Long Island newspaper *News-*

day had published the telephone number of the KGB headquarters in Moscow to let Americans register their complaints.

The paper had neglected to include information on how to dial an overseas number, and the Marras just happened to have the same number that the KGB Moscow office had.

What Check List?

BIRMINGHAM, ENGLAND—An Orion Airways chartered jetliner had taken off with one hundred passengers, taking them to a vacation on the Greek island of Crete. Takeoff was on time and smooth, and minutes later at cruising altitude of thirty thousand feet, the pilot's voice came over the intercom.

"This is the captain speaking. Sorry, but we are returning to the Birmingham Airport. We forgot the luggage."

Psst. Want to Buy Some Tickets?

SANTA MARIA, CALIFORNIA—Officials of the Pacific Conservatory of Performing Arts of Hancock College had been expecting a shipment of box office tickets from a printing company in Arkansas. They received instead several cases of tickets to the World Series, thousands of field and loge box seat tickets.

College president Gary Edelbrock estimated the value at several million dollars. He said, "This is better than winning the state lottery."

They returned the tickets. All of them.

And It Won't Happen Again

WANTAGH, LONG ISLAND, NEW YORK—The weekly newspaper *Wantagh-Seaford Citizen* printed an apology for a mistake in a previous issue.

Our typographical error was pointed out to us by a number of readers. We are embarrassed and contrite that our proofreading let such a error escape us.

How's That Again?

WASHINGTON, D.C.—An Associated Press headline sent on the wires to radio, TV stations, and newspapers across the country:

THIS YEAR'S DROUGHT IN THE NORTHEAST COMES 20 YEARS AFTER THE SAME REGION SUFFERED THRWORDS.

A few minutes later the AP sent the following correction:

THIS YEAR'S DROUGHT IN THE NORTHEAST COMES 20 YEARS AFTER THE SAME REGION SUFFERED THRTIES.

Well, that clears that up.

The AP ran this story from its Paris bureau about an armed robbery at a museum:

Police said at least four men with guns drawn, including five by Claude Monet and two by Auguste Renoir...

We can picture that.

Which Pedal Is This One?

RICHMOND, CALIFORNIA—Lily Fowler drove her car into an automatic car wash and kept going straight through to a busy street where she hit a car, bounced into a wire fence, and then knocked a gasoline pump off its base. The gasoline spilled onto the ground as Fowler's car kept going, back toward the line of cars waiting to get into the car wash, where she hit another

car. The spilled gasoline ignited and set Fowler's car
and three others on fire. No one was hurt, including
Lily Fowler, eighty, the mother of the town's fire captain.

"I stepped on the wrong pedal," she said.

Well, It Was Close

CHARLESTON, SOUTH CAROLINA—The United States
Conference of Mayors voted in favor of this Southern
city as the nation's "most livable" city. And so conference officials printed up news releases and a letter of
praise and congratulations, and sent it to the mayor of
the town. Mayor Joseph Riley was pleased but puzzled, because the news releases and letters were sent to
Mayor Michael Roark of Charleston, West Virginia.

Did We Forget Anything?

ORLANDO, FLORIDA—Everyone who had worked on
the three-hundred-million-dollar airport was proud of
the new facility. Just before construction began, officials made a last-minute check and noticed a few
errors. The most obvious was on-the-ground shuttle
cars that people would ride to and from flight gates. At
each end of the tracks were shiny glass partitions almost like mirrors. People in the shuttles would have
seen the image of their own trains, giving the impression of a head-on collision.

Officials noticed another mistake on the mezzanine,
where the airport restaurant was located. There were
two escalators between the mezzanine and the ground
floor, and both were "up."

The most glaring error was on the ground floor.
There were no rest rooms.

The plan was not exactly commodious.

What We Meant, Was...

NEWHAM, ENGLAND—Authorities in this east London
borough received numerous complaints from people

about a campaign to encourage the use of seat belts.
The posters read: Drivers, Belt the Wife and Kids.

An Acronym by Any Other Name

DES MOINES, IOWA—The people who run things in
Iowa decided to reorganize the state bureaucracy and
streamline a few things. The Iowa Development Commission became the Department of Economic Development, or, as one official decided, DED.

When employees began answering the phone, they
noticed a little trouble with the acronym, as in, "Good
afternoon. DED office."

DED spokesman Phil Thomas said, "People now
answer the phone, 'Economic Development,' or 'The
department.'"

How about, "Hello?"

Just One Day Off

RALEIGH, NORTH CAROLINA—The state Wildlife Resources Commission's calendar for 1986 was perfect.
Almost. Wednesday, February 19, was followed by
Thursday, February 21.

Well, time flies when you're having fun.

She Was Here a Minute Ago

INTERSTATE 70, MISSOURI—It had been a relaxing vacation in Oklahoma for William and Frances Norris,
and they were driving back home to Swartz Creek,
Michigan. They had a nice lunch at Shorty's Restaurant in Columbia, and Frances decided to take a nap in
the back seat. Thirty miles down I-70, at a service stop
in Mineola, William pulled over for a rest stop. Forty
miles later he pulled into Al's Standard Service in
Warrenton for some gas. He was just pulling out when
he noticed his wife wasn't in the back seat, so he
stopped, got out, and looked around.

Half an hour later he called police to report a missing wife. State police showed up, and they began a methodical search of the area, but found no trace of the woman. Then the troopers got a call that a Mrs. Norris had filed a missing husband report with police back in Mineola. That's where Frances had left the car to use the rest room, minutes after William got out.

They had been celebrating their twenty-fifth wedding anniversary. Any bets on a twenty-sixth?

Hoist with Their Own Petard

ALLENTOWN, PENNSYLVANIA—Three federal officials of the General Services Administration in Washington arrived in town to discuss the city's problems in collecting nearly ten thousand dollars in unpaid parking fines run up by U.S. servicemen and women.

When the three officials returned to their car, they found a parking ticket on the windshield.

Testing, 1–2–3

WARSAW, POLAND—President Wojciech Jaruzelski's New Year's Eve message, broadcast live on Polish television, could barely be heard above loud crackling and shuffling noises. It was a twenty-minute interview with two journalists.

The director-general of Polish TV, Aleksander Perczynski, took the blame and resigned. No one had noticed that the microphones were under the table.

Try It Again

NEW YORK CITY—The author of this book has had his share of embarrassing moments on the air. While broadcasting a story about a trial, he tried to say, "Hypodermic needle." It came out, "Hypodeemic nerdle." He tried again. "That is, hypodeemic nerdle." And once more. "I mean, hypodeemic nerdle." And finally. "Uh, syringe."

II Politics

One Can Never Be Too Sure....

WASHINGTON, D.C.—During a rehearsal for the oath of office ceremonies for President Ronald Reagan's second term, First Lady Nancy's Chief of Staff, James Rosebush, wanted to be certain about protocol. A Presbyterian minister explained that after the president took his oath, the minister would give the benediction.

Rosebush asked, "How will we know when the benediction is over?"

An aide whispered to Rosebush, "When they say 'Amen.'"

...Can One?

AQABA, JORDAN—Vice President George Bush's second tour of the Middle East in August of 1986 took him one afternoon to a dusty bluff overlooking the Golan Heights. Mr. Bush looked at a Jordanian general accompanying him and asked, "How dead is the Dead Sea?"

"Very dead, sir," the general replied.

It Might Come in Handy

WASHINGTON, D.C.—The U.S. Department of Agriculture recently issued a booklet titled, "What To Do With Your Fertilizer During An Enemy Attack."

The "Iron Lady" Packs a Heavy Verbal Punch

LONDON, ENGLAND—Nicholas Fairbairn, Scotland's flamboyant former attorney general, astonished everyone with this story during a public session of the House of Commons:

"A gentleman, who out of chivalry I will not name, but who occupied grand office and had taken grand wine, went up to Prime Minister Margaret Thatcher and said words that I will not use...that he had always fancied her. To which the prime minister replied, 'Quite right. You have very good taste, but I just don't think you'd make it at the moment.'"

A spokesman at No. 10 Downing Street denies it.

Doggone

JAFFREY, NEW HAMPSHIRE—Folks were enraged when Charles Vaitiskis was appointed the town's dog officer. They circulated a petition demanding that the appointment be withdrawn, on grounds that two months before his new job, Vaitiskis was found guilty of cruelty to animals and fined for shooting and killing a neighbor's dog.

Policy

WASHINGTON, D.C.—There is occasional rivalry between the White House and the State Department, which White House spokesman Larry Speakes was thinking of when he explained news policy to some reporters.

"The way questions are answered by the Administration," Speakes said, "depends on how we rate it on a scale of one to ten. If it's something really big, the president would come out and say it. If it was semibig, I'd come out and say something. If it was teeny-tiny, we'd give out a piece of paper (a news release). And if it was teeny-tinier than that, we'd let the State Department do it. If it's bad news, we'd let the Interior Department do it."

A Blank Check

LANSING, MICHIGAN—City officials weren't moving fast enough for Jeffrey Blank, so he decided to make a statement about all the potholes around town when he paid his city taxes. He wrote his check for twenty-six dollars on a lump of asphalt weighing nine pounds. It cost him seven dollars to mail it to the city treasurer.

The post office accepted it. So did the city. They turned it over to a bank, where paper was substituted in the transaction.

End of protest.

No Parking

SAN JOSE, CALIFORNIA—About sixty people who had parked illegally one day in December returned to their cars expecting tickets, but they found greeting cards under their windshield wipers. The cards read, "Merry Christmas from your friendly meter maid. Your car is in violation, but this is only a warning. Be good and have a happy day."

City officials weren't happy, though. One official said the meter maid had violated traffic department policy, which apparently is the bureaucratic equivalent of, "Bah, humbug."

On the Campaign Trail

PHOENIX, ARIZONA—Remember when it was great sport to mail a letter without a stamp? The post office doesn't deliver unstamped mail these days, but that didn't stop Richard Adams in his campaign for a seat in the Arizona State House of Representatives. He said he'd been saving postage for years by keeping certain envelopes from his mail, inserting his reply and writing "Return to sender, please" on the outside of the envelope.

Postal authorities said it's illegal.

"I didn't know that," Adams said.

MIAMI, FLORIDA—Does the name "Campbell" sound familiar? As in soup? Jack Campbell ran for a seat in the Florida House of Representatives by using the Campbell's soup logo in his campaign. But the folks at Campbell Soup Company were boiling mad and sued the candidate, saying he hoped to benefit from the company's long-established image of "traditional all-American values and wholesomeness."

Candidate Campbell agreed to comply with a court order to stop using the trademark, and said it was his mother's idea in the first place.

It occurred to her one day during lunch.

ANNAPOLIS, MARYLAND—George Haley ran for a seat in the U.S. Senate, but had trouble getting voters to notice him. He was a Republican, so he decided to ride an elephant at all campaign appearances. He called city officials to track down an elephant permit, but no one had ever heard of such a thing. He said they just laughed at him. Haley decided to go ahead without permission, risking getting arrested.

The next step was a little harder, though. Hertz and Avis rented only cars. He called all over town looking for an elephant. Even used the trunk line.

Oh, *That* Millard Fillmore

BUFFALO, NEW YORK—People usually get together during the first week of January to celebrate the birth of Millard Fillmore. In case you've forgotten, he's famous for his lack of fame and most remembered—if at all—for things people usually forget.

Millard Fillmore became our nation's thirteenth president in 1850 after Zachary Taylor died of typhus. He was the last president of the Whig party and was not renominated in 1852. He ran in 1856 on the Know-Nothing ticket and carried only the state of Maryland.

Fillmore is credited with being the first president to have a bathtub installed in the White House.

You Don't Say

TOKYO, JAPAN—The Health Ministry of Japan released a survey showing that the people who live the longest are those who talk the most.

Or so it seems.

The Check Is Where?

DALLAS, TEXAS—The U.S. Postal Service had occupied a building in suburban University Park for thirty years when the building was sold. The new landlord raised the rent, but postal officials objected and withheld payment. The landlord sued them, and they decided to pay up. But the check failed to reach the landlord on time, and a federal judge signed an eviction notice.

The check had been delayed in the mail.

Illegal Signs

CUMBERLAND, RHODE ISLAND—Town officials decided to call a special meeting to deal with an unusually high number of traffic accidents, as many as seventy per month. Motorists knew that most traffic signs were invalid because the town had never passed the ordinances required to accompany each traffic prohibition.

Maybe "please" would help.

Would a Note from My Mother Be Okay?

LAPLACE, LOUISIANA—Nine councilmen from Saint John the Baptist Parish have been ordered to repay more than thirty thousand dollars they received for meetings they failed to attend over a period of three years.

The Great Pothole War

BURLINGTON, VERMONT—Are you fed up with all the potholes in your city? Bruce Ploof was, too. So he began a campaign to persuade city officials to do something, a campaign that got news coverage all over the country in major newspapers and on network TV.

He planted a tree in every pothole he found.

Diplomatic Immunity

OSLO, NORWAY—A Russian diplomat had a little too much vodka at a party and had some trouble maneuvering his car home. Witnesses say the diplomat did his best in trying to avoid numerous obstacles, but he hit a dozen parked cars, a lamppost, and a brick wall. "Nonsense," said another Soviet official. "Those reports are highly exaggerated." He claims the diplomat hit only two parked cars and a house.

Peace Talks

PARIS, FRANCE—There were times when the negotiations to end the Vietnam War seemed as interminable as the fighting itself. In September of 1970, U.S. Ambassador David K. Bruce came out of the eighty-fourth peace conference to tell reporters about America's response to the latest Viet Cong proposal to end the war.

"Their plan is like new wine in old bottles."

A short time later an aide came out to explain that the ambassador really meant to say, "The plan is like *old* wine in *new* bottles." But several journalists wondered which version was correct and official. The next day another U.S. official said that he was authorized to correct the record.

"It's old wine in new bottles," he said.

Then everyone made plans for the eighty-fifth peace conference.

Let Me Make This Crystal Clear

OTTAWA, CANADA—Deputy Prime Minister Erik Neilsen is known affectionately as "Velcro Lips," because reporters have a hard time getting him to say anything. And when he does speak, he has a reputation of saying nothing in many words. During a visit to Ottawa in the summer of 1986, Vice President Bush made some comments about that during a speech he delivered at an official state dinner, directing his comments to Neilsen.

"I picked up a lot watching you during that question-and-answer period in the Parliament today. I must smile (when facing tough questions) and be more relaxed. And in the face of a controversial question, I'm going to try to say absolutely nothing."

Presidential One-liners

RALEIGH, NORTH CAROLINA—President Reagan, on the campaign trail for Republican candidates, took aim at Terry Sanford, a Democratic nominee for the Senate.

"He was raising taxes back when I was making movies," Mr. Reagan said. "Believe me, when it comes to reruns, *Bedtime for Bonzo* is better than tax time with Terry."

Maybe Next Time

LITTLE MOUNTAIN, SOUTH CAROLINA—Most of the three hundred residents went to the polls in a local election, and officials were pleased at the heavy voter turnout. The only problem was a light candidate turnout. No one had met a filing deadline to be on the ballot.

Well, nobody's perfect.

It's Easy Being Green

MONTGOMERY, ALABAMA—The race for governor ran into a few legal hurdles. Judges had to make more than fifteen legal decisions involving candidates in a runoff election. There were also charges of illegal votes cast. This caught the attention of some students at Auburn University, and they began a write-in campaign for their favorite candidate, the cartoon character Gumby. Campaign organizer Shirley Beske said, "Gumby's lovable and well dressed, and we think he'd make a perfect governor."

The candidate showed up in person at one rally, a student named Neal Green, dressed in a seven-foot green costume.

One campaign slogan was, "The best things in life are green: money, grass, and Gumby."

Follow the Bouncing Bill

WASHINGTON, D.C.—A few years ago, when the U.S. Ping-Pong team was returning from Hong Kong after a successful tour overseas, Senators Hiram Fong of Hawaii and William Spong of Virginia asked that bells be played in Honolulu when the team came home. They introduced a bill for this in the Congress, and it became known as the Spong-Fong Ping-Pong Hong Kong Dingdong Bell Bill.

Trick or Treat

ABOARD AIR FORCE ONE—During the fall of 1986 President Reagan flew all over the country campaigning on behalf of Republican candidates in the off-year election. On Halloween, after a day of appearances in Washington State and Idaho, Mr. Reagan walked toward a rear cabin of the presidential jetliner and came face-to-face with someone in a ghoulish mask, a horrible apparition with long hair and fearsome fangs.

It was an Air Force steward. The president laughed and said, "I thought it was Sam (Donaldson of ABC News)."

More Presidential Humor

ON THE ROAD WITH MR. REAGAN—At local rallies during the president's campaign swing across the country on behalf of his G.O.P. colleagues in the Senate and the House of Representatives, the president often repeated certain stories.

"Did I ever tell you the one about the little boy who was seen in front of the Democrats' headquarters, selling 'Democratic' puppies?" Mr. Reagan said. "Well, a few days later, the same little boy was seen in front of the local Republican headquarters selling 'Republican' puppies. Someone said to him, 'Son, these look like the same puppies.' 'Yessir,' he replied. 'But now they've got their eyes open.' "

Reporters traveling with the president heard that story over and over and over and over. One day Mr. Reagan noticed some signs in the press corps: No More Puppy Jokes.

"Very well," the President said. "Did I ever tell you the one about the little boy, standing in front of the local Democrats' headquarters, selling kittens?"

A Politician's Dictionary

LITTLE ROCK, ARKANSAS—Richard Allin began collecting words that state legislators used, and printed them in a column for the *Arkansas Gazette*. The list of words grew lengthy, and Allin put them all in a book titled, *The Southern Legislative Dictionary*. He said it would help people understand what their lawmakers were saying.

"Gubment bidness," was translated to "government business." "Chimbley" was a "smokestack," and a "mayter" was a "round, red vegetable" often sliced, garnished with "maynaze" or "mayonnaise" and used in a sandwich. "Markin" was a patriotic citizen, as in "a true-blue Markin."

The book was published just in time for a special, or "spatial," session of the state legislature dealing with improving education.

A White House Directive

WASHINGTON, D.C.—President Gerald Ford was never able to get rid of an undeserved image that he was clumsy, often stumbling or bumping into things. But he was dexterous about many things, including the proper use of words. And during the Ford Administration, Robert Funseth, a spokesman for the State Department, said that the State Department would follow Mr. Ford's directive not to use the word "detente." The president objected to the word, on grounds that it did not reflect the true state of affairs between the United States and Russia: peace through strength.

The word "detente" was then expunged from the official lexicon. But there was little truth to subsequent reports that the president also prohibited the use of "expunge," which sounded like something "icky," and he didn't particularly care for "icky," either.

"Lexicon" would have to be used sparingly, and "sparingly" was never to be used. Neither was "never," which was too negative.

President Ford urged all State Department officials to abide by his wishes and not fall down on the job.

III Crime

The Key Is Prevention

DALLAS, TEXAS—City Councilman Rolan Tucker was active in crime prevention and supported an ordinance that would make it illegal to leave a key in the ignition of an unattended car.

But Tucker lost all of his research material on stolen cars and other crimes. It was in his car. Someone stole it. He had left the car unattended with the key in the ignition.

A Potpourri of Purloined Pontiacs, et al

STATEN ISLAND, NEW YORK—Mr. and Mrs. Arthur Robinson rented a car so they could drive around and look for their car, which had been stolen. They had a slight collision with another car—theirs.

LAS CRUCES, NEW MEXICO—Police arrested two kids, fourteen and fifteen, on charges of stealing a car. But they said they were only doing someone a favor and pointed to the rear bumper. It had a sticker that read: Answer My Prayers. Steal My Car.

BURBANK, CALIFORNIA—A man told police that he was wiping down his car after going through a do-it-yourself car wash when a strange man jumped in, rolled up the windows, and locked the doors. Then he started the ignition and drove away.

SEATTLE, WASHINGTON—Roy Williams went to a police department auction of used cars and bid sixty-five dollars for a nice station wagon. A few days later a policeman pulled Williams over, arrested him, and took him to jail on charges of stealing a car.

It took a while to sort things out, but police finally dropped the charges and released Williams after finding out that the car had been stolen, sold to someone, and then confiscated by police during a drug raid. Authorities tracked down the original owner and returned the car. They also refunded Williams's sixty-five dollars.

BUENA PARK, CALIFORNIA—Patrick West needed a car in the worst way, so he decided to steal one. He chose a car parked at a corner service station, jumped in, turned the key in the ignition, and drove away. West, unfortunately, didn't notice that the car had been on a jack and had one front tire missing.

The service station owner, Carl Rozatti, jumped in his pickup and drove after the car thief, who had managed to get up to sixty m.p.h. on three wheels trying to get away. Along the way, Rozatti enlisted the help of several other drivers, and the posse was bearing down on the culprit. Once, at a red light, Rozatti jumped out and pounded his fists on the roof of the car, demanding that the thief get out. West noticed all the people chasing him and drove off again, looking for a safe spot. He pulled up in front of the Buena Park police station and ran inside to get away from the posse.

Stop or I'll Throw

LANESBORO, MINNESOTA—The entire police department in this community consists of a police chief and a part-time officer. And when Jack Munns was chief, he asked the City Council to approve the purchase of another pistol. The police department had only one gun. Munns complained that he had to hand over his pistol at the end of his shift to the part-time officer who took over, but the council turned down his request.

It caused a lot of publicity, and as a result, someone donated a powerful .357 Magnum to the chief. Munns liked the gun so much that he took it with him when he retired. But the council asked him to return it, and he did. The new police chief, Richard Meier, decided that the new gun was, by now, historical because of all the publicity, and refused to wear it. It was too powerful anyway, he said. City Clerk Keith Burmeister put it in the safe at city hall, and Chief Meier borrowed a pistol from the Fillmore county sheriff's office.

Burmeister said they don't really need heavy fire-power in Lanesboro.

"All you really need," he said, "is five rocks in your pocket and a good arm."

Meese: Mea Culpa

LOS ANGELES, CALIFORNIA—He's often called the nation's Top Cop, and Chief Prosecutor. But Attorney General Edwin Meese was once a fugitive from justice. It began on June 11, 1980, in Century City, when a police officer issued a summons to Meese for jay-walking, a ten-dollar fine that he failed to pay. Five years later officials reviewed court records, saw the unclosed case, and issued an arrest warrant. Well, the law is the law.

But Police Chief Daryl Gates decided to call the White House, and later that day Meese mailed off a check for $130.50, which included the original fine of ten dollars plus penalties, and Chief Gates rescinded the arrest warrant. A spokesman for Meese explained that Meese had just assumed that someone had taken care of the ticket.

Meese was with two other people who were also issued summonses for jaywalking—William E. Timmons, a former Reagan campaign official, and the late William Casey, CIA Director.

Timmons, a Washington lobbyist in 1985, was quoted as saying, "Uh-oh. I better not go back to that jurisdiction again. I thought I'd paid the dadgum thing."

End of the Line, Pardner

MILWAUKEE, WISCONSIN—Have you ever been annoyed at someone for pushing ahead of you in a line? Zettie Mae Scaggs, sixty-three, was in a line at a grocery store when a man shoved in front of her, so she reached into her purse and pulled out a .32-caliber revolver.

A security guard called police, and they charged the woman with felony possession of a firearm.

Save a Little Here and There

NEW BRUNSWICK, NEW JERSEY—Signs on the New Jersey Turnpike read: Stop At Toll Booth. Take Ticket. Other signs read: Warning. Only One Ticket Per Vehicle.

Gordon Hector of the Turnpike Authority explained that some drivers will take a ticket from the automated machine, drive ahead a foot or so to trigger a device that ejects another ticket, and then back up and take a second one. The toll fees are based on where a motorist enters the highway, so it's possible to save a few cents on a longer trip by handing over the other ticket on a trip another day.

"There are all kinds of people in this world," Hector said. "Some people will steal a nickel."

Sting Sting

MIAMI, FLORIDA—A policeman disguised as a drug dealer was arrested on charges of stealing ninety dollars from an undercover cop pretending to be a drug buyer.

One Hamburger and All the Cash, to Go

ARLINGTON, WEST VIRGINIA—A man walked into a tavern and ordered a hamburger from counterman Steven Seaman, then ordered him to open the cash register and hand over all the money. He warned that he had a gun.

Seaman grabbed a plastic bottle of ketchup and squirted it in the man's face, knocked him to the floor, and sat on him while he called the police.

That order again: One hamburger, hold the perpetrator.

But I'm a Star

CENTRAL CITY, COLORADO—A film crew was shooting a scene for the CBS miniseries, *Dream West*, in this historic gold-mining town, and Patrick Burke of Denver thought it would be fun to sign on as an extra. Not only fun, but also a few bucks, and he might even become famous.

Back in Denver, Rosetta Anderle saw the TV show and decided to get in touch with Burke. She wasn't exactly a fan. Federal marshals had been looking for Burke for five years in connection with a cocaine charge. Anderle, the county sheriff, tracked Burke down and arrested him.

How fleeting is fame.

Close, but No Cigar

ARLINGTON, TEXAS—Two plainclothes police officers pretending to be customers at a yard sale were checking over the merchandise carefully and confirmed that some items were stolen in a rash of recent burglaries, so they decided to question the seller.

But the officers were from a nearby town of Dalworthington, and there were some legal questions. Their chief said later that his two officers made a slight departure to straighten out questions of proper evidence gathering and jurisdiction, but unfortunately the suspect had made a slight departure, too.

How to Rob Banks

DENVER, COLORADO—A man walked into a bank and told a teller to hand over all the money. But the man suddenly began searching his pockets and said, "Wait a minute. I forgot my gun. I'll be right back."

He returned a few minutes later, but the teller said she didn't have his money ready for him yet, so he walked out in disgust and ran into a policeman who had not forgotten his gun. The man was arrested on charges of attempted robbery.

PHILADELPHIA, PENNSYLVANIA—It didn't take long to track down a suspect who had tried to hold up four banks within twenty minutes. Employees at each bank said the robber was well dressed and an absolute gentleman. He handed tellers notes that read, "Please hand over your money. Thank you."

No one did, and each time the robber simply turned and walked out. But police caught up with him minutes later at a check-cashing agency and arrested him.

Politely, of course.

PITTSBURGH, PENNSYLVANIA—A man held up a bank and escaped with a bag of money such as banks often use to discourage robbers. It's a package containing a mild explosive, colored dye, and tear gas. The man dropped the bag after it blew up, and he escaped.

The next day the same man went into another bank, announced a holdup, and you guessed it, the teller gave him another bag of bills that went bang.

Later that day the man tried a third bank. This time he told the teller to hand it over, "But don't give me any of that exploding money. I hate it." He got it and got away.

The third time is the charm.

LYONS, FRANCE—No one paid attention to the young man who walked into a bank carrying a long loaf of French bread under his arm. But he suddenly split the loaf apart and pulled a .22-caliber rifle, announced a holdup, and got away with several thousand dollars.

HOUMA, LOUISIANA—It was a slow day at the First Federal Savings and Loan, until a woman with a gun walked up to teller Nicky Blanchard and demanded money.

"I can't," she said. Then she jumped over the counter and grabbed the bank robber, bit her on the arm, shoved her into the front door, and grabbed her gun. The holdup woman ran to a pickup truck and drove away, but police tracked her down a short time later.

Nicky knows how to put the bite on crime.

A New Approach

CORDELE, GEORGIA—A teller at a bank answered the telephone and heard a woman's voice. "This is a stickup. I have a gun. Put some money into a bag and leave it by the front door. I'll pick it up later. Don't call the police, or you'll be sorry."

A teller at another bank got the same call, and both alerted police. Detective Tommy West said one teller remembered hearing the sound of a railroad-crossing bell, and since Cordele is a small town, West knew the approximate location. There was one more call, and it was traced to a small frame house near the railroad tracks. Inside the house, West said, was a ten-year-old girl making the calls. Her eight-year-old friend in another house had helped her, according to police. Detective West said he believes it was the result of boredom and too much TV.

Just another phony scam.

How to Break Out of Jail

HUNTSVILLE, TEXAS—It was a great idea, brilliant in its simplicity. Two inmates of the Texas Department of Corrections, Hercules Gann, forty-nine, and Billy Battenfield, thirty-two, planned their great escape by hiding inside a tractor trailer that had pulled into the prison compound to make deliveries. It worked. Guards failed to check the truck when it left the prison, and fifteen miles down the road, where the truck stopped, Gann and Battenfield eased the door open and stepped out. The truck had stopped at another prison, where the two inmates were taken into custody.

WHEELING, WEST VIRGINIA—Raymond Matheny was serving a sentence at the county jail for grand larceny, but he was a model inmate and soon became a trusty. One day he asked officials for permission to go jogging and jogged right out of town. But sheriff's deputies were in shape, and they caught up with Matheny a few days later. He was told he could continue his jogging —in place in his cell.

MONTVILLE, CONNECTICUT—Inmates of the Community Correctional Center were playing a softball game, and Joseph Lyman was the left fielder. The batter hit a foul ball that curved into a wooded area, and Lyman ran after the ball. And kept going.

Three weeks later he struck out. Police found him at a nearby fast-food outlet.

CARSON CITY, NEVADA—The warden objected to a project that three inmates were busy with. They were building a helicopter.

MEMPHIS, TENNESSEE—Everyone was proud of the brand-new, modern Shelby County Justice Center, known as the Glamour Slammer. It had private cells, gyms, and other amenities, and all the latest state-of-the-art equipment that made the jail "escape proof."

Two months after it opened, officials reported that three inmates had escaped. Chief Deputy B. J. Smith said, "We are shocked that this could happen." Smith added that it really wasn't an escape, just "an unauthorized departure."

A Streak of Bad Luck

BUFFALO, NEW YORK—About thirty-five thousand people were in War Memorial Stadium on a pleasant summer night watching the Beach Boys sing. Right in the middle of "California Girls" a man took off his clothes and ran nude across the field. Police caught up with him, wrestled him to the ground, and handcuffed him. As they led him off the field, they discovered that he was an off-duty police officer. He said it wasn't really his fault that he took off his clothes. He claimed that his drink was spiked.

Obviously with a dash of something.

Never Leave a Trail

EL MONTE, CALIFORNIA—Police who responded to a call about a stolen paint truck had no trouble tracking down their suspect. The paint buckets came loose and left a multicolored trail for fifteen miles. The driver, Virginia Quinonez, thirty-eight, hit at least fifteen cars and nearly hit a pedestrian. Police caught up with her in a parking lot and charged her with auto theft and drunk driving.

Never Heard of Such a Thing

CHICAGO, ILLINOIS—Two teenagers with previous arrest records appeared in court on charges of burglary.

Police caught them because a third teenager—posted as a lookout—had failed to alert his friends that police were on the way.

All three teenagers were deaf-mutes.

Oh

NEW YORK CITY—Floyd Flow, twenty-four, showed up in a Manhattan court to face charges of illegal possession of a handgun. But he was arrested on new charges when police checked a paper bag he was holding and found seventy-four vials of crack.

"I forgot I was carrying it," he said.

Crime doesn't pay. He should remember that.

IV Courtroom

Everyone Needs a Hobby

BOULDER, COLORADO—Have you ever wanted to take someone to court? Albert Carter is an old hand at suing people. Authorities say he has filed more than 225 federal lawsuits in Colorado and other states. When Carter is offended by someone, he files a suit, and if the judge dismisses the case, Carter sues the judge and files the suit in a different court.

U.S. District Court Judge Sherman Finesilver said Carter used the legal process, "to harass innocent citizens and made bald assertions with complete disregard for their accuracy." Judge Finesilver concluded that, "the vast majority of these cases have been found to be frivolous or vexatious," and he ordered Carter to stop filing lawsuits, particularly because he was doing it without a lawyer.

Carter filed an appeal of Judge Finesilver's action, without using a lawyer.

Next Case

NEW YORK CITY—The Internal Revenue Service is ready for questions and complaints under the recent tax reform bill that Congress approved and President Reagan signed into law. One tax judge, Howard Dawson, is prepared for many arguments. He recalls one case in which the taxpayer claimed, "As God is my judge, I do not owe this tax."

The judge's reply was, "He isn't. I am. You do."

I'd Love to, but . . .

DENVER, COLORADO—Bill Deveraux once said he was ready to write a book about excuses that people gave him when he was jury commissioner. One man said he couldn't serve on a jury because he had bad breath and didn't want to offend anyone.

Another said he worked nights, slept late, and was too grouchy in the morning to hear someone else's troubles.

There was one excuse that had to be accepted, though. The return letter said, "Since September of 1944, the potential juror has been in residence at Crown Hill Cemetery."

Jurisprudence Updated

COLUMBUS, OHIO—Professor Steven Jones of Ohio State University studied fairy tales to find out how certain characters would be dealt with in the modern criminal justice system. Jones said Goldilocks would face trespassing charges, the wolf in "The Three Little Pigs" would face charges of breaking and entering and murder, and Jack of "Jack and the Beanstalk" would be guilty of theft and manslaughter.

But with plea bargaining, all would still live happily ever after.

Bored with Board Games?

SAN BERNADINO, CALIFORNIA—If you're tired of Monopoly and Trivial Pursuit, try a new board game called "U B the Judge." Superior Court Judge John F. Ingro has come up with the new game, in which lawyers, judges, and prosecutors play against each other while collecting fees and salaries. The crimes range from manslaughter to petty theft, and defendants are named Rummy Ralph, Brawler Billy, Desperado Dan, and Call Girl Candy.

Judge Ingro said there are many outcomes for each case, just as in real trials. "But unlike real cases, guilt or innocence is determined by a roll of the dice."

Sounds like an honorable game.

Sounds Fishy

PORT ANGELES, WASHINGTON—A trial had to be held to resolve a dispute in a fifty-thousand-dollar Salmon Derby. The biggest fish would get the biggest prize money. But judges wondered about a man and his wife who brought in the two top entries, a salmon that weighed forty-three pounds and another one that weighed thirty-six pounds.

Other fishermen were skeptical, too, and claimed that the two fish had been caught earlier, frozen, and then thawed out for the contest. Officials impounded the fish, arrested the couple, and sent the fish to a lab for analysis. A court hearing was then set.

It was an unusually weighty problem for the scales of justice.

Another Step for Justice

AMBERG, WEST GERMANY—Three West German soldiers used a ladder to sneak into a girls' boarding school, but a nun caught them and called police. Later, in court, the judge decided the evidence was slim, but he did fine each man $1.37 for violating a law against leaving ladders in the street.

Maybe they could take their case to a higher court.

Offer May Be Withdrawn at Any Time

CLEVELAND, OHIO—Judge James Devine decided to run a half-price sale on parking tickets. He would retire at the end of the year, and he wanted to close the books on all outstanding traffic violations by then. Ten-dollar tickets, for example, would be gaveled down at five bucks each.

Some of the judge's colleagues were skeptical and didn't expect many scofflaws to take advantage of the offer. "They'll have to be arrested and brought to the bar," one official said.

Maybe Judge Devine could send them to a halfway house.

Supply and Demand

HACKENSACK, NEW JERSEY—A Superior Court judge sentenced two tow truck operators to jail for a year, plus five years probation, for a novel con game. The two men poured oil on an entrance to an interstate highway, and when a car skidded off the road, the tow truck operators just happened to be there to offer help. At a price, of course.

They were really slick operators.

Everyone Got Taken for a Ride

WASHINGTON, D.C.—Ralph Rinzler was minding his own business, getting out of a car he had bought recently, a 1981 BMW, when two men who identified themselves as FBI agents stopped him and said that he was driving a stolen car. They impounded it as evidence, and Rinzler sued the dealer who sold him the car. He was awarded twenty-eight thousand dollars. The dealer then sued the man who sold him the car and was awarded thirty-three thousand dollars. That man, who lived in Cockeysville, Maryland, then sued a car dealer in Roswell, Georgia, where he had bought the car. And that dealer filed a suit against a car rental firm that sold him the car.

This twisty trail finally led to Aaron Cohen of Atlanta. He had totaled his BMW two years before all this started, and his old license plates somehow ended up on a car that had been stolen in New York City. That car was finally returned to its original owners.

And Ralph Rinzler, who started the whole legal process, used his court-awarded money to buy a new car, a brand-new Toyota.

It's too bad that car didn't turn out to be stolen, too. It would have made a much better story.

V Animals

Miss Who?

BAL HARBOUR, FLORIDA—Bert Parks was ready to sing, and the audience waited, anxious to hear the decision of the judges at the beauty pageant, wondering who would be crowned the most beautiful of them all.

It was Leona, long-legged and covered with soft fur, a four-year-old cat from Norfolk, Virginia. She was named All-American Glamour Kitty Queen, and Parks began to croon, "There she is, the Glamour Kitty Queen of America. There she is, the kitty cat queen of the year."

It was—as you may suspect—a contest sponsored by a firm that made kitty litter. And why Bert Parks?

"It's just a big spoof," he said, "me being the master of ceremonies at the Miss America Pageant and all that jazz. If I can't poke at myself, I don't know who can."

Parks doesn't like cats, but he said he was chosen because, "I'm just marvelously talented."

Blackout

HARTFORD, CONNECTICUT—It was a day most dreary for thousands of people when the electricity went out, along with the telephones. Power wasn't restored until late in the day. People were inconvenienced, and the business loss was estimated in the hundreds of thousands of dollars.

A utility company spokesman said the trouble had been traced to a crow, or a raven, that got tangled up in some wires and landed on a circuit breaker. Everyone else will recover, but, quoth one official, "The raven is no more."

It's a Bird. It's a Plane. It's a Dog?

BERLIN, WEST GERMANY—A man was taking a walk along the street, minding his own business, when he was hit by a flying dog. Emergency medical teams say the dog fell out of a window four stories high. Neither the dog nor the man was seriously hurt.

No word on what kind of dog it was. Probably an Airedale.

Unrequited Love

DEVON, ENGLAND—Sheila Court had a problem with a young gander named Rodney. She had introduced him to several young eligible female geese during the breeding season, but Rodney wasn't interested. He had his own true love, a sprinkler can with a long graceful pouring spout. He sat next to it for hours, gazing adoringly.

Why the infatuation? Court said the only thing she could think of was that Rodney was "so young that he didn't know what a real goose looked like."

Silly goose.

The Sweet (?) Smell of Summer

TROY, ILLINOIS—You know all about those harbingers of spring, the swallows that return each year to Capistrano in California. And you probably have heard about the buzzards that return each spring to Hinckley, Ohio. But folks in Troy know summer is near when the skunks show up.

It has become an annual problem, environmentalists say, because the skunks are losing their natural habitat as surrounding woods vanish to make room for people and homes.

Police chief Clarence Quinley said the complaints

get worse each year, and there are times when a mother skunk, trailed by her babies, can be seen parading down the middle of Main Street.

Chief Quinley said if people just leave the skunks alone, they'll eventually take their babies back to the woods. Sometimes he has to shoot them, but he said skunks usually spray after being shot. "My wife complains when I walk into the house, so every once in a while I eat my dinner on the porch."

Oink If You Love Pigs

GREENVILLE, SOUTH CAROLINA—Mayor Bill Workman once said, "People are just pigs with short snouts." And that was just what Jack Tate had been waiting for. Tate, the director of a Greenville organization called the Short Snout Society, was dedicated to improving the image of pigs. So Tate named Mayor Workman, "Mr. Short Snout, U.S.A."

"We had looked all over the nation," Tate said, "for the top pig booster. But the mayor is number one."

The Short Snout Society raises money for charity and urban improvement and has press clippings from the *Atlanta Constitution*'s weekly magazine; the *Wall Street Journal*; and at least two mentions on NBC's *Today* show.

And the book you're now reading.

What? No Toasters?

HOUSTON, TEXAS—The First City Bank wanted to offer a premium to attract new depositors, so they came up with a novel approach. For every one-hundred-thousand-dollar CD, you get a free Arabian colt. That's a small horse, by the way. A real one.

Before you give them the horse laugh, consider that they got word from potential depositors from as far away as Connecticut, New York, Virginia, and Florida.

Seize the Moment

SAINT PAUL, MINNESOTA—Gigi the orangutan was sitting on a tree branch in her compound at Como Zoo when the branch gave way and tumbled her to the ground. She wasn't hurt, but she looked at the broken branch, gave it a good heft, and then propped it against the twelve-foot-high concrete wall around her compound, climbed up and over to freedom.

Talk about a lucky break.

Full House

SANTA ANA, CALIFORNIA—An unemployed clown named Johnny Whiteriver got into trouble with police because of overcrowding in his trailer home. He lived in there, neighbors complained, with three bears, a burro, two possums, a monkey, three peacocks, and Mrs. Whiteriver.

Actually, the neighbors didn't mind Mrs. Whiteriver, but the others, they said, were noisy, smelly, and dangerous. Except for Mr. Whiteriver, of course.

Time and Other Things Pass

YORK, NEBRASKA—An Oklahoma man, Mickey Bohannon (no relation to the author) was at the county fair with his trained elephant Butch, when Butch decided to eat the contents of his trainer's shirt pocket. That was the last that Bohannon saw—for a while—of one thousand dollars in cash. He gave the elephant a massive dose of mineral oil, and after a close watch of Butch and other things, he eventually collected pieces of bills, which he sent to the Federal Reserve in Washington, D.C. Bohannon soon received a check for $760.

Fortunately, the money wasn't counterfeit, so Butch was able to pass it.

By the way, Mickey. Nice name. And stay in show business.

A Real Dog

AMSTERDAM, HOLLAND—Dutch artist Wim Schippers was nervous, and so was his cast at the municipal theater. It was opening night of *Going to the Dogs*, the premier of a drama featuring half a dozen German shepherds. No people. Just six dogs.

Shortly after the curtain went up, a few members of the audience walked out in disgust, including the theater manager.

Maybe they were cat lovers.

Racing Porkers

DALLAS, TEXAS—The Texas State Fair featured a pig race, young pigs dressed in racing silks running on a track for a prize at the finish line, an Oreo cookie. But the Humane Society demanded that the race be called off, on grounds that the pigs were under stress.

Probably all that talk about ham sandwiches for lunch.

Gosh. There Goes Another One

LARGO, FLORIDA—Karen Smith doubted her twelve-year-old daughter's claim that their pet chicken had eaten a diamond earring. So Smith offered the other earring to the chicken. She ate it.

Is anyone interested in Chicken McNuggets with a prize?

Man Bites Dog

HINGHAM, MASSACHUSETTS—Police arrested a man on charges of biting off part of an ear of a German shepherd guard dog.

Dog Shoots Man

HELSINGOR, DENMARK—A hunter told police that he was wounded after he put his shotgun on the ground and his hunting dog stepped on the trigger.

Dog Runs over Man

TWIN FALLS, IDAHO—A man was treated at a hospital after being run over by his own van. He told police that his dog, a terrier, jumped on the gear shift and threw the van into reverse.

VI Achievements

Did I Ever Tell You?

BOSTON, MASSACHUSETTS—Most people were warm and cozy in bed around 4:30 one cold morning in January. But Paul Mooney had staked out a choice spot in a parking lot to wait for an explosion.

City officials had decided to demolish a twelve-story parking garage to make way for a new building. They detonated 320 pounds of dynamite, and in seven seconds the garage was reduced to a pile of rubble.

Mooney had shivered in the bitter cold for hours waiting for the brief blast, but said it was worth it. "It's something I can tell my children about someday."

Often, no doubt.

Wait Till Next Year

CHATTANOOGA, TENNESSEE—Edna Brewer hates to fly in airplanes, but on her birthday she decided to go for a ride in a hot-air balloon. It was her 103d birthday. She said she's been doing something different for each birthday since becoming 100.

"Old? I don't *feel* old," she said. "I don't even *think* old."

Retired in the Fast Lane

BOOTHBAY HARBOR, MAINE—Move over for Edgar Reed II. He put on a pair of water skis and skied forty-three miles down the coast of Maine from Boothbay Harbor to Portland Head and into Falmouth. The trip lasted two hours. Reed, sixty-one, said, "I wanted to prove that you don't slow down, ever, if you're in good condition."

Now's the Time

NASHVILLE, TENNESSEE—Mary Matthews had always wanted to ride a motorcycle ever since she could remember. And one day she finally achieved her lifetime goal by actually riding one. She said she was happy about doing it before she got older because, "It would be silly for a seventy-year-old woman to ride a motorcycle."

Matthews went for her ride just in time, a month before her seventieth birthday.

Never Too Late

OAKLAND, CALIFORNIA—When Arthur Reed reached his 123d birthday on July 4, he said he wanted to get married again. He was looking for a special woman between eighteen and thirty-five.

Reed didn't say much about the secret of a long life. But the trick is to have been born a long time ago.

Be Picky

NATICK, MASSACHUSETTS—When Dr. Henry Godfrey died at age 105, he had the distinction of being the oldest living graduate of Harvard. He was once asked for his secret of a long life.

"Pick out your ancestors."

A Peaceful Protest

TACOMA, WASHINGTON—Two members of the Greenpeace environmental organization wanted to make a statement about acid rain and air pollution in a certain neighborhood, so they camped out on the catwalks of a smelter smokestack. They climbed up early one morning. But it was around noon before anyone saw them up there. There was too much smog.

Out Is In

LAKEVIEW, OREGON—If you're a collector, you'll appreciate Jim Schmidt's hobby. He collects outhouses. So far he has about eighty, including several dating back to 1880.

"They range," he said, "from a simple one-holer to a substantial four-holer that once served a local stagecoach stop."

Most of his outhouses are on display at his roadside museum on Oregon Highway 140. Kids, he said, are fascinated by the outhouses. "They always ask how you flush it."

Schmidt said he's just doing his part to preserve the nation's agricultural past. "You can't collect barns, they're too big."

Time After Time

BRAINERD, MINNESOTA—The alarm clock rings at 1:00 A.M. in Lorraine Schultz's bedroom. Then another alarm clock goes off. And another. Within ten minutes about fifty alarm clocks will have gone off. No, Schultz doesn't hate to get out of bed. She collects clocks. At last count she had six hundred clocks. Clocks that ding, clocks that dong, clocks that beep, buzz, bang, clang, and speak. One even reminds you to wind it, so it can wake you up the following morning. It takes her half an hour to wind up all her spring-driven clocks. And twice a year, once in April and again in October, she spends more than two hours resetting her clocks in the change from standard time to daylight saving time and back again.

Schultz, who has been collecting clocks for twenty years, has run out of outlets to plug in her electric clocks. But there's always room for one more battery-powered or windup clock.

She never oversleeps.

Undiscovery Day

OCEAN SHORES, WASHINGTON—In 1792 the British explorer George Vancouver sailed along the coast of what would one day become the American Northwest, but he never stopped at a site now known as Ocean Shores. And each year the folks there gather to celebrate Undiscovery Day. They have a big party and wade into the surf and shout, "Hey, George."

J. K. "Bun" Lewis, the first mayor of Ocean Shores, established the "Holler" in 1973, but some folks say the current parties aren't what they used to be. Lewis's wife, Janie, recalls one year when a busload of women came down from Vancouver, British Columbia.

"The youngest one must have been sixty," Janie said. "I never saw such a bunch. They carried on all night and went clam digging at four in the morning."

Zany Madcaps

TACOMA, WASHINGTON—Radio station KNBQ-FM sponsored a wacky contest to find out what outrageous things people would do in public if they had a chance of winning one thousand dollars.

Quite a few people volunteered. One man ate twenty live worms. A woman dressed head to toe in yellow lay down while three assistants covered her with eight gallons of ice cream, several bowls of split bananas and pineapple chunks, topped off by huge amounts of whipped cream and cherries.

But the judges decided the winner was Chris McDonald, who wore a diaper, lathered himself with shaving cream, and had himself shaved with a straight razor.

A spokesman for the contest said McDonald was shaved head to toe, "Except, of course, for his eyebrows and, um, the, uh, area under his diaper."

Tellers of Tall Tales

BURLINGTON, WISCONSIN—Members of the Liars' Club get together annually to choose the World Champion Liar of the Year, and that's the truth.

Is This Thing Leaking?

CARBONDALE, ILLINOIS—Thousands of people gather each spring along the shores of Campus Lake at Southern Illinois University for the Annual Cardboard Boat Race. These are huge crafts, big enough for several people as crew members. And some of the boats are quite elaborate, such as a pirate galleon and a Mississippi paddle wheeler.

Yes, all the boats are made of cardboard. And, yes, all of them usually sink or tip over and then sink. And, no, we don't know why they've been doing this each year since 1973.

Maybe it's because reporters have been talking about it each year since 1973.

Kids

WASHINGTON, D.C.—Congressional researchers came up with astounding figures showing that the average American child watches about three hours of commercial TV each day, beginning at age two. By the time high school is over, that comes to more than twenty thousand hours spent watching TV, more time than spent in the classroom.

But at least you know where they are.

Tempo! Tempo!

SEATTLE, WASHINGTON—It was a concert to end all concerts. William O. Smith wrote a composition titled "Line Up," a little ditty for one hundred clarinets. They stood single file, lined up in a field for one mile with twenty guest conductors, each leading five clarinetists. And they did two performances of three minutes each.

Smith, a former soloist with Dave Brubeck, and now a music professor at Washington State University, had no trouble finding a hundred clarinet players. At least three hundred clarinetists were at the university to attend the International Clarinet Society Conference.

Encore

NEW YORK CITY—One weekend in August about three thousand flutists and flute lovers gathered in Manhattan for the annual convention of the National Flute Association. Several hundred flutists took part at Lincoln Center in a "Flute In" and a brief concert of several songs. Flutist James Galway led the group.

Jacob Berg, principal flutist with the Saint Louis Symphony Orchestra, explained that the high turnout was because flutists are congenial and love to socialize. "This would never happen with violinists," Berg said.

Camilla Hoitenga of Cologne, West Germany, added, "Flutists are more sanguine. You'll never find flutists who are melancholic or phlegmatic."

And One More Time

AMHERST, MASSACHUSETTS—While the flutists were tooting in New York, serpent players got together for their own celebration. A serpent is a Renaissance instrument that sounds like a combination tuba, bassoon, and French horn. "But the sound isn't as boring," according to Christopher Warren, leader of the London Serpent Trio. "A serpent's sound is more uneven and bumpy."

The instrument looks like a drainpipe designed by a committee, but serpent players love it. There aren't too many, unfortunately. During the convention Warren led players in a special composition titled, "Suite for Eight Serpents."

Why eight?

Warren said, "That's how many serpent players we could find."

A Gospel Truth

PITTSBURGH, PENNSYLVANIA—If you should see kids on a beach throwing marshmallows at a man wearing a lopsided visor, don't worry. It's all part of the act. He calls himself Mr. Mudd, and he hangs around beaches all over the country at the invitation of local churches, to preach the Gospel to idle kids. He gets their attention with puppet shows and by inviting the kids to pelt him with marshmallows.

Mr. Mudd is really Reverend Richard Patterson, Jr., thirty-seven, director of the Children's Surf and Sand Ministry.

"Fun is the world that kids live in," according to Mr. Mudd. "If you want to teach them the Gospel, you've got to have fun."

If You Don't Know the Words...

NEW YORK CITY—Several hundred people gathered one Sunday in October in a tunnel in Central Park, to hum. Bonnie Barnett, thirty-nine, of Los Angeles, held a successful "Hum," as she calls it, earlier in the year in Berkeley, California. "Most tunnels," she said, "respond best to hums in E-flat." But she has led hums in the keys of F, C, and D, of course.

Hmm.

All Things Are Relative

NEW YORK CITY—ABC-TV, in 1986, gave the state of Texas two hours of prime time to celebrate its 150th anniversary. When Rhode Island marked its 350th year, ABC gave it ten seconds.

At Last

NEWPORT, ENGLAND—It was something he had wanted to do all his life, according to Sidney Guest. And one day he got his chance to become a member of the town's official band, even though he didn't read music and couldn't play an instrument. Guest became the new drummer's mate. His job is to walk in front of the bass drummer, carrying the heavy drum on his back.

The guy who retired from that job had to quit because of a heart condition, a hernia, deafness, and a skull fracture.

A Famous First

BAY VILLAGE, OHIO—This suburb of Cleveland is the home of the most patriotic baseball fan in the country, Rocco Scotti. He travels around the country to sing the national anthem. Scotti said he began singing it at Cleveland Indians' baseball games around 1973 and performs the song at least three hundred times a year.

One day he decided to have his dentist make him a front tooth in the shape and colors of the American flag.

Now, there's a patriotic smile.

News Is News

LONDON, ENGLAND—When Prince William, the infant son of Prince Charles and Princess Diana, took his first wobbly steps, the weekly tabloid *News of the World* ran a story about it. The newspaper said that neither of the youngster's parents was present for the event, which was described as "the Prince's staggering achievement."

British humor.

Why Not?

JUNCTION CITY, OREGON—James Bails spent years of trial and error and finally accomplished his dream. He was able to teach a mule to roller-skate. His mule, Abragail, wears a skate on each foot and seems to enjoy it.

"It's something I've always wanted to do ever since I was a kid," he said.

Stubborn persistence.

May the Best Chip Win

BEAVER, OKLAHOMA—Each year the folks in this town get together for their Annual Cow Chip Throwing Contest. A cow chip is a dried out chunk of—well, what you'd expect.

This is the major leagues, by the way. Winners are those who can toss a cow chip well over 150 feet. The contest is open to men and women. There is one restriction, however. Politicians aren't allowed to enter. One observer said, "That would be a redundancy."

The Real Dirt

LANSING, MICHIGAN—Remember the Pet Rock? And other similar gimmicks that made millions? Do you often think there's nothing new in the gimmickry department? Then meet Barry Gibson. He sells small vials of "Celebrity Dirt," which he claims is from the yards of stars such as Johnny Carson, Sylvester Stallone, Joan Collins, Paul Newman, and many others.

Gibson says he travels around the country and gets the dirt from front yards, sidewalks, and from around shrubbery. He packages each vial in a wooden block and includes a certificate of authenticity. Each vial sells for $5.95, and Gibson says he has made about $10,000 so far.

"Dolly Parton sells the most dirt," he said.

Now there's a man with a scoop.

Another Famous First

DOVER, ENGLAND—Bill Neal sailed across the English Channel in a bathtub. He was the first to do it, so naturally he was showered with praise.

A Body of Artwork

GRESHAM, OREGON—One day back in 1946 Elizabeth Weinzirl got a tattoo, a small butterfly on her left thigh. Today she's covered with tattoos from her neck down to her ankles. She's festooned with birds, flowers, cherubs, slogans, all in vivid colors. Weinzirl, eighty-three, lives in a retirement home. She had herself covered with tattoos over the years, she said, because her husband liked it.

Obviously, he had designs on her.

VII   Well, It Seemed Like a Good Idea

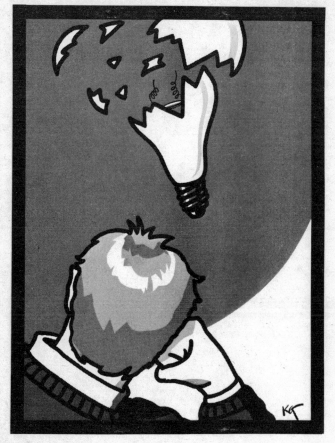

Make My Day

TUCSON, ARIZONA—Police insist this really happened. Noah Dotson showed up in a hospital emergency room for treatment of a gunshot wound. He explained that a fly kept pestering him, and when it landed on his left hand once too often, he took out a pistol and shot at it.

I Paid for It and I Want It

DEL CITY, OKLAHOMA—Harold Arnold, a security guard at city hall, said all he wanted was a sandwich from a vending machine. He put in his money, but nothing happened, so he stuck his hand inside to try to reach his sandwich. The machine, Arnold said, grabbed his hand and wouldn't let go, so he pulled his revolver and shot it. The machine let his hand go, but he never got his sandwich and didn't get his money back, either.

Recidivism Revisited

SEATTLE, WASHINGTON—No names are given in this police report about a man who decided to take the law into his own hands after being held up twice by the same three men. Unfortunately, the robbers caught the man off guard and held him up for the third time. They got away in a hail of gunfire by the victim. But there was one casualty. Police say the victim shot himself in the hand.

This Is War

RICHMOND, TEXAS—Residents called police to report a shoot-out in a quiet neighborhood. Witnesses said five men in a car ganged up on one man and took turns shooting at him with a shotgun. The victim grabbed his own shotgun and returned the fire. By the time police officer Buddy Sanders arrived, there were a number of casualties. "They shot up four houses and one truck. But nobody was hurt," he said. "I guess everybody was a bad shot."

Take That ...

NASHVILLE, TENNESSEE—A clatter-crash-bang noise woke John Brooks up early one morning. He looked out the window and saw movement near his garbage cans and thought it was a dog, so he got his pistol—but not his glasses—and took a shot. He wounded the garbage collector.

... And That

ROCHESTER, NEW YORK—Robert Enright found a skunk living in his basement, so he grabbed his .22-caliber rifle and shot at it. Unfortunately, he missed the skunk and put a bullet hole in his gas meter. Fumes filled the basement, and, afraid of an explosion, Enright called the fire department, and the fire department alerted the police.

There was no explosion. Police officer Leon Wilson said, "The skunk got away. He couldn't stand the smell of the gas."

He Did What?

NASHVILLE, TENNESSEE—John Burnett, a thirteen-year veteran on the police force, was showing his pistol to a visitor at the Criminal Justice Center. He put the revolver back into his holster and shot himself in the leg.

VIII Department of Great Comments

True

NEW YORK CITY—Brooke Shields, quoted in *Omni* magazine:

"Smoking kills. If you're killed, you've lost a very important part of your life."

A 50-50 Chance of Being Right

DENVER, COLORADO—"Like Venus from the head of Zeus..." said Judge John P. Moore of the Tenth U.S. Circuit Court of Appeals. It was related to his court decision on a mail-fraud case.

But Assistant U.S. Attorney Robert Streepy of Kansas City, Kansas, sent the judge a letter reminding him that "Zeus was the Greek supreme god. The goddess that sprang from his forehead was Athena, the goddess of war and peace as well as wisdom."

Judge Moore inserted a corrected version into the court record. He said, "I was sure it was either Venus or Athena; I just picked wrong, I guess. I can't remember names. Anyway, it's all Greek to me."

Beware of New Enterprises That Need Remodeling

CONCORD, MASSACHUSETTS—The state approved of six hundred thousand dollars to restore the natural beauty of Walden Pond, which inspired philosopher Henry David Thoreau in the mid-1800s. Bathhouses and piers had been built years ago to accommodate thousands of tourists who swim and boat in the pond, which covers sixty-two acres.

Some visitors expecting natural beauty were disappointed to find touches of the modern world encroaching on Walden Pond, so the restoration work is to make the bathhouses and piers blend in with the environment. And naturalists want the pond turned into a sanctuary where boating and swimming would be banned.

One visitor, Edward Goldman, thirty-seven, of Boston, opposed that idea. "Walden Pond is for people to use, not just look at," he said. "If you want solitude, you can go somewhere else."

Amen

ELIZABETH, NEW JERSEY—Mayor Thomas Dunn was opposed to a proposal to rename one city block "Praise the Lord Plaza."

"As long as I'm in charge," he said, "the plan doesn't have a prayer."

It Could Have Been Worse

PHOENIX, ARIZONA—A private plane crash-landed after taking off following a golf tournament, but none of the seven people aboard was hurt. Entertainer Glen Campbell was among the passengers. He said, "The crash landing wasn't much worse than my golf game."

Did I Really Say That?

BUFFALO, NEW YORK—Students at the State University of New York complained to police that four hundred women's panties and bras were stolen from dormitory laundry rooms.

A campus security officer said, "We'll get to the bottom of this."

Well, What I Meant Was...

PORTLAND, OREGON—Watermelons contaminated by pesticides were blamed for at least three hundred illnesses in four Western states during the summer of 1985. State officials knew where the tainted watermelons came from and urged consumers to buy only those approved by health inspectors. Sales were brisk everywhere. In Portland, produce buyer Karl Najdek said, "People are dying for them."

Lord, Can You Spare a Strike

RANTOUL, ILLINOIS—Billy G's is a bowling alley and bar on Route 136. And on Wednesday nights, members of the Christian Life Church hold services there.

"Our church is a divine manifestation of the Lord's sense of humor," the Reverend John Bonacorsi said. "In this location we can help people get out of the gutter."

And rapt? You can hear a pin drop.

IX Love & Sex

Love on the Wing

LAWRENCE, KANSAS—Orley Taylor gets a lot of invitations to present his lecture, titled "Sex at Fourteen M.P.H." But some people may be disappointed when they find out that Taylor, a biologist at the University of Kansas, lectures on the mating habits of honeybees.

"It can be a split second affair with no discernible courting," he said, adding, "It's not unlike singles bars."

Do you buzz here often?

X-rated Village

STOCKHOLM, SWEDEN—What to do with a four-hundred-acre estate? Bengt Granberg decided to turn it into a group-sex village. But he had to give it up because Swedish officials weren't pleased, and the only ones who showed up on opening day were five elderly men and two reporters.

All Aboard, Anyone

LONDON, ENGLAND—British railroad officials were enthusiastic about a special train between London and Manchester. It had a bar car, continuous rock music, and uninhibited young woman dancers. Two people bought tickets the first day, an old man and a reporter.

Ladies, Start Your Bids

PEORIA, ILLINOIS—They held an event called "Rent A Gent," to raise money for a local charity, an auction of forty-nine of the city's most eligible bachelors. About six hundred women attended to bid for an evening out with their favorite man. The high bid of the night was for Dr. William Hayden, a forty-three-year-old pediatrician, who promised a University of Illinois football game, followed by dinner and dancing in Chicago. The bidding went as high as $1,100.

Kevin Greves, twenty-five, a casket salesman, offered dinner at Burger King, a few arcade games, and an evening of TV reruns at his apartment. High bid was $230, and reportedly still open.

Do You Come Here Often?

NASHVILLE, TENNESSEE—Are you single? Want to meet someone nice? Skip the bar scene, and never mind the personal ads, just give some blood. The Red Cross began a Thursday-night special drive for single donors between seventeen and sixty-five. They offered valet parking, romantic music, and fancy hors d'oeuvres. And sharp needles.

Remember, now. It's not "What's your sign?" It's "What's your blood type?"

Bare Facts I & II

LONDON, ENGLAND—A young woman appeared in court after causing a disturbance at a Laundromat. A London bobby charged her with indecent exposure, on grounds that she took her clothes off and washed them in the Laundromat. The judge suspended sentence with his admonition: "For goodness' sake, young lady, don't repeat the performance, because it provokes comment and bothers the London police."

NEW YORK CITY—A reporter could wait a lifetime for the following story. It was lunchtime, with a temperature of thirty-five degrees and gusting winds that made it feel even colder. But an attractive young woman strolling along Fifth Avenue didn't mind the weather. She was nude.

Police arrested her and took her to a psychiatric hospital for observation.

Keeping Abreast of the Competition

DES MOINES, IOWA—Business was terrible at Darrell's Grease & Go, a fast-lube-and-oil-change spot, so owner Darrell Lafon hired two beautiful women to work topless. It worked. Cars began lining up outside the place.

One of the topless women, who gave her name only as Peggy, said, "If you want a standard lube and oil change, it's $14.80. But for $29.88, you get the Boob Lube."

WEST PALM BEACH, FLORIDA—Business was also slow at Doughboy Donuts, so owner Jerry Gallagher hired a waitress to work topless. Several months later Gallagher filed for bankruptcy.

It appears that he lost his shirt when the business became a bust.

X Weddings

You Look Familiar

GREECE, NEW YORK—Lori Sidoti and Chuck Krause had been dating for about two years when they discovered that their mothers had known each other thirty-three years ago. They had met in a hospital maternity ward where they had their babies just minutes apart.

Lori and Chuck decided that since they were born together, they might as well spend the rest of their lives together, so they got married.

Oh, Why Not?

CHELMSFORD, ENGLAND—When Arthur Hill proposed to Alice Brothers, she said she wanted to think it over. Four years later she said yes, and they trudged down the aisle. The blushing bride was ninety-one; the nervous groom was ninety-four.

One More Time

GREEN BAY, WISCONSIN—John and Genevieve Rousseau remember their wedding day in 1938. They also recall the day they got divorced in 1957. And they will never forget the day in 1986 when they decided to get married again. John, seventy-four, said, "We decided to try it again." Genevieve, seventy-five, said, "This time it's for keeps."

Man and Wife and Easy Payments

GREENSBORO, NORTH CAROLINA—If you want to get married in an unusual spot, how about the Dallas Furniture Store? Lots of folks have exchanged their vows there, according to manager Darrell Freedle. It costs only one hundred dollars, plus various fees and tests, and the furniture store handles everything. Freedle said they have two physicians on call, along with a local magistrate, and he said they can complete all arrangements in two hours.

"We've handled more than thirty-four hundred weddings since 1968," he said. "There's one man we've married three times. At the last ceremony, he was seventy-two."

I now pronounce you husband and wife, and we have a special this week on sofas.

Keep Up

PITTSBURGH, PENNSYLVANIA—Steve Hines and Mary Gwaltney were really enthusiastic about jogging—and each other—so they decided to jog before their wedding. They also invited their guests to join them in a short jog through a suburban area, just a few miles, to speed the newlyweds to marital bliss.

It seems only natural for two people with a long-running relationship.

Don't Look Down

RENO, NEVADA—Alan Fox and Ronnie Palm met at work, began dating, fell in love, and decided to get married. They were both window washers, so they held their ceremony on a platform outside of the fifteenth floor of a hotel casino.

That's taking marriage vows to a new height.

Speaking of New Heights

JACKSON, MISSISSIPPI—Bob Provine was a helicopter pilot, and he met Cindy Allen during an assignment for some aerial spraying. They fell in love and chose a helicopter for their wedding ceremony. Their best man flew the helicopter. Also on board for the ten-minute ceremony was a maid of honor, who helped transmit the service by two-way radio so that the family and friends on the ground could hear it.

The minister who performed the ceremony felt right at home. He was also a pilot.

Happy landings.

Deep Love

MORGANFIELD, KENTUCKY—The bride wore white overalls and a white hard hat, and the groom wore dark bib overalls and a black hard hat. It was most appropriate for Nancy Robertson and Roger Adamson, who worked in a coal mine. That's where they met, and that's where they got married. The ceremony was held in a mine shaft seven hundred feet below the surface, which is one way to take the plunge.

A Doubleheader

PORTLAND, OREGON—Sherry Otos and Jamie Reynolds are baseball fans, so it was a natural to hold their wedding ceremony at the ballpark. They exchanged vows at home plate at Civic Stadium, just before a Pacific League game.

MILWAUKEE, WISCONSIN—Eden Clorfene and Thomas Elieff met during a World Series game one year and decided to get married at County Stadium.

Both couples can boast of a wedding party with thousands of guests, although that's only a ballpark estimate.

Some Things Are Final

BROOKFIELD, WISCONSIN—Lorie Herold and Rod Craig held their wedding ceremony in a funeral home. Both are funeral directors and decided it was the only appropriate place to start their lives together. Craig said, "This reflects our personal lives and the types of individuals we are."

They covered up all decorations that could identify the chapel as a funeral home, and the wedding was held on a day when no funerals or wakes were scheduled, so it wasn't a grave ceremony.

Let's Do It

DALLAS, TEXAS—It was a decision on the spur of the moment for Bill Dawkins and Donna Bradshaw, who live in Lithonia, Georgia. They decided to get married, so they let their relatives in Texas know and said, "Meet us at the Dallas County Courthouse." Then they jumped on a plane. They had an hour and a half to catch a plane back home, and criminal court judge Ed Kinkeade was walking out of the elevator on his way to lunch, but he agreed to perform the ceremony.

"I almost—out of habit—asked them if they wanted to enter a guilty plea," the judge said. He couldn't remember the traditional matrimonial phrases, so he improvised. "Do you promise to take care of her and not to leave her?" He asked the bride the same thing, then pronounced them husband and wife.

After exchanging their vows, the groom kissed the bride, the judge kissed the bride, and a few relatives cried. Then the bride and groom rushed back to the airport, and the judge went to lunch.

When the waitress asked the judge if he wanted his usual, he said, "I do."

Stay Tuned

PAMPA, TEXAS—John Pascarella and Lori Maxwell had a lot in common, including their love for country music. They both worked as disc jockeys at radio station KSZN and decided to get married on the air. A local minister performed the double-ring ceremony on

Valentine's Day, and the 6:00 P.M.-to-midnight show on the station was the newlyweds' reception.

A commercial idea that was self-sustaining.

A Rebroadcast

EUGENE, OREGON—Disc jockey Billy Pilgram of country music station KEED wanted to hold a wedding ceremony on his program and asked for volunteers. Georgia Wilcox and Robert Ball were ready to say "I do" anyway, so they said it on the air in a live broadcast. After a twelve-minute ceremony the newlyweds segued to their honeymoon.

A Valentine's Day Tradition

PHILADELPHIA, PENNSYLVANIA—A young couple wandered into a Common Pleas Court on Valentine's Day in 1977, looking for a judge to perform a marriage ceremony. A judge who thought of himself as a romantic said yes. The following year another couple asked the judge to marry them on Valentine's Day.

It then became a tradition for the judge to perform Valentine's Day weddings in his courtroom. He hit a new record in February of 1986 when he held separate ceremonies for twenty-five couples.

The judge's reputation became well known, and he even performs wedding ceremonies throughout the year. People just love to see his name on their marriage licenses. It's Judge Bernard J. Goodheart.

A Honeymooners' Spat

HONOLULU, HAWAII—They looked like a typical young honeymooning couple, holding hands, gazing into each other's eyes. But police say the groom got angry later in their hotel room and ordered his bride to leave. She did, but came back a little later with two men she had met on the beach. The two men beat up the groom and took his money—nearly a thousand dollars. He escaped by jumping over a third-floor railing to the ground.

How to Make Marriage Last

HADDON HEIGHTS, NEW JERSEY—When Albert and Catherine Rhoads celebrated their seventieth wedding anniversary, they said it was just another day. Albert, ninety-two, and Catherine, ninety, were the center of attention, though, as people wondered if they had a secret for staying married.

"We just get along," Albert said. "We never fight, and we don't throw things at each other."

I Do, But I'm Sorry I Did

BASINGSTOKE, ENGLAND—The young couple, Daniel and Susan Stockwell, had exchanged their vows and were mingling with their guests at the reception when Susan saw Daniel talking to an ex-girlfriend. Susan, as one guest said, "blew her top."

"It's all a mistake," the bride said. "I want a divorce."

The groom said, "I must have been mad to go through with it. I'm better off without her."

Well, nothing lasts forever.

XI Food

Smart Cookies

WORCESTER, MASSACHUSETTS—Customers at the Ding Ho Chinese Restaurant complained about the messages in their fortune cookies. One read, "A fortune awaits you with a Baybanks IRA." Another read, "You are heading in the right direction with a Baybanks IRA."

Owner John Ng said it was a mix-up in an order from the company that supplied the cookies. The fortune cookies had been a special order for the bank as a promotional gimmick, and some of them got mixed in with the restaurant order. The company apologized to the restaurant, and after a slight delay sent a new supply of real fortune cookies.

Mr. Ng checked one just to be sure. The message said, "Patience pays."

Truth in Advertising

FORT YATES, NORTH DAKOTA—A Sioux Indian, Benny Left Hand, said his wife was cutting up a chicken for dinner and found a lump of metal about the size of a pea. It was a lump of gold, appraised at five hundred dollars.

Now that's *really* Chicken McNuggets.

Things Are Seldom What They Seem

DETROIT, MICHIGAN—An official at the Stroh Brewery confirmed that Old Milwaukee Beer is brewed in Longview, Texas; Van Nuys, California; Memphis, Tennessee; Saint Paul, Minnesota; and Winston-Salem, North Carolina.

Who Said There's Nothing New?

RICHMOND, INDIANA—Penelope McJunkin had to wear braces on her teeth and soon became tired of eating virtually nothing more than milk shakes and mashed potatoes. Her husband, Jack, started experimenting with recipes that were easy on her choppers, and soon they had a new cookbook: *The I Hate To Chew Cookbook: A Gourmet Guide for Adults Who Wear Orthodontic Braces*.

It has a lot of substance, but not much of a bite.

What's for Dinner?

TORRE DEL MAR, SPAIN—Officials of the town spent more than fifteen thousand dollars to put together the world's biggest paella, a Spanish rice-and-seafood dish. It took forty cooks to make it, and they served it up to more than fifteen thousand people on hand for the town's Tourist Day.

So, what's for dessert?

No Vanilla Ice Cream Left?

PHELPS, NEW YORK—Folks in this upstate village held their annual Sauerkraut Festival, where they also featured sauerkraut chocolate cupcakes.

It's an acquired taste.

Bon Appétit, Pal

CORDELE, GEORGIA—The nation's newest French restaurant, Mon Petit, popped up in south Georgia. It featured white linen tablecloths, filet of beef Richard III, and a Château Mouton-Rothschild Premiers Cru at $145 a bottle. Owner Leon Perlis said his chef, Richard Gerow, has always loved French cooking. And after an expansion and remodeling program at the Perlis Truck Stop, they had an extra room, so they turned it into the Mon Petit French restaurant.

Friday and Saturday evenings only. Reservations suggested. And it's formal; you'll need a napkin.

It Pays to Advertise

JACKSONVILLE, FLORIDA—When the United States attacked Libya in April of 1986, some newspapers carried an Associated Press picture of a Navy jet fighter flying above the Mediterranean off the Libyan coast. In the window of the plane was a sign: Send Cookies.

John D. Gavin, a retired rear admiral, and Frank Gibbs, a retired executive of the Winn-Dixie grocery chain, led a drive that resulted in one hundred cases of cookies being sent to the crew of the USS *Saratoga*.

Can't Be Too Careful

LONDON, ENGLAND—Security officials at Heathrow Airport thought they had found a terrorist with sticks of dynamite around her waist. But it wasn't dynamite, it was Italian sausages. A spokesman said, "It was just an elderly, portly Italian grandmother on her way to see her relatives in America."

The airline allowed her—and her sausages—on board. And they kept it a secret until after the woman had cleared customs in the U.S.

Never Mind a Better Mousetrap

BLOOMINGTON, MINNESOTA—Jim Bever came up with a gimmick that sold well, a metal stencil you attach to a slice of bread before it goes into the toaster. When the bread pops up you have a slice of golden-brown toast, and a gleaming white message: Good Morning.

Just what we need in the morning. Toast that talks back.

What's Next?

PEEKSKILL, NEW YORK—Folks in this town are proud of their Famous Firsts or World Records. They're known for making an omelet with ten thousand eggs; a hero sandwich more than a thousand feet long; a cake eighty feet long and forty feet wide; a popcorn ball twelve feet in diameter; a serving of lasagna forty feet long and four feet wide; and a brownie forty-five feet long.

And what do they do with these king-size dishes? Stand around and look at them for a few minutes, then eat them.

XII The Bizarre & the Mysterious

A Lot of Extras

CHICAGO, ILLINOIS—James Motycha bought a brand new car but took it back to the dealer six weeks later with a complaint. He showed the dealer two dozen mushrooms growing in the carpeting.

"The missus," he said, "doesn't particularly care for mushrooms."

Fate

BUFFALO, NEW YORK—A man who had recently recovered from cancer was walking down the street with his family when he was hit and fatally injured by a nude man who was running from the police.

Maybe Later

LONDON, ENGLAND—The Reverend Donald Sherriff kept his clothes on while he conducted a special service for a hundred members of a nudist club. He said, "I wasn't embarrassed at all."

There was a slight problem when the collection plate was passed around, though.

The Sky Is Falling

EVANS, COLORADO—People who live on Pleasant Acres Drive have had a mystery on their hands for at least four years. Kernels of corn keep falling out of the sky. Sometimes, they say, they also get a sprinkling of pinto beans. One resident, Gary Bryan, said, "If I picked it all up, I'd probably have a ton of the stuff."

Several reporters have confirmed it, including Mike

Peters, a reporter for the *Greeley Tribune*. Asked if he thought it was just a practical joke, Bryan said, "That would be a lot of corn to buy and a lot of time for a prank."

There are no cornfields near the homes, and the closest grain elevator is five miles away.

So far, there's no explanation.

It's Around Here Somewhere

EUFAULA, ALABAMA—Everyone had always talked about the building with a marble plaque inscribed, "Time Capsule Placed, May 29, 1885." Historian Doug Purcell even found a newspaper dated June 2, 1885, with a story about the time capsule being placed in the building. One hundred years later they removed the plaque and found a brick wall eleven inches thick. Workmen smashed through the wall and found more bricks. Then they tried all four corners of the building but found nothing. After that they used metal detectors but again found nothing. Purcell said, "It sure has us baffled. Really strange."

The building, by the way, is the Odd Fellows Lodge.

Waterloo

GAUHATI, INDIA—Villagers had been terrified for months because of a rampaging elephant that raided crops and granaries in this region of Assam State. According to authorities, the elephant, about thirteen feet tall with tusks measuring five feet, had killed at least ten people. But the reign of terror ended when the elephant pulled down an eleven-thousand volt power line and electrocuted himself.

New Warden

OTISVILLE, NEW YORK—The Federal Correction Institution here recently got a new warden: Jesse James.

Objection Noted

PROVIDENCE, RHODE ISLAND—Members of a rock group known as Alarm became upset when they found out they had to share the bill with a band calling itself Rash of Stabbings.

"Sounds too violent," Alarm members said.

Hydrants

NEWARK, NEW JERSEY—Twelve-year-old Rahina Hoffman and her friends were cooling off one summer afternoon in the spray of an open fire hydrant. The kids had been squealing in delight, but suddenly they began to shriek in horror. Rahina ran inside her apartment and told her mother that fish were coming out of the hydrant.

Rahina's mother went outside and saw four large fish that looked like baby sharks. The woman ran back inside and called authorities, and while she was inside, a fifth baby shark, about two feet long, came out of the hydrant, and it appeared to be still alive.

The city's health and welfare director, James Buford, arrived and verified that the five fish were indeed baby sharks.

Daniel N. Berardinelli, chief municipal water engineer, said he was convinced that it must have been a prank. He said there was no way that sharks could live outside of salt water, and the turbulence of the city's water lines would destroy them anyway.

"That size fish couldn't even get past the valve opening," he said, "which is only about three and a half inches." And even if the fish had somehow got into the city's water supply, he said it would have been unlikely that all five would come out of one hydrant in a city with six hundred miles of water pipes.

The kids insisted they saw the baby sharks come out of the hydrant, and officials said they had to accept their story. But no one ever came up with an answer.

Just when you thought it was safe to go wading . . .

Mint Condition

BRUNSWICK, MAINE—Workmen were remodeling a brick building that had been a grocery store and then a catalog store. As they removed bricks from one wall, they saw something inside, something quite large. More bricks came away, and soon they could see that something had been hidden inside a vault made of bricks. That something was a 1954 Corvette.

Cynthia Sampson, thirty-seven, remembered the car. She had ridden in it when she was a kid. Inside the car, on the floor, was a small measuring cup that Sampson remembered playing with.

The car was in perfect condition, except for the white exterior paint, which had blistered and turned yellow with age. But the car's interior was like new.

Sampson's father, Richard Sampson—who had died some years before—had sealed the car in the brick vault. But Sampson said she didn't know why her father did it. No one else did, either.

What would Stephen King say about this?

No Peeking

HUNTINGTON, WEST VIRGINIA—It's traditional for the circuit clerk of Cabell County to hand over to his successor a yellowed, tattered envelope. It has been handed down among circuit clerks for eighty-three years. A typed statement on the envelope reads: "Please do not open until September, 1990."

No one knows what's in the envelope.

And no one will open it until September, 1990.

XIII   It's Nice to Go Traveling

How's That Again?

INDIANAPOLIS, INDIANA—Did you ever get a ticket for speeding? And did you ever try to talk your way out of it? Indiana state police have been saving the best ones, including the one about the man who insisted that he was in a hurry because he was late for an important appointment. He was on his way to receive an award from the Safe Drivers of America.

The Law Is the Law

CHARLESTON, WEST VIRGINIA—A patrolman gave a fellow officer a ticket for driving a police car with an expired safety-inspection sticker on the windshield. But the chief of police said that was the wrong way to handle it, so both men were reassigned to scooter patrol.

Keep Moving

DENVER, COLORADO—There was a terrible traffic jam on a major parkway during the height of the rush hour, and many drivers blamed it on the police department. A patrol car ran out of gas, and a second patrol car was dispatched to the scene so the officers could siphon gas into the first car.

By then a third patrol car had to be dispatched to the scene so that officers could divert traffic around the first two police cars.

An Arresting Color

MINNEAPOLIS, MINNESOTA—The state police department had always had Fords and Chryslers. That was the way it had been for at least thirty years. But one day someone decided to add 146 new Chevrolets to the fleet. It's policy—or at least tradition—for the cars to match the officers' maroon uniforms, so patrol chief Roger Ledding checked over a color chart and compared samples to his uniform.

When the cars were delivered, everyone was surprised to see that the color was not quite maroon, but *bright* maroon.

"Looks red to me," Ledding said. "A lot more red than maroon."

Dave Thomas, a fleet sales manager, explained, "When you look at a one-square-inch color sample chip and compare it to a fifteen-foot long car, there's a considerable difference."

Many motorists agreed, including one man who was stopped after passing one of the new patrol cars.

"I thought it was a fire department car," he said. "Who in his right mind would pass a state trooper?"

Each new car cost $10,400. But state officials said there are no plans to repaint each one. They'll go on the auction block in a year or two.

Until then, where's the fire?

Turn Right at the Living Room

CLAY, NEW YORK—Daniel Allison, twenty-two, was sound asleep in his bedroom, minding his own business, when something woke him up. It was part of his bedroom wall, lying on his chest.

"I didn't hear a sound, but I woke up because I felt something on top of me," he said.

Then he saw a car, its wheels spinning, the engine racing, in the middle of what had been his bathroom and his kitchen. Water from broken pipes sprayed in all directions. The car had smashed into his house through his bathroom and continued into the kitchen.

Hazel Mascato, seventy, explained that she had lost control after hitting a parked car in front of Allison's house.

Neither Mascato nor Allison was hurt. But Allison had a little trouble explaining to his boss why he was late to work that morning.

Accidents Will Happen

MOSCOW, IDAHO—Gregory Umbright was driving along a deserted road when he found himself in a ditch. He said later that he had fallen asleep at the wheel and had driven off the road. Umbright wasn't hurt. Neither was Mort Bliven, the prisoner Umbright, a deputy sheriff, was transporting to a nearby jail. This was just one of a series of accidents involving police cars, and Sheriff Ken Buxton wasn't pleased. It was the third such accident in recent weeks. So the sheriff ordered all his deputies to attend driver-training classes.

Pull Over, If You're There

DUNDEE, SCOTLAND—The officer in the first patrol car to begin the chase radioed for help in what turned out to be a long, high-speed chase. Soon, half a dozen police cars were in hot pursuit. The officers in the lead cars kept radioing that they couldn't see the driver. In fact, they said, it looked as if there was no one at the wheel.

Finally, they pulled the car over to the side of the road and surrounded it. But there was no sign of a driver as the officers moved cautiously toward the car. The reason they couldn't see the driver was because he was quite short, only three feet. He was also six years old. It was Stephen Peters, who had taken his father's car out for a joyride. It was the third time that day that Stephen had "borrowed" the car.

Stephen's father said, "I just don't know why he does that."

That kid had a driving determination.

Hero Worship

LONDON, ENGLAND—Chris Lloyd wanted to be just like his father, so one day he sat down and had a few drinks. Chris, nine years old, didn't know which bottle to choose, so he poured drinks from several bottles. He had at least a dozen glasses of gin, rum, and scotch before his father found him and called for help.

They rushed Chris to the hospital to pump out his stomach. He said he felt okay, a little sick to his tummy, but strong, really strong. The ambulance attendant confirmed that. He said he had to sit on Chris in the ambulance to make sure he wouldn't jump out on the way to the hospital.

This Is the Captain Speaking....

MIAMI, FLORIDA—The passengers were settled into their seats on board Eastern Airlines flight 141, which was finally on its way to Tampa. There had been several delays, first for refueling, then another delay because the pilot was late. And then, after the plane was on the runway, there was another delay because of a runway backup. That's when the pilot's voice came over the intercom.

"You know, there's a saying that when you die, you have to change planes in Atlanta."

This brought a few chuckles and some murmuring from the passengers. Then the pilot's voice was heard once more.

"I'm fed up with it. I'm sick and tired of the delays, tired of the waiting. You can have it. This flight will be my last flight."

Then he taxied the plane back to the gate and got off. Eastern eventually found another pilot for the flight, and company spokesman Glenn Parsons, who didn't identify the pilot who quit, said only, "This was a significant departure from standard practices."

Wonder how the airline felt being bumped.

Just Need a Little More Experience

OMAHA, NEBRASKA—North Central Airlines began a nonstop service in the fall of 1970 between Omaha and Minneapolis. But the inaugural flight drew little attention. It left with one passenger and ninety-eight empty seats. And when the jetliner landed in Minneapolis, the passenger discovered that his baggage was still in Omaha.

But think positively. At least the plane didn't get hijacked.

Bad News. Good News. Bad News

DEKALB, ILLINOIS—Student pilot Jasper Plazza was on his first solo flight in a small private plane, and everything was going well. But Plazza noticed that he was running dangerously low on fuel and decided to make an emergency landing. He chose the only spot available: a busy highway. It was tricky, but he landed safely, just missing several cars.

A state trooper showed up a few minutes later and gave Plazza a ticket for entering the highway at the wrong place, and for failing to pay the thirty-cent toll.

Just one of those days.

On the Road

TOKYO, JAPAN—When you travel in a foreign country it's important to know local customs and traditions. The Japanese, for example, seldom hitch rides on the highway. But one expert on such matters says that the Japanese recognize that many foreign visitors are without adequate means of transportation. So a Japanese driver will often stop and give a hitchhiker a lift.

But be prepared. This expert says, "When a Japanese driver stops to accommodate you, he will assume responsibility for your comfort and well-being. A Japanese driver will go out of his way to deliver you safely to your destination, often buy you lunch or at least offer a snack, and even flag down another car to speed you on your way."

It's a rule of thumb.

Stars Wars Closer to Home

TRENTON, NEW JERSEY—Motorists were warned not to speed and also not to rely on those "fuzz busters," or radar detectors to dodge police speed traps. They're illegal in certain states. New Jersey state police superintendent Clinton Pagano said many patrol cars would soon be equipped with "beam interrupter switches," which make radar detectors useless.

The cops are so proud of the new devices, they're beaming.

Life in the Fast Lane? Pshaw!

KANSAS CITY, MISSOURI—The mayor's annual Christmas Tree Fund was underway, and donations to help the needy were coming in slower than usual, so a local car dealer decided to help increase donations by offering a new car to be raffled off among the contributors. Someone reached into a barrel of names and picked the winner, Pauline Darrah, sixty-seven, a great-grandmother. She had won a new Jaguar worth thirty-four thousand dollars.

But Darrah said she didn't want it. "I don't need a car. I don't want a car. I walk or take the bus." She said she couldn't give it to one of her grandchildren because she had eight, and no matter who she picked, "the other seven would be mad at me."

At last report someone had offered to buy the car from her, and she said she would think about it.

On the bus.

Lots of Extras

SEATTLE, WASHINGTON—A firm that makes jetliners got a special order from a good customer who wanted a top-of-the-line model. It had to have a few homey touches, such as Waterford crystal lamps and a 24-karat-gold shower rod. A few other extras would make the price just under six million dollars, but the customer thought that would be a bargain. It was for a Saudi Arabian sheik.

Just a little something to think about next time you "fill 'er up."

XIV 911

Out on a Limb

NASHVILLE, TENNESSEE—The fire department got an urgent call requesting the rescue squad for a man who was stuck in a tree. He was a foreigner and had never seen such tall trees, especially one thirty feet tall. He wanted to see what it was like to climb the tree, but when he got up there, he saw it was pretty high but also scary because he saw the ground far away and couldn't see how to get back down.

Soon, he saw red flashing lights and a fire department cherry picker with a snorkel bucket at the end, but the fire chief saw power lines nearby and ordered the cherry picker back down. After a delay, they used a fifty-foot ladder, and two firemen helped the poor guy back to solid ground.

He was heard muttering, "I think that I shall never see/me/again, in a tree."

It didn't scan, but it made a lot of sense.

We Know, We Know

TIPTON, IOWA—Things never were the same at Robert and Betty Thumma's farm after their silo caught fire. They called the fire department, but firefighters just couldn't get it out. The fire seemed to go out, but it smoldered and burst into flame several times. The chief decided the best thing to do was just let it burn itself out, which it did for at least three weeks.

And that's when people driving past the farm started stopping to tell the Thummas that their silo was on fire. It happened all day and all night. Finally, the

Thummas decided to put up a large sign at the side of the road near the silo: YES, WE KNOW THE SILO'S BURNING. THANKS.

You Can't Be Too Careful

INDIANAPOLIS, INDIANA—About a dozen employees at a United Parcel Service building noticed skin irritations and rashes while they were unloading packages from a truck, so they called the fire department. The department's hazardous materials team turned out in full force, wearing chemical-protection suits and carrying special equipment. But they couldn't find any chemicals or corrosive materials that might have leaked out of the packages.

After a more thorough search officials found evidence of an earlier spill from a previous truckload. It was chili powder.

So much for hot news.

How Embarrassing

FRAMINGHAM, MASSACHUSETTS—Firefighters were enjoying their annual banquet at a restaurant when fire broke out in the kitchen. No one was hurt, but there was a lot of damage at the restaurant, the Burnam House.

You'll Get Used to It

BUHL, ALABAMA—Fire Chief L. A. Marlowe had a great idea. He designed a combination fire station and tornado shelter to be built at least six feet underground. It would be just like any other fire station, with plenty of modern conveniences and all the comforts of home for the firefighters. But there would be one thing missing: a fire pole.

Well, it would be hard to slide *up* a fire pole.

A Big Order

BRISBANE, AUSTRALIA—Police were called to a home
where a woman had broken her leg. The woman's husband said his wife's thigh bone had just snapped, apparently because of her weight: 727 pounds. The
police ambulance team couldn't lift the woman to get
her out of the house and discovered that even if they
could, she wouldn't fit through the door, or a window.

The police called for help from some workmen, who
cut a hole in the side of the house. While the workmen
were busy, the ambulance team removed all medical
equipment from their ambulance so that the woman
would fit inside. They drove slowly to the hospital, the
ambulance creaking and groaning under the weight.
And at the hospital they had to arrange several mat-
tresses on the floor—the ground floor—because there
were no beds strong enough to support the patient's
weight.

A police spokesman said they often got calls to that
house to settle domestic disputes between the woman
and her husband, who weighed 112 pounds.

Open Wide

IDABEL, OKLAHOMA—They talked for weeks about
the saga of the Determined Dentist and the Persistent
Patient. The patient, a woman, called police and said
her dentist had showed up at her home demanding six
hundred dollars for a set of dentures he had made for
her. She refused to pay him, on grounds that the teeth
didn't fit properly, and the dentist decided on an im-
mediate extraction. He grabbed the woman's teeth
right out of her mouth.

The woman fought back and bit the dentist's hand
before he escaped with her—or his—teeth. The dentist said he would never again make dentures on credit.
The woman said she planned to file a lawsuit against
the dentist and really put the bite on him.

Au Naturel

GAINESVILLE, FLORIDA—Two couples went to a secluded cove for a picnic, and one young woman wandered off to be alone for a while. Her friends went to
look for her and found her clothes piled on the bank.
They assumed that she had decided to go for a swim in
the nude, but they became alarmed when they didn't
see her in the water, so they called the police.

Several patrol cars arrived, sirens blaring, lights
flashing. The convoy included a medical emergency
unit and half a dozen police scuba divers. The divers
searched the cove for nearly three hours but found no
trace of the woman. Everyone thought that she had
drowned and that her body, caught by an undertow,
would eventually turn up.

A short time after everyone left, police got another
call from a man who lived near the cove. He said a
nude woman was knocking on his door.

Later, police said they believed that the woman had
seen all the police cars and the divers, and hid near the
cove until everyone left. She told police that she just
couldn't remember a thing.

It's the Latest

LOS ANGELES, CALIFORNIA—The National Association of Uniform Manufacturers and Distributors chose
L.A. police as the best dressed in the country. The
judges said they based their decision on uniforms that
projected a favorable image, professionalism, neat-
ness, and authority.

Designer Jeff Hamilton said the L.A.P.D. look was,
"neat and trim, projecting just the right tone of authority without menace."

Their uniforms are a nice blue. Quite arresting.

Jackpot Litter

NEW YORK CITY—It's against the law to litter the streets of New York. You can be issued a summons and fined. But Sherri Noorian, twenty-seven, denied that she was guilty. A sanitation officer stopped her and said that she had dropped something on the street, then gave her a summons calling for a fifty-dollar fine.

The sanitation officer said Noorian had dropped a state lottery ticket. But Noorian was furious, saying that she had obviously dropped it by mistake. "Who would throw away a lottery ticket that might be a million-dollar winner? Especially one for a drawing that particular night." Noorian said she would fight it in court and hoped she would win. "I also might win the lotto jackpot," she said.

She didn't.

Show and Tell

AUGUSTA, WISCONSIN—Eleven-year-old Kevin Pettis was worried about what to take to class for the show-and-tell session coming up that week. His mother had suggested a few things from his room, but Kevin said, "Naw. That's old stuff." Then one day he came home with a strange-looking piece of metal that he said he had found in a vacant lot. He tossed it around, poked at it, hammered on it, and threw it in the corner.

His mother said, "We don't need any more junk around here. Take that thing to class for show-and-tell." So he did. And the teacher nearly fainted. She ran for the principal, who called the police bomb squad.

That piece of metal turned out to be a 75-mm artillery shell with a live detonator, and it could have exploded.

A police spokesman said it was an old one, probably from the 1920s or 1930s, but potentially dangerous.

Show-and-tell turned out to be a bomb.

Is Something Burning?

MONMOUTH, OREGON—It was just another day plowing the fields at Walter Conley's two-hundred-acre farm. Back and forth and back and forth on his tractor, and he thought he felt a bump, but kept going. He was near the barn a few moments later, and he stopped for a drink of water. That's when he noticed the flames and smoke in the middle of the field, so he called the fire department.

Firemen showed up, took a close look, and the chief ordered everyone back and radioed for help from the bomb squad. Conley had run over an old World War II bomb that had been buried in his field all those years. His farm was adjacent to Camp Adair, which had been a training center during the war.

An Army bomb squad arrived and blew the bomb up, leaving a crater the size of a pickup truck.

So much for a blast from the past.

XV Science & Progress

There Go the Good Old Days

BRYANT POND, MAINE—Train service to this lakeside glen in the mountains of western Maine stopped one day. Then the clothespin mill shut down. The local print shop closed. So did the drugstore and the hardware store. The general store remained, though, as many people moved away. But the lake was polluted, and those who were left couldn't easily pay increasing taxes. But there was something of the past that remained, even though it appeared destined for the dust heap.

Folks in Bryant Pond used hand-cranked telephones, the last in the country. A turn of the crank rang the switchboard in the living room of Elden Hathaway, who had owned the local company for thirty years, a family business. But it had been sold to the Oxford Telephone and Telegraph Service, which planned to replace the old system with new electronic circuitry and dial or touch-tone phones.

Well, at least it'll eliminate all those crank calls.

A Microchip Scarecrow

BRISTOL, ENGLAND—Three high school students have invented an electronic scarecrow. They say it has a computer that hears and analyzes calls of approaching birds and then selects an appropriate distress call from its recorded library of bird sounds.

Emma Boyce, Andrew Gillions, and Mark Hill say the sound makes the intruding bird think danger lies ahead, so it flies away.

There is no truth to a story that an American farmer in Iowa bought one of these new high tech scarecrows and reported success. He is alleged to have said, "It scared the crows so much they brought back the corn they stole last year."

Just Needs a Little Work

HOBBS, NEW MEXICO—School officials at the local high school spent one hundred thousand dollars for a sophisticated fire alarm system. But they had a lot of trouble with it in the first year. There were at least thirty false alarms. Local fire officials finally decided they would stop responding automatically to the alarm and would wait for a follow-up phone call saying there was a real emergency.

Investigators tracked down the trouble in the system. Tiny roaches were crawling into the system and triggering the alarm.

Obviously, they have to get all the bugs out.

Uh-huh

MOSCOW, RUSSIA—Soviet scientists claimed they have taken the uncertainty out of fishing by training trout to be caught voluntarily. The scientists say they used sound waves instead of flies and worms, and the trout became accustomed to responding by swimming into small cages.

Sounds like a pretty big one to us.

They Could Dance All Night

ZURICH, SWITZERLAND—You might not notice anything different or unusual about a certain disco in this city. There's the usual garish glow of multicolored spotlights and loud music, with crowds of young people dancing enthusiastically. You would never guess that the kids are deaf. But they have no trouble feeling the music. They feel it in their feet, literally. The floor was designed specifically to transmit the rhythmic sounds through vibrations. A spokesman said this was a good way to get handicapped kids out in public for some social contact.

Anyone with normal hearing would, of course, have to shout to be heard above the din. But the deaf kids have even another advantage. They can communicate in sign language.

What If...?

STAMFORD, CONNECTICUT—A man who reads a lot of science fiction said he came up with a great idea for a book, a story about a spaceflight to Mars. The crew, he said, was two astronauts and five live dolphins, who would make the flight inside a huge water tank.

"I had one slight problem, though," he said. "Why dolphins?"

He said he wrote to NASA and asked for opinions from experts. Several scientists passed the man's letter around, but no one could find a solution. NASA replied to the man's letter, wishing him success and asking that if he ever figures out "Why dolphins?" to be sure to let them know.

Hey, he just comes up with ideas. The details are someone else's problem.

XVI   The Occult

Hexes Banned

BOGOTÁ, COLUMBIA—The Communications Ministry banned radio stations from broadcasting programs by witches and mind readers.

"There are clairvoyants and so-called witches," a ministry spokesman said, "who deceive people and do unscrupulous business over the airwaves." Any station broadcasting such programs would lose its license.

Officials also decided to extend the broadcasting ban to magicians. Obviously they didn't want to sleight anyone.

Web of Spider, Wiggle of Worm...

CRAB ORCHARD, TENNESSEE—Folks who want to know what kind of winter to expect usually check with Helen Lane, a weather soothsayer.

"Nature itself reveals the future," she said.

She began her weather predictions in 1959, based on the number of spider webs, woolly worms, and how much noise katydids made. One fall she predicted heavy snow for the coming winter, another year, a mild winter. What if she's wrong? Do people blame her and get angry?

"I don't believe that anyone will ever get mad at me," she said, looking ahead.

A Sacred Snake

BANGKOK, THAILAND—Albino elephants are common in this country, but an albino cobra? Manit Sikaya found the snake one day and took it to a local spiritualist, who claimed that it was a holy snake. Manit returned to his home and put up a shingle, so to speak, inviting people to visit his holy snake for a fee, of course.

People soon began lining up to pay homage—and the equivalent of $1.30—to the snake. Manit said the snake learned to sip tea and sleeps in front of an electric fan.

Cobras can usually sleep anywhere they want.

I See

TARASOVKA, RUSSIA—Soviet authorities were concerned about a woman who called herself, Lyuba, the fortune teller. She made her own fortunes, charging the equivalent of $13.50 per person, giving her a monthly income of as much as six thousand rubles. The average Soviet citizen makes about two hundred rubles a month, and one Soviet official said, "We must look quietly on her conscienceless deceit."

When reporters tried to interview Lyuba, she gave them what was described as "lethal stares." Reporters then tried to pretend they were customers, but Lyuba spotted them and became enraged.

Soviet authorities also tried to interview her, but she sent them away, too, with "a volley of censored epithets." She also punched several officials in their noses.

Lyuba is not a happy medium.

Trust Me

NICE, FRANCE—Seers and mediums are common in France and often advertise in local newspapers. One, who called himself Grand Sorcerer and Seer Seydou Diaby, said he was from Africa and offered his services—for a price, of course.

A man who visited the seer was told to drop a fifty-centime coin into a pot of boiling water and secret herbs. He did; the seer placed a top on the pot, uttered a few incantations, and removed the lid. The coin had vanished, but floating on top of the bubbling herb water was a five-hundred-franc bill.

The man was impressed and promised to return later with a colleague. A few days later the man and his colleague showed up for another "consultation" with the seer, who was unaware that the two men were national police officers.

The seer repeated the miracle for both men, again turning a coin into a bill. A few days later the two men returned with sixty thousand francs (about $7,600), a combination of savings and borrowed money, ready to drop it into the magical water and retire on what would surely be an astronomical sum.

This time the seer put the money into a suitcase, closed it, muttered incantations, and told the two men to take the suitcase back, keep it safe for three days.

"But do not open it," the seer warned, "or the spell will be broken. Return it to me in three days."

Three days later the men opened the suitcase and found shredded newspaper. When they returned to the seer's office, they discovered that he had obviously looked ahead, anticipated trouble, and had left town.

I Predict

NEW YORK CITY—Around Halloween, an organization known as the New York Center for the Strange releases its annual list of predictions for the year ahead. Executive director Richard Blaine describes the organization as "dedicated to the exploration of prognostication, prophecy, soothsaying, and divination."

Predictions are based, according to Blaine, on a nationwide survey of 290 American witches. Among the center's correct predictions, Blaine listed President Nixon's resignation, the success of the TV game show *Wheel of Fortune*, and the 1986 summit in Iceland between President Reagan and Soviet leader Gorbachev.

Among the misses: Richard Nixon would write an

erotic novel, and rock star Prince would win a Nobel Prize.

Looking ahead to 1987, Blaine predicted that Edward Koch, the talkative mayor of New York City, would join an obscure cult and take a vow of silence; a new James Bond movie would feature villains played by Ruth Westheimer, Henry Kissinger, and Walter Cronkite. Also predicted was the invention of a car that would run on orange juice and vodka.

But that might give you a headache in the long run.

Proof

SUNRISE, FLORIDA—James Randi is known professionally as the Amazing Randi. He has performed magic for many years and has also written books and held lectures and demonstrations to prove that "real" magic doesn't exist. In 1965 he offered ten thousand dollars to anyone who could demonstrate paranormal powers under controlled conditions.

The money is still in a bank.

XVII People

A No-no

LITTLETON, COLORADO—You can see those "vanity" license plates everywhere these days. And most states have a strict policy about initials or words that might be offensive or in bad taste. No one thought twice about Brad Thomas's recent request for OUI OUI, which is French for "yes yes."

But somewhere out there someone else was offended and complained to the motor vehicle bureau. The complainer said that the letters could also be read as "wee-wee," and that was offensive, at least to the offended person.

The state ordered Thomas to return the plates.

You can't please everyone.

A Short Story

BEECH GROVE, INDIANA—Connie Lee Smith, seventy-four, looked back on his five years as a school-crossing guard with no complaints. He had worked as a circus clown for years and got the part-time job to keep busy after he retired. Smith said most of the kids he helps across the street tower over him. "I'm four feet four on a good day," he said. "But there's no trouble. I respect them. They're like family to me. Oh, I'm strict, but I love them like they were my own, and I make darn sure nothing happens to them."

The kids respect Smith, too. They sort of look up to him.

Some Friends, Indeed

MILWAUKEE, WISCONSIN—Manuel Garcia had lost his hair because of radiation treatments for cancer. But he had a lot of moral support from more than fifty relatives and friends. They had their heads shaved.

Those folks were just a cut above the rest.

A Neighborly Response

HOLYOKE, COLORADO—Linda Heerman became a widow at thirty-two, after her husband was killed in an accident, and she was worried about trying to handle their farm alone. She had three hundred acres of sugar beets ready for harvest, so she put an ad in a local newspaper for some help. About two hundred people volunteered and went to work in the fields. They finished in a day and a half what would have taken several people two weeks.

Linda said she had tears in her eyes over the response. "It was beautiful," she said. "The people in this community are so nice. A small town has its advantages, and this is one of them."

One volunteer said, "It's just a response to a neighbor in trouble."

No one missed a beet.

Need a Little Help?

HOUGHTON, MICHIGAN—They were all set for the Woodfield Winter Carnival one year, but there was one thing missing: snow. A slight dusting came, but it wasn't real snow. So the folks in Michigan's Upper Peninsula helped out. They loaded up five huge trucks with snow—one hundred tons—and sent them to Houghton in time for the festival.

Take that, Mother Nature.

How Do I Remember Thee?

WAUKESHA, WISCONSIN—Mary MacDonald Anderson had a big family, but she kept track of everyone with a simple rhyme in order of their birth.

> Rosemary and Eleanor and Jack and Pauline.
> Bill and David and Elaine and Maureen.
> Mary and Michael and Gloria Jean.

But one day her brother turned up after a disappearance of thirty-four years. And now her family poem is:

> Rosemary and Eleanor and Jack and Pauline.
> Bill and David and Elaine and Maureen.
> Mary and Michael and Gloria Jean.
> And Patrick.

Anderson said she was glad to see her long-lost brother. But it just doesn't scan anymore.

Correction

NEW YORK CITY—Minutes after broadcasting the above story we received a telephone call from some folks who politely but firmly informed us that the town was pronounced "Waukasha," and not "Waukeesha." We took note and corrected the pronunciation, but wondered on the air what you would expect from someone in New York City where Houston Street is pronounced "Howston," and a popular drink known as an egg cream has neither egg nor cream?

We're Sinking

BROOKLYN, NEW YORK—People who lived in a twenty-square-block region of Sunset Park were upset when their apartment buildings and brownstone houses began twisting, buckling, and sinking slightly.

Officials came in and checked everything but could find no cause. One investigator said it could have been vibrations from heavy trucks causing subsoil to sink. Another said maybe it was the result of deteriorating sewers. Still another theorized that it was a geological tilt.

Whatever is causing it gives new meaning to the phrase, "Well, there goes the neighborhood."

A Very Special Delivery

RIO RANCHO, NEW MEXICO—The mail that day in October of 1986 brought the usual. Anne Dreher Feindel, eighty-nine, found bills and junk mail. And a postcard from her mother. That was odd, since Emma Hallet Dreher had died in 1958. The card was postmarked from Stroudsburg, Pennsylvania, on June 11, 1954, when Anne's mother was eighty-seven. And there was another postmark, September 29, 1986, next to a new stamp.

Anne said it appeared that the original stamp had fallen off, and whoever found the card thirty-two years later put another stamp on it and dropped it in the mail.

Who?

CAMP HILL, PENNSYLVANIA—James H. Smith is the founder and president of the Jim Smith Society. Anyone can join. Anyone named Jim Smith, that is. Members began getting together in 1969 for their annual Jim Smith Fun Festival.

Founder Jim Smith said the society has a membership of about twelve hundred Jim Smiths all over the country. And he said, "I never met a Jim Smith I didn't like."

Not to be overlooked, however, is the Bob Joseph organization that began in 1985. This is a much smaller group, thirty-six at the start. But Robert Joseph of Brooklyn, New York, the founder, hoped to sign up at least a hundred Bob Josephs before the second annual get-together. Roberta Josephs are invited, too.

At their first get-together they had a picnic that included a one-mile Bob-A-Thon. They had a Bob-a-que, ate shish-ka-Bob, and Bobbed for apples.

And, of course, a lot of jokes. Probably a lot of Bobbed humor.

The Perfect Community

PLEASANT RIDGE, MAINE—The population of this town in the northern part of the state is about one hundred. And they reap the benefits of the Central Maine Power Company, which operates the hydroelectric dam there. The company pays the town about $225,000 a year in tax assessments. So where does the money go?

Each household has free cable TV and a free movie channel. When it snows, all driveways are plowed at no cost. Lunch in the school cafeteria is free, and all kids under eighteen are automatically covered by accident insurance. The town also picks up the first thousand dollars for each year of college.

Sounds like a great town, but don't move there. Most of the undeveloped land belongs to the Scott Paper Company, which uses it to grow trees. And there are no homes for sale anyway.

Some luck. We find Shangri-la, and it's standing room only.

Taxing Questions

JACKSONVILLE, FLORIDA—People everywhere call their local Internal Revenue Service office with questions, but officials in this city have gathered a few of their state's most unusual queries.

One man who raised earthworms wanted to know about a depreciation period for a worm. No one knew.

A goldfish dealer wondered if he should keep the corpses of his dead fish as proof of loss. Not advisable.

A woman called to explain that her daughter's recent marriage had been a disaster, and wedding expenses ought to be classified as a casualty loss. Nope.

A man became indignant when he was told that he couldn't claim his dog and his mother-in-law as dependents. "But I spend fifty dollars a year more on the dog than on my mother-in-law," he said. Uh-huh.

Another man had lost his false teeth and wondered if that was a casualty or a medical deduction. Either one.

A woman called to say that she was "simply not in the mood to file an income tax return this year," and promised to file two returns the following year. Get back in the mood.

One taxpayer sent a letter with a request. "Please remove my name from your mailing list." Nice try.

And one irate and indignant man called the IRS office demanding to know why they had sent him a letter.

"What does the letter say?" a representative asked.

"I don't know," he yelled. "I haven't opened it yet."

Want a Bargain?

LOUDENVILLE, NEW YORK—Everyone loves a bargain. And once a year the New York state police hold an auction of all unclaimed property. There are always bikes, boats, lawn mowers, TV sets, cameras, safes, jewelry, and often quite a few unusual items. One year there was a concrete lion with one paw missing, and an old tombstone up for bidding.

There was also a deed to a half-acre chunk of Terrapin Point that was last seen going over Niagara Falls. And a hay baler made out of corsets and shoe trees.

There was one more item of interest. How much would you bid for thirty-eight gallons of water that was displaced from Lake George on a day that Dolly Parton jumped in for a swim?

Neither Wind nor Rain nor Court Battles...

LAKE WORTH, FLORIDA—Some people never give up. John Fleckner, Jr., was a member of the U.S. Postal Service when he had a motorcycle accident and lost his right leg below the knee. The post office ruled that his artificial leg made him medically unsuitable for his job as a letter carrier. But Fleckner filed a lawsuit and persisted in court battles until he won his job back.

Fleckner said he could do the job as well as before he lost his leg. And he said his artificial leg gave him an advantage over other letter carriers.

"I have only a fifty percent chance of getting a dog bite."

Speaking of Dog Bites

SPRINGFIELD, MASSACHUSETTS—Frank Bacon retired after thirty-four years as a mailman. And he claimed to hold the record for being bitten by dogs: twenty-three times.

On Bacon's last day at work his supervisors came up with a cute publicity picture. They had Bacon hold three adorable puppies in his arms.

One of them bit him.

XVIII Show Biz

Round and Round It Goes

LOS ANGELES, CALIFORNIA—The movie and TV series *Fame* was based on the New York High School for Performing Arts (now known as the La Guardia High School of Music and the Arts), but it was filmed in Los Angeles, which didn't have such a school. But in 1985, L.A. opened the brand new Los Angeles County High School for the Arts, and hundreds of teenagers auditioned, hoping to be chosen as students.

One of the first students to apply had recently moved to California from New York.

Casting Call

HENDERSON, KENTUCKY—It seemed like a great idea. Members of the Friends of Audubon, Inc. wanted to put on a play as part of the celebration of the anniversary of the 200th birthday of John James Audubon. They advertised for an actor with special abilities, a clean-shaven man with long blond hair, muscular build, and a French accent. He would also have to be able to draw birds, of course, and play the violin or flute, ride a horse, and shoot a muzzle-loading rifle.

On audition day they looked over the candidates. First in line was an unemployed carpenter. Next came a rock musician. Then an actor who said he was afraid of horses, but a pony might be all right. And the last person to audition was a man who hesitated when asked about his acting background.

"Well, I was a sheep in a school play."

Don't call us, we'll call you.

Just for the Heck of It

LONDON, ENGLAND—One day a group of actors, in between roles, decided to proclaim National Hello Day. They were curious to find out how many people would return a hello from a stranger.

The actors said most people answered, even though the friendly strangers were a bit out of place on the busy London streets that spring day. There were twenty-two Santa Clauses, four Eskimos, five aliens from outer space and one penguin. And King Charles II.

Famous Fuzz

NEW YORK CITY—The National Hairdressers and Cosmetologists Association recently voted for the ten men with America's all-time greatest beards and mustaches.

Clark Gable topped the list, followed by Groucho Marx and Tom Selleck. Others included Buffalo Bill, Teddy Roosevelt, baseball pitcher Rollie Fingers, Oliver Hardy, Jesse Jackson, Mark Twain, and wrestler Hulk Hogan.

One panel member said, "Actually, Hulk Hogan's mustache isn't all that great. But we couldn't find anyone who wanted to tell him."

Those Lips

HOLLYWOOD, CALIFORNIA—Who has the best lips in the movies? Ask S. Clay Campbell. He began collecting pucker prints many years ago as a movie studio makeup artist. Campbell would apply the lipstick and then make a careful impression so he could duplicate the exact makeup for the following day's scenes.

He began saving the lip samples and listed some of his favorites. "The best lips of all," he said, "belonged to Donna Reed, Marlene Dietrich, and Rita Hayworth. But Hayworth's were the most intoxicating.

Ann Sheridan's were the most glamorous, Janet Blair's the most petulant, Olivia De Havilland's the most angelic, and Claire Trevor's the most inviting."

Campbell's collection became quite famous. Spread by word of mouth, of course.

A Nearly Great Pretender

HOLLYWOOD, CALIFORNIA—Actor John Mackey looked the part, so he got the role as Prince Charles. A Hollywood publicity agent dreamed up the stunt to take advantage of the interest in Prince Charles's marriage to Lady Di.

Mackey needed a little help from a makeup man who put putty behind his ears, and he had to stand on his tiptoes to appear taller than the actress who played the part of Lady Di.

But the stunt didn't return much of a princely sum, so Mackey bowed out. He said he would go back to his old job as a look alike for Stan Laurel, which might turn out to be another fine mess.

It's a Good Start

PITTSBURGH, PENNSYLVANIA—The Pittsburgh Laboratory Theatre put out a special casting call for Tom Stoppard's comedy, *The Real Inspector Hound*, a satire of Agatha Christie type mysteries. The director needed a "guest corpse" for each performance, a man twenty-five to forty, who had to wear a suit and lie on his stomach for an hour and a half while the actors performed.

The cast was professional, but the guest corpse could be filled by an amateur. Director Bill Roylston said he got more calls from people who wanted to be guest corpses than from ticket buyers.

Some people are dying to get into show business.

Now This

HAMBURG, WEST GERMANY—A TV news anchorman ended his news broadcast one night by saying, "All lies." But a spokesman at the station said later that it was merely a misunderstanding, and a reference to the length of time of the program's final film clip. "He (the anchorman) didn't know his microphone was still on," the spokesman said. And he insisted that's the way it really was.

Sure.

And This

LAGOS, NIGERIA—A news anchorman at a government-owned TV station here stopped reading in the middle of a news story, threw the script down, and said, "I'm fed up with this false information. I quit. I can't continue with this stuff."

And then he walked out of the studio.

And that's the way that was.

Write Right

ST. LOUIS, MISSOURI—If you have a kid who scribbles a lot, it's best to encourage it, according to Stevie Hoffman, an education expert at the University of Missouri. During a recent symposium, she said that "scribbles are the first step toward good writing."

Unless your kid is in high school, of course.

No More Kumquats

ADA, OKLAHOMA—There was quite a crowd one afternoon on the campus of East Central State College. It was a protest against the kumquat. Students handed out leaflets, held banners and signs, and shouted anti-kumquat slogans. A spokesman for the group made a speech, showing irrefutable evidence that the artichoke is obviously superior to the kumquat.

Later, the student organizers met with reporters and admitted that the whole thing had been a hoax to prove that campus demonstrations can be formed against almost anything.

They said they really weren't bitter toward kumquats.

Where Unwanted Maps Go

JACKSON, MISSISSIPPI—The National Geographic Society had some leftover maps on its hands, and rather than throw them away, they gave them away to the state Department of Education. The maps—of the Southeastern United States—were then distributed to schools and tacked up on classroom walls.

"The maps are a valuable tool for teachers and students. It puts lessons into perspective," said Nancy Brown, a spokeswoman for the education department. "There are all types of ways to use them. Even for creative gazing."

And the kids can get a better view of the state they're in.

A New One

ATHENS, GEORGIA—Students of all ages often use the old excuse: "The dog ate my homework." But Christine Swartout, a student at the University of Georgia, told her professor she was forty minutes late for class because a dog with three legs had held her hostage inside her home. She claimed that she was just leaving her campus apartment when she saw a very mean, three-legged dog in front of her door snarling at her. She called campus security, and they dispatched a dog-catcher to Swartout's apartment, but the beast had left.

Some doggone story.

A Textbook Case

MAZOMANIE, WISCONSIN—Jim Newton's fourth-grade class was learning all about a math problem from a new textbook. The question was: If you have four square blocks, how many different ways can you arrange them on a flat surface? The answer, according to the book, was four.

Wrong, said several students, and they proved it with a fifth way. The same students also found at least three typographical errors in the textbook. They wrote a letter to the Macmillan Publishing Company, which wrote back thanking the students and promising to correct the errors.

Kids.

Drive Carefully

CARROLLTON, TEXAS—Student drivers are often edgy, but the students at the Classic Driving School in this town may be more nervous than the average new driver. They learn to drive in a brand new Porsche.

The owners of the school have three 1986 models, each one equipped with a Student Driver sign. It costs $310 to take the course, only slightly more expensive, the owners say, than other driving schools. And there's not a scratch on any of the cars.

No one wants to be the first nervous wreck.

Dress Code 101

PATERSON, NEW JERSEY—Officials of the school district imposed a dress code on teachers, enforcing a new rule that male teachers cannot take off their jackets and loosen their ties unless the outside temperature hits eighty degrees.

Most of the schools are not air conditioned, so the teachers are really hot under the collar.

Writing as Punishment

SYRACUSE, NEW YORK—Many people have memories of those good old school days, writing on the blackboard, "I will not talk in class" five hundred times. But the National Education Association of New York took a dim view of that as a punishment for students. Members adopted a nonbinding resolution banning such punishment on grounds that it takes the fun out of words and inhibits desired attitudes and essential communication skills.

Union spokeswoman Linda Rosenblatt said she had heard of one student who had to write his name two thousand times simply because he had forgotten to put his name on a homework assignment.

Some English teachers said if the resolution is

adopted, they will retaliate by making certain students do math problems or build bookshelves.

The resolution carried no enforcement power.

The resolution carried no enforcement power.

The resolution carried no enforcement power.

XX A Mixed Bag

The Ultimate Gadget

HARODSBURG, KENTUCKY—Just when you think there are no other gadgets to think up, someone comes up with a new one. Two brothers, Dalton and Connie Hendren, conceived and designed a device they called the Octopus, a battery-powered gizmo for people who need more hands.

The device was a combination AM-FM radio, flash camera, flashlight, alarm clock with a dual time-zone indicator and stop watch, and a storage compartment to hold keys and small change.

Great for consolidating things. But what do you put it in to carry it?

A Showcase

PITTSBURGH, PENNSYLVANIA—A four-day exposition opened recently to showcase new inventions along with their inventors. Organizers of the event said it was the first convention ever to combine private inventors and large corporations.

Everything went well at the convention. But many delegates were reluctant to answer the question, "What's new?"

Some Things Are Certain

HIBBING, MINNESOTA—Many people hold down two jobs to make ends meet. But Jim Steele is unique. He's the town's deputy tax assessor and also a grave digger.

"I'll see everyone in town," he said, "sooner or later."

We hope it's later.

It May Rain. But It Might Not

LOS ANGELES, CALIFORNIA—If you get annoyed about weather predictions that fall short of the mark, you may want to consider what the other side has to say.

"Laymen think," said meteorologist Chuck Conway, "that with all these satellites and computers we should be right one hundred percent of the time. But the fact is, we've oversold the technology." Conway said that scientific equipment is merely a tool to increase accuracy. "The accuracy of short-range forecasts is up from zero percent forty years ago to as high as eighty percent today," he added.

Forecaster Dion Hamilton said, "Sometimes we just can't tell what the weather will do. I can be right or I can be wrong. Either way, I get paid."

It's plain that the rain can be a pain if it's not predicted.

Oh, There's Plenty of Time

BERKLEY, CALIFORNIA—Psychologists Jane Burka and Lenora Yuen studied procrastination and organized a treatment program to help college students who get into trouble because they put things off. Their study was comprehensive and revealing, and they were invited to present their conclusions to an annual meeting of the American Psychological Association in Los Angeles.

Unfortunately, Burka and Yuen failed to complete their presentation in time to meet the APA deadline for accepting papers.

This took place, by the way, in September of 1981. But we never got around to reporting it until December.

There's No Place Like an Auction

NEW YORK CITY—Remember the scene in *The Wizard of Oz* where the good witch magically put ruby slippers on Dorothy's feet so she could go back home? MGM had nearly a dozen of those slippers made, but one pair believed to have been the only ones that Judy Garland wore for close-up scenes was auctioned off at Christie's East.

The bidding was fast and furious and included an anonymous bidder on the West Coast who bid via telephone, and that person won.

The final price was twelve thousand dollars, in toto.

The New Kid

BURLINGTON, VERMONT—Bernard Sanders came out of city hall and found a parking ticket on his car. He had parked in the mayor's parking space. But Sanders *was* the mayor.

"I've been in office only six months," he said. "Guess I'm still not an insider."

Perhaps he never talked much about being mayor. You know how reticent those New Englanders are.

A Promise Is a Promise

SHORT HILLS, NEW JERSEY—Mike LaMorgese usually came up with unusual Christmas presents for the whole family each year, but by the time his daughter Kristin was fifteen, he had run out of ideas. He asked her what she would like to have this time and she said, "A white Christmas."

"You've got it," LaMorgese said, even though the weather forecasts seemed to indicate otherwise. It was almost Christmas, and the skies were still clear, but LaMorgese said, "Don't worry. I'll think of something."

Then he called a ski resort in Monticello, New York, and rented a snowmaking machine, which he had shipped to his home and set up in his backyard just in time for Christmas.

The snow machine started making snow on Christmas Eve, the day it started to snow.

Mother Nature just needed a little reminder.

Don't Worry and Deposit Another Quarter

WASHINGTON, D.C.—In most major cities you can pick up the telephone and dial for virtually any product or service ranging from a pizza to a steak dinner, the weather, jokes, prayers, and even counseling.

Telephone psychologists are everywhere. In New York you can dial Shrink Link; in Los Angeles it's Dial-a-Shrink; and in Minneapolis it's Tele-Psych Inc. But David Mills, the ethics director of the American Psychological Association, doesn't approve of counseling over the phone. One phone shrink said many clients are male executives who just don't have time to visit an office for counseling. Mills said, "Our ethics code is that psychotherapy is best done in a personal visit."

In other words, don't take any phony advice.

A Family Reunion

PEKING, CHINA—Members of the Rong family were important as industrialists until the late 1940s, when Chinese leaders ruled that the private development of industry was wrong. So many of the Rong clan moved to Canada, West Germany, and the United States. But not long ago Rongs all over the world were invited to return to China for a family reunion.

About two hundred Rongs made the rite.

So That's Where They Are

ROBERTA, GEORGIA—Remember bronzed baby shoes? Virtually everyone had a pair on the mantelpiece. But, like all fads, it faded in popularity. And you can imagine Doug Spillers' surprise when he was cleaning out a house and found three hundred pairs of bronzed baby shoes. The house had been the center of the Bronze-Rite Baby Shoe Studio for about twenty years, but the studio went out of business when the owner died.

Spillers said he found work-order tags attached to most of the shoes, indicating that the shoes came from all over the Southeast. He said he hoped to find at least some of the owners, but he had his doubts.

That man has a lot of soul.

Something Different

SOUTHHAMPTON, ENGLAND—Ian McGregor said he had found the perfect Christmas gift, the ultimate executive toy. He had sixteen of them for sale, sixteen slightly used Sherman tanks.

"All in good condition," he said, "and complete with instructions." He offered them for sale at a little over eleven thousand dollars. But there were a few disadvantages. Tanks aren't allowed on British roads, and they're not exactly great on mileage at one mile per gallon.

But it's perfect for the person who has everything. Something to guard it with.

Strike

MADRID, SPAIN—It was a grim time when there were no *olés* in Spain because of a strike by bullfighters' assistants. The matadors had the responsibility of hiring their own assistants, who demanded a twenty-percent raise. But the matadors said they just didn't have the extra money.

Everyone was on the horns of a dilemma.

The Real American West

WASHINGTON, D.C.—What's your image of a cowboy? Most likely he's a handsome guy with light brown or blond hair, muscular build, voice like an angel when he sings. He has a colorful wardrobe and carries a huge pistol in a holster hanging from his belt and always gets the girl. Right? Wrong.

That's merely a popular and romanticized view of the American cowboy of the late 1800s. When the Library of Congress opened a new exhibit to show us what the cowboy was really like, it was quite a revelation. The genuine cowpoke was usually young, single, Southern, quite poor, and often black or Hispanic. His clothes included a cheap wool hat and a pullover shirt with no pockets. And he never carried a gun and never sang. The work was hard, under miserable conditions.

And he used lots of discouraging words.

About Your Sense of Humor

PEORIA, ILLINOIS—For twenty years Michael Zinman sold Caterpillar Tractor Company equipment, and for twenty years wondered why the firm showed no sign of a sense of humor. One day Zinman created the Raterpillar Tractor Company, thinking it would tickle their funnybones. They were not amused. They threatened to file a lawsuit charging Zinman with infringement of their trademark.

Things were eventually resolved after the giant firm of Caterpillar agreed to pay five hundred dollars to take over the smaller firm of Raterpillar.

Richard Stober, a spokesman for Caterpillar's trademark division, said, "It's an insignificant matter. A trivial matter. It deserves no further attention. And it deserves no further time on our part. We are not going to make any further comment."

Did it upset them? Naw.

Semantics

TAMPICO, ILLINOIS—Folks in this town are proud to say a famous person was born here. The key word, though, is *here*. What does it mean, precisely?

Helen and Paul Nicely know. They own the two-story brick building where, on February 6, 1911, during a blizzard, Ronald Reagan was born.

Now, we checked an advertisement in *Yankee* magazine, a New England monthly, and read: "President Reagan's birthplace, Tampico, Ill., two-story brick building, formerly a bank, downtown corner lot, $40,000."

Mr. and Mrs. Nicely were nice about it when a woman from Tennessee showed up and said she wanted to buy their building. "It's not for sale," they told the woman. She insisted it was, and showed them the ad.

The ad was traced to real estate developer Joseph Leach of Glasgow, Kentucky, who owned a two-story brick building across Main Street and a half block down from the building where the president was born. Leach said he told all callers that the word "birthplace" referred to the town of Tampico, and not to any specific building. "I wasn't trying to deceive anyone," he said. "I just didn't know how to word that ad. At six dollars a word, you haven't got time to tell a long story."

Well, that's his story.

Musical Floors

SEATTLE, WASHINGTON—Have you ever walked into a shopping mall parking lot or a garage and wondered where you had left your car? At the Seattle First National Bank garage building it's easy to remember. Each parking level has its own theme song, a recorded tune playing outside the elevator.

One floor is Tony Bennett's "I Left My Heart in San

Francisco." Another is "New York, New York" sung by Liza Minnelli.

The Standard Parking Corporation has one other musical garage, the Transportation Center in Chicago, where one floor's theme is Frank Sinatra's "My Kind of Town."

And if you can't remember the words, just fake it and hum a few bars.

The Parade Passes Quickly

BOULDER, COLORADO—Many cities have parades on St. Patrick's Day, but this town is unique. It's a tradition that began in 1978. Their parade route is only fifty-two feet. Floats, clowns, bagpipers, and motorcycle escorts line up and march toward J. J. McCabe's Bar, where the celebration really begins.

Even Royalty Needs a Little Extra

LONDON, ENGLAND—Prince Charles, next in line to the British throne, has an income of about a million dollars a year from his real estate holdings. He had always taken half and given half to the state. But shortly after his marriage to Lady Di he increased his share to three-quarters.

A spokesman at Buckingham Palace said it was because the Prince's expenses had gone up with an additional residence and more servants.

And, of course, when the prince and the princess dine out, there must be a tip in the heir.

XXI Practical Jokes

It's About Time

TOLEDO, OHIO—Ninth-grade general science students at Libbey High listened attentively as their teacher, Dave Bourland, told them they would be required to send their watches and calendars to the state capital for conversion when the United States switched to the metric time system.

No one said anything, but there were a few murmurs and gasps, so Bourland continued.

"The system," he said, "would mean that clock faces would have to be changed to all tens, hours would have one hundred minutes, and there would be ten hours of daylight and ten months in a year." The only sounds were feet scuffing the floor, a notebook snapping open, a pencil clattering to the floor.

"Only ten months in the year," Bourland said, "means that summer vacation would be reduced to twenty days, and those of you born in July and August would have your birthdays canceled."

Bourland had been ready for questions—lots of questions—and even a challenge from at least one or two students. He said he had come up with the plan to instill a spirit of scientific skepticism in his students. But he was shocked and dismayed that no one questioned it.

"Not one student," he said, "sat down with a pencil and tried to figure it out. No one came up with the fact that it would not have worked. They said later that some questions had crossed their minds, but they didn't ask. And if they had, I would not have been able to answer."

Bourland said this is a problem that teachers everywhere face. "Students don't think. That's the biggest thing that educators are fighting against."

The students weren't the only ones who bought the concept. Some parents called the school to ask when metric time would start.

A few days later Bourland told his class it had been a hoax. The students said they liked the whole thing, that they had actually learned something from it.

The students should have been skeptics. Bourland once told another class that people didn't have the ability to see colors until color TV was invented.

Good Night, David

ESSEX, CONNECTICUT—David Brinkley of ABC-TV may not want to remember his visit once to a quaint New England inn, the Griswold. He had been looking forward to a few days off, resting and relaxing in the solitude, the peace and quiet.

When he signed in, he was informed that he would have to pay in advance, and the desk clerk seemed to be speaking louder than necessary. In the dining room that evening he was seated at a secluded table surrounded by potted palms, and a person who weighed nearly three hundred pounds shouted at him all through dinner, asking for his order.

Brinkley was unaware of a letter that one of his colleagues had sent to the owner of the inn, saying that "Mr. Brinkley is quite deaf and very sensitive about it. So sensitive, in fact, that he prefers to have people shout at him at all times." The letter also said that "Mr. Brinkley has been known to withhold tips from those who serve him because of his inability to hear. He is also fond of setting up gambling games, and many establishments prefer to try to keep him from mingling freely with the other guests."

Two off-duty state troopers—pretending to be waiters—were assigned to keep an eye on Brinkley, and the three-hundred-pound person who yelled at him during dinner was a teacher of the deaf.

Brinkley was also served watered-down drinks and then, as the letter had suggested, locked in his room at night with a guard posted outside.

There was one casualty. One of the troopers, inexperienced as a waiter, spilled soup on Brinkley's suit, and the innkeeper agreed to pay for a new one.

As Brinkley was ready to leave, the owner of the inn began to suspect that it had all been a joke, and told Brinkley about the letter. Brinkley, reportedly, laughed more than anyone else. He also said he knew the person who had written the letter and said that he (the prankster) had a great sense of humor. That person most likely has spent all the days following his little prank, looking over his shoulder, wondering what might happen. And when.

A Long-standing Run

SALT LAKE CITY, UTAH—Fred Finlinson and Richard Carling, both state senators, liked to jog together. And one day while the senate was in session, two state troopers walked onto the floor and arrested them for jogging, on grounds that they were "public nuisances."

Someone read a resolution, backing up the arrest. "Joggers create a safety hazard, as motorists passing by are dangerously distracted and horrified by the sight of nearly naked bodies flailing wildly down the road."

The two senators began to suspect a practical joke, and they were correct. But the reading of the resolution continued. "If Carling and Finlinson continue in this dangerous practice, the legislature will not hesitate to hold them up to public disdain and ridicule by displaying photographs of them taken from behind while jogging around the capitol."

An observer was heard muttering, "Is this any way to run a state government?"

And Finally

TV anchormen and anchorwomen seldom—if ever—write their own news broadcasts. But when you hear a radio network anchor, you're listening to someone who has written everything that he or she is reading on the air. Of course, it's not supposed to really sound as if it's someone reading. A true professional broadcaster will be talking just to you, communicating in a friendly, warm, personal style rather than aloof announcing.

All written copy that's broadcast must go through the editor's desk for a final check for accuracy before it gets on the air. And since we deal in the bad news, all the doom and disaster, twenty-four hours a day, seven days a week, we often include—in addition to the "Kickers"—what's known as a "Gotcha" story to catch the editor. These stories never get on the air. They're meant to take the sting out of the day's bad news, a chance to laugh, even though we're constantly surrounded by news of wars, riots, greed, disasters, pollution, et al.

One such story was based on fact, a man who claimed to have successfully crossbred a cat and a dog. The offspring was a strange looking critter that he called a "pupkit."

I wrote the story and added this fictitious line: "The man was astonished to see the pupkit chase itself up a tree."

My editor raised his eyebrows at that line.

Another story involved a legitimate report about a flood in North Dakota. But I embellished it a bit.

"A dramatic event this morning. Wilbur Zarf, a musician, floated to safety on his piano. He was accompanied by his brother, George, on bass."

Another raised eyebrow from my editor.

There was a survey in London showing that the sales of chocolate had dropped to their lowest level in five years. And again I added a bit of whimsy.

". . . The survey also shows that card playing is declining in popularity, particularly bridge. So you might say that London bridge is falling down."

My editor's eyebrows raised even higher.

A well-known bird-watcher, Fred Evenden, once made a study of birds living on the grounds of the White House and concluded that the bird population had dropped significantly over the years. Evenden said he had spotted only nine different types of birds, including starlings, sparrows, and robins. Among the unusual types of birds he found, I wrote, were a fish-crow, a red-bellied woodpecker, (and here I added my own fictitious birds) a morning peewee, a cross-eyed blearypatch, and a bleary-eyed crosspatch.

This time there was no reaction. The editor didn't bat an eye.

And I damn near read it on the air. Sometimes editors play Gotcha with their anchors.

And if you'll pardon one final fling of things whimsical:

Officials at the London Zoo reported a gnu had been born in captivity, the first gnu born there in several years.

And that's the latest gnus. Stay tuned for the weather.

About the Author

■ ■ ■

JOHN BOHANNON, born in North Carolina in 1936, has been a professional broadcaster for thirty years, mostly in New York City. He has been a network radio correspondent, reporter, and anchorman for ABC and CBS, and he is now heard regularly on the NBC Radio Network.

He writes his own news broadcasts, and his articles and humor have been published in *Grump*, the *Newsday Sunday Magazine*, the New York *Daily News Sunday Magazine*, *TV Guide*, and *McCall's*.

When he is not broadcasting or writing, he works as a professional magician and is a former president of the New York City chapter of the Society of American Magicians, an office once held by Houdini. He is now chairman of the S.A.M. Occult Investigation Committee, a post also held by Houdini and more recently by magician-author Milbourne Christopher, who wrote *Houdini: The Untold Story*.

Some of his previous jobs: maker of hand-rolled cigars; picture framer; Hollywood bed manufacturer; salesman in a shoe store; disc jockey; newspaper columnist; actor; and Monback—a truck driver's helper, the guy who stands on the curb behind the truck and says, "Mon back."

His wife, Barbara, is a Ph.D. in mathematics, an assistant professor at Hofstra University on Long Island. His son, Adam, is a computer expert, crazy nuts about the News York Mets and the New York Rangers, and several inches taller than his old man. And a helluva good kid.

John Bohannon is the only book author extant who has never been photographed by Jill Krementz, and he has always been suspicious of anyone who uses the word extant.

'**What are you** [ ] **murmured in So**[ ] **her; she hadn't rea**[ ]

'"Playing at", my lord?[ ] [ ]. What can you mean?'

'You know very well what I mean. You manoeuvred Miss Malthouse to sit beside me at supper; it was so obvious I wondered others did not notice it.'

'Now, how could I, a mere slip of a girl, manoeuvre you, of all people? And why *would* I?'

'I do not know, but it was unkind of you. I had to endure her idle chatter throughout supper, and afterwards while we walked. Listening to her is exhausting. I am persuaded you must have some motive.'

'My lord, I have been accused of being a hoyden and a flirt, and Cassie is convinced that I am trying to put her out with you. I had to make her see otherwise.'

'And you wouldn't be doing anything of the sort, of course?'

'Certainly not. I should be wasting my time, would I not? Have you not declared you are not looking for a second wife?'

'Indeed I have.'

'And I am not prepared to be one, so let us be friends.'

He laughed. 'Oh, Sophie, if anyone could make me change my mind it would be you.'

Born in Singapore, **Mary Nichols** came to England when she was three, and has spent most of her life in different parts of East Anglia. She has been a radiographer, a school secretary, an information officer and an industrial editor, as well as a writer of some sixty novels and a biography. She has three grown-up children, four grandchildren and three great-grandchildren.

**Visit the author profile page
at millsandboon.co.uk for more titles**

THE HUSBAND SEASON

Mary Nichols

Published in Great Britain 2015
by Mills & Boon, an imprint of Harlequin (UK) Limited,
Eton House, 18-24 Paradise Road, Richmond, Surrey, TW9 1SR

© 2015 Mary Nichols

ISBN: 978-0-263-24778-7

Printed and bound in Spain
by CPI, Barcelona

THE HUSBAND
SEASON

Chapter One

1819

Miss Sophie Cavenhurst was not renowned for her patience or tact. Nor, come to that, for her common sense. This lack was balanced by a comely face and figure, a soft heart and a sunny disposition. Young gentlemen frequently proposed and were as frequently turned down. 'You see,' she would say with a smile meant to soften the blow, 'it just would not do.' Which, according to her fond papa, showed she had more sense than she was generally credited with.

The trouble was that Sophie measured all prospective husbands against the husbands of her two older sisters, and her swains had always been found wanting. Mark, Lord Wyndham, who was Jane's husband, was gentle and kind and dependable; Isabel's husband, the recently knighted Sir Andrew Ashton, was dashing and exciting and was always taking Isabel off to foreign climes to have adventures. They were both wealthy, though their wealth came to them in very different ways: Mark's through inheritance, Drew's through international trade. None of the suitors who had asked for her hand in marriage came anywhere near them.

One thing she did not want was a scapegrace like her brother, though she loved him dearly. It had taken a really bad shock and a spell in India for him to come to his senses. To give him his due he had saved the family bacon when it looked as though they would lose everything, including their home, and for that she would forgive him almost anything, even the way he teased her.

'Sophie, you have exhausted all the eligibles in the neighbourhood,' he told her one day in April. 'You are fast earning a reputation for being hard to please.'

'What is wrong with that? Marriage is a big decision. I don't want to make a mistake like Issie very nearly did.'

'And as a consequence will likely end up an old maid.'

'That's why I want a Season in London. I would meet new people there.'

'A Season?' he asked in surprise. 'When did you think of that?'

She could not tell him she was afraid she was falling in love with Mark and that simply would not do. She had decided that the best cure was to leave Hadlea for a time and try to find a husband to equal him. What better way than a Season in London? 'I have been thinking about it for a long time,' she said. 'Lucy Martindale is having one this year and she talks of nothing else.' The Martindales had an estate ten miles from Hadlea and Sophie had known Lucinda since they were at school together. They corresponded frequently and often visited each other.

'I can quite see you would not want to be left behind, but what does our esteemed father say to the idea?'

'I haven't asked him yet.'

'I doubt you will persuade him to take you. You know how coach travel always makes Mama ill, and he would not leave her behind.'

'I know that,' she said with a sigh. 'But if Papa won't take me, you will, won't you?'

'Good heavens! Whatever gave you that notion?'

'Well, who else will?'

'Ask Jane.' No one in the family seemed to have given up the habit of saying, 'ask Jane,' whenever a problem raised its head.

'Jane is too wrapped up with her baby to leave him, you know that, and Issie is on the high seas somewhere. If you agree to take me, then Papa can have no objection, can he?'

'Ask him first.'

She found her father in the morning room reading the newspaper, sent down every day from London. He liked to keep abreast of the news, though very little of it was good. There was unrest everywhere, especially in the industrial north, and frequent demonstrations for parliamentary reform, not to mention the unpopularity of the Prince Regent and rumours that he was about to divorce his wife, from whom he was separated. Such a thing was unheard of and set a very bad example to the populace. There was a rumour that, since the death of his daughter and her baby, he was anxious to marry again and produce a legitimate heir. His brothers, none of who had legitimate heirs but plenty of illegitimate ones, were all hastily trying to marry and have children. So far only the Duke of Kent had made any progress in that direction; his duchess was *enceinte*.

He laid the paper aside when his youngest daughter tripped into the room, all winning smiles. 'Papa, dear Papa,' she wheedled, 'I have a request to make.'

He smiled. 'And I have no doubt it will cost me money.'

She squatted down on a footstool near him. 'Yes, I suppose it must, but I know you would not like to disappoint me.'

'Go on,' he said patiently.

'I should like a Season in London.'

'A Season,' he repeated. 'I expected to be asked for a new gown or some such frippery, but a Season! Where did you get that idea?'

'All young ladies of any standing have come-out Seasons. It is how they find husbands. You would not wish me to be an old maid, would you?'

'I doubt there is any fear of that.'

'It is what Teddy said. He said there were no eligibles left hereabouts, so I must look farther afield. He will take me, if you cannot.'

'I would not lay such a burden on his shoulders, Sophie.'

'Then, will you and Mama take me?'

'Sophie, there is no question of you having a Season this year or any other,' he said. 'We are not so well up in society as to aspire to such heights. It would cost a prodigious amount of money, which I am afraid cannot be spared. Neither of your sisters had a Season…'

'But they did go and stay with Aunt Emmeline in Mount Street.'

'Sophie, they stayed with her for two weeks, and the purpose of the visit was not a come-out as you know very well. They both found their husbands without recourse to balls and assemblies and tea parties.'

'Yes, but where am I to find another Mark or Drew if I don't go where I might meet them?'

'Mark and Andrew are estimable young men, but why would you want a husband like them?'

The reason was her secret, so she simply said, 'They are my ideal.'

He laughed. 'Sophie, you will find the right man for you, all in good time. There is no hurry. You are but nineteen years old. Indeed, too much haste could very well end in disaster.'

'So you will not let me go?'

'I am afraid not. Now leave me to my newspaper.'

Drooping with disappointment, she left him to find her mother. Lady Cavenhurst was in the garden cutting daffodils from the hundreds that grew there. Sophie poured her woes into her mother's ears. 'You will persuade him, won't you, dearest Mama? You know how important the right connections are to a young lady. There is no hope that I will find a suitable husband in a backwater like Hadlea.'

Her ladyship continued to cut the flowers and lay them in a trug on her arm. 'Why this sudden urge to be married, Sophie?'

'It is not sudden. I have been thinking about it ever since Jane and Issie were wed and I felt I should make a push to find a husband like Mark or Drew.'

'You have set your sights very high, child.'

'Why not? Is that a fault?'

'No, dear, of course not.'

'So will you speak to Papa? Aunt Emmeline would have me, would she not?'

'Your aunt Emmeline is old, Sophie. I doubt she goes out and about very much nowadays.'

'Teddy said he will escort me, so you will speak to Papa?'

Her mother sighed. 'I will talk to him, but if he has made up his mind there will be no shifting him and I will not press him.'

'Thank you, Mama.'

Having obtained that concession, which would have to do for the time being, Sophie went back indoors. If the answer was still no, she would have to marshal further arguments. She hurried to her room, put on a bonnet and shawl and set off to call on her sister at Broadacres.

Broadacres was a magnificent estate about three miles' distant from Greystone Manor. It was not as old as the manor, but much grander. A long drive led to a carriage sweep and a truly magnificent facade with dozens of long windows. Cantilevered steps led to a massive oak door. The vestibule had a chequered marble floor and a grand staircase. She was admitted by a footman. 'Her ladyship is probably in the nursery,' he said. 'Shall I go tell her you are here?'

'No, I will go find her.'

Sophie was perfectly familiar with the layout of the house and soon found her way up to the nursery suite, where her sister was playing on the floor with her ten-month-old son, Harry. She scrambled to her feet when Sophie entered. 'Sophie, what brings you here? There is nothing wrong at home, I hope.'

'No, everyone is well. Can't I visit my sister when I feel like it?'

'Of course, anytime. You know that.' She rescued Harry from a cupboard he had crawled into to investigate. 'I was thinking of wheeling Harry out for a little fresh air. Shall you come, too?'

'Yes, I should like that.'

Instructions were given to the nursemaid to put warm clothes on the infant and bring him down to the back hall where his baby carriage was kept.

'Now, tell me what goes on at Greystone,' Jane said as they went to her room for her to put on outdoor shoes, a shawl and bonnet.

'Nothing. It is as boring as ever. I want to go to London. I asked Papa for a Season.'

'And you think that might relieve your boredom?'

'Well, it would, wouldn't it? And I might find a husband.'

'So you might. You might find one here in Norfolk, too.'

'Teddy says I have exhausted all the eligibles from here.'

Jane laughed. 'How many proposals have you had?'

'Well, there was Mr Richard Fanshawe, who

is as ill mannered as anyone could possibly be and stormed off in a huff when I rejected him. Then Sir Reginald Swayle, who affects to be a dandy but only succeeds in looking ridiculous, and Lord Gorange, who is positively ancient and has two motherless children. I wonder at Papa even allowing him to speak to me. I can't marry anyone like that, can I?'

'I can see your point. What did Papa say about a Season?' Jane had finished putting on her shoes and was looking in the mirror to tie the ribbons of her bonnet, and her remarks came to Sophie through her reflection.

'He said no.'

They left the room and went downstairs to where the nursemaid waited with Harry, who was sitting in his carriage beaming at everyone. 'He will soon be walking,' Jane said as she wheeled him out of doors and down a path that led into the surrounding park and gardens. 'He can already pull himself up on the furniture. And I heard him say *papa* the other day when Mark came into the nursery. Mark is a doting father, you know.'

'Yes, I do know, and you are a doting mama. I declare that nursemaid has too little to do.'

'I love being with my son, Sophie, and would be with him all day, but I do have duties which require me to be from him, and then Tilly has plenty to do.'

Sophie knew one of her sister's abiding passions beside her husband, child and home was the orphanage she had set up in nearby Witherington. She often spent time there herself, helping with the children. 'You would not leave him to come to London for a while?'

'No, Sophie, I would not. Is that the reason you are here today—to persuade me to take you?'

'I guessed you would not. Teddy would take me, but Papa says he is not up to the responsibility.'

'Papa has a point.'

'I don't know why you are all so against Teddy. Since he came back from India, he has been the model of decorum.'

Jane laughed. 'Hardly that. He seems to have dissipated most of the money he had left after he saved Greystone.'

'At any rate, he has done nothing untoward, and if we stayed with Aunt Emmeline…'

'You have worked it all out, haven't you? What do you want me to do?'

'Persuade Papa that Teddy can be trusted to look after me. Mama said she will do what she can, but if you spoke to Papa, too, it would help.'

'Why this sudden urge to go to London?'

'It is not sudden. I have been thinking of it ever since you and Issie first went, but there were always reasons why I could not. First there was that business over Lord Bolsover, and then the court was in mourning for Princess Charlotte and her baby, and last year old Queen Charlotte died, but I cannot see why I shouldn't go this year. I have never been to London. You have been several times and Issie has been all over the world. It just is not fair. I shall end up an old maid.'

'Oh, Sophie, that is highly unlikely,' Jane said, laughing. 'There are not many young ladies can boast of having turned down three offers at your age.'

'But not from the right man.'

'So, tell me, what would the right man be like? Bear in mind perfection is unattainable.'

'I don't want to him be perfect, that would be boring, but he must love me and I must love him, just as you and Mark love each other.'

'That goes without saying, but what will make you love him, do you think?'

'He must be tall and handsome and have a fine figure…'

'That, too, goes without saying.'

Sophie was well aware that her sister was teasing her, but carried on. 'He must be kind and generous and dependable.'

'Admirable traits. I commend your good sense.'

'But on the other hand, I should like him to

be exciting, to make my heart beat faster, to take me by surprise sometimes…'

'Surprises can sometimes not be pleasurable.'

'I meant pleasant surprises, of course. You are not taking me seriously, Jane.'

'I am, indeed I am. But you might well find that when you do fall in love, he will be none of those things or perhaps only some of them. Falling in love is not something you can order, like a new bonnet or a new pair of shoes, it just happens.'

'I know that, but it is never going to happen in Hadlea, is it?'

'It did to me.'

'Yes, but there is only one Mark.'

'I know that.' Jane smiled. 'You are quite set on this, I can see. I will ask Mark's opinion and if he says he can see no harm in it, then I will speak to Papa.'

'Oh, you are the best of sisters. Thank you, thank you.'

Confident of success, Sophie turned to other subjects: gossip and clothes, Harry's newly acquired accomplishments, the latest doings of the children at the Hadlea Home and speculation on where Isabel might be and how long before they would see her again.

'The last letter I had from her was written in India, but she and Drew were about to leave for

Singapore,' Jane said. 'Have you heard anything
more recent?'

'No, Mama received a similar letter. According to Teddy, Drew has his eye on trade with
the Orient and will very likely buy another ship.
If he and Issie were to come home by the time
the Season begins, they might sponsor me.' A
statement that proved her come-out was never
very far from her thoughts. 'But I cannot de-
pend upon it.'

'No, better not.'

They turned back the way they had come,
Harry was returned to his nursemaid and Jane
ordered tea to be brought to the drawing room.
'Mark has gone to Norwich,' she said to explain the absence of her husband. 'I had hoped
he would be back by now, but his business must
be taking longer than he thought. I will speak
to him, Sophie, I promise you, but do not expect miracles.'

Half an hour later Sophie set off for home
with a light step.

Two days later, Mark and Jane brought Harry
to visit his grandparents. There was nothing unusual in this; they were frequent visitors, but Sophie immediately assumed they had come on her
behalf and joined them in the drawing room. 'I
am so glad to see you,' she said, taking Harry
from his mother and sitting down with him.

'Naturally, we all are,' her mother said. 'But I suspect your enthusiasm has something to do with this idea for having a Season. Am I right?'

'I thought Jane might help.'

Lady Cavenhurst turned to her eldest daughter. 'Were you planning to go to London for the Season, Jane?'

'No, Mama, I would not leave Harry or the Hadlea Home for so long, but I gather Teddy has agreed to escort Sophie.'

'I don't know how she managed to talk him into it,' her ladyship said. 'It is not something I would have expected of him.'

'Why not?' Sophie asked.

'He might find the responsibility tedious. Besides, he is too young. You need someone mature enough to be aware of how a young lady should behave in society and to look out for all the pitfalls that might attend her, of being unknowingly lured into a situation that might reflect badly on her reputation, for instance.'

'I know that and can look out for myself,' Sophie insisted. 'And I am sure Teddy knows it, too. Besides, Aunt Emmeline will chaperone me and see I meet the right people, won't she?'

'What do you think, Jane?' their mother asked.

Jane was thoughtful. 'I really don't know. Have you spoken to Teddy about it?'

'He has said he will do it, but of course there is the cost of a come-out.'

'Money is not a problem.' Mark spoke for the first time. 'I will happily sponsor Sophie, but only if you and Sir Edward agree that she may go.'

'Oh, Mark,' Sophie said, eyes shining. 'Would you really?'

'Yes, if your parents say you may.'

'That is more than generous of you, Mark,' her ladyship said. 'I suggest you find my husband and see what he says. You will find him in the library. Tell him I have ordered refreshments and would like him to join us.'

Mark rose and left them.

'Oh, I can't wait,' Sophie said, hugging the child on her lap. He squirmed to be put down and she set him on the floor and he crawled rapidly to his mother, who picked him up.

'It is not a foregone conclusion,' Jane said. 'There is Aunt Emmeline to consider. She may not be well enough to have you. I recall when we were there she tired easily and she is so very deaf. If she agrees to have you, you must be very mindful of that.'

A maid brought in the tea tray and set it down on a table at her ladyship's elbow. She left the room as Sir Edward came in followed by Mark and Teddy, who was in riding coat and buckskin breeches, having just returned from a ride.

'Excuse me, Mama,' Teddy said. 'I'll go up and change. I won't be long.'

'Well?' Sophie asked of her father. 'May I go?'

He sighed as he sat on the sofa next to his wife. 'It seems you have marshalled your forces very well, child. I have been outmanoeuvred.'

'You mean, you agree?' She jumped up and went over to put her arms about him and kiss his cheek. 'Oh, thank you, thank you, Papa.'

He gently disengaged her. 'It is Mark you should thank. He tells me he has to go to London on business next month and will take you and Teddy in his carriage and see you safely to Lady Cartrose's house. After that it will be up to your aunt and your brother to see you come to no harm.'

She turned to Mark. 'Oh, you are the kindest, most generous of brothers-in-law. If I could find a husband like you, I should be well content.'

'Sophie!' admonished her ladyship.

Mark laughed to cover his embarrassment. 'You will find the right man for you,' he said. 'Do not be too impatient.'

Teddy came back into the room, dressed more fittingly for a drawing room in a single-breasted tailcoat and light-coloured pantaloon trousers. 'Is it decided?' he asked, looking round the company.

'Yes,' his father said. 'Provided you know what is expected of you.'

He found a seat and accepted a cup of tea from his mother. 'Look after my little sister and see she don't get into any mischief.'

'Precisely. And keep out of mischief yourself. No gambling.'

'What, none at all? That's a bit hard on a fellow, ain't it?'

'In a social situation, it is permissible,' his father said. 'With counters or low stakes, and only if Sophie is being chaperoned by her aunt at the time. But no gambling hells.'

'Of course, that is what I meant.'

'Then, if Lady Cartrose agrees, you may take your sister to London at the convenience of Mark. Bessie will go with you.' Bessie Sadler was her mother's maid. She had been with the family many years, but was close to retirement and had been training a young successor. Apart from the family, no one knew Sophie better than she did and she would spot trouble before Aunt Emmeline or Teddy.

Sophie, always effusive, be it through happiness or misery, jumped up and ran to everyone to thank them. She was so happy, she had them all smiling, too. After that, they moved on to how the Hadlea Home for orphans was growing and, as always, was in need of more funds. It was one of Jane's main tasks to secure those. Mark, with his standing and influential connections, was a great help to her in that and it was the reason he was going to town. He was in the course of arranging a concert to raise funds, an idea borrowed from the Foundling Hospital where they had been doing it for years.

Lady Cavenhurst wrote to Lady Cartrose and a reply soon arrived, saying her ladyship would be delighted to have Teddy and Sophie to stay. She did not often go out and about herself, but would undertake to introduce Sophie to friends who might invite her to join them for outings, if that would suffice. Sophie agreed that it would and her ladyship's offer was accepted.

It was a month before they were to go and Sophie passed the time impatiently dreaming of what she would do, the outings and balls she would attend, the beaux she would meet and planning what she would take in the way of clothes. She was not short of garments, but when she came to review her wardrobe was cast down to think nothing was good enough for a come-out Season when it was absolutely essential she look her best at all times. Her day dresses were perfectly adequate for Norfolk but, in her view, useless for town and would do nothing but let the *ton* know that she was a country bumpkin. She did have one very fine gown that she had worn at Jane and Issie's double wedding and an afternoon dress of blue crepe decorated with pale-blue-and-white embroidery that she had worn for Harry's christening, but that was all. It was nowhere near enough.

Fortunately her sister came to her rescue before she could summon the courage to approach her papa with yet another request. 'Mark is so generous,' Jane told her one day when Sophie had walked over to Broadacres to bemoan the lack. 'He is constantly encouraging me to buy new clothes. I have a wardrobe full of garments I shall never wear again. We can alter some to fit you and bring them right up to date.'

This was the next best thing to having a new wardrobe and they were soon busy with scissors, needle and thread, lace, ribbons and silk flowers. Jane was an expert needlewoman, and as one gown after another was transformed, Sophie lost her regret that she was not to have a completely new wardrobe. No one could possibly know they were not made especially for her and in the latest styles, too. Shoes, boots and slippers would have to be bought because Jane's feet were larger than Sophie's, but Sir Edward, thankful that his expenses would be no more than providing her with a little pin money, agreed to pay for those.

'I have a little present for you,' Jane said as if a wardrobe fit for a queen were not enough. 'Wear this with your blue gown.' She handed Sophie a small box. It contained a silver necklace studded with sapphires and diamonds. 'It is just the right colour for it.'

'Jane! It's lovely, but should you really be giving it to me if Mark bought it for you?'

'It was his idea, Sophie. When he saw the material I was working on, he said it would be just the thing. I have so much jewellery I can easily spare it.'

Sophie flung her arms around her sister. 'Oh, that is so like Mark. Tell him thank you from me. I shall be the belle of the ball, thanks to you both.'

'I hope you may but, Sophie, I must caution you to behave with decorum while you are with Aunt Emmeline. Too much pride will not help your cause. On the other hand, do not be too submissive. Remember you are a Cavenhurst.'

'Oh, I will, dearest Jane.'

It was a very happy Sophie who said goodbye to her parents and Jane one morning at the end of May and climbed into Mark's travelling coach. She was on her way at last. The only disappointing thing was the weather. It had turned bitterly cold and she had perforce to wear a warm coat over her new carriage dress and a fur muff to keep her hands warm, while her feet were set upon a hot brick wrapped in flannel.

The journey took two full days, but as the carriage was a very comfortable one and new horses had been ordered for the frequent stops along the way, where Mark also procured more hot bricks, the time passed agreeably.

They arrived in London in the evening of the second day, having spent the previous night at the Cross Keys in Saffron Walden. There were flags flying from all the public buildings and from some private houses, too, in honour of the birth of a princess to the Duchess of Kent on the twenty-fourth of May. In Sophie's view that augured well for her visit. The city would be *en fête*. Mark sent his coachman on to his town house in South Audley Street and accompanied them into Lady Cartrose's Mount Street home.

Her ladyship, rounder than ever and deafer than ever, greeted them warmly. 'Welcome, child,' she said, taking both Sophie's hands and holding her at arm's length to regard her from top to toe. 'My, you are a pretty one. We shall have no trouble firing you off.'

Sophie giggled. 'That sounds painful.'

She was obliged to repeat what she had said twice more before it was heard, and by then the repartee had lost its wit.

Emmeline turned to Teddy and subjected him to the same scrutiny. 'I cannot remember the last time I saw you, young man. It must have been at your sisters' weddings. What a happy occasion that was, to be sure. You are not affianced yet?'

'No, Aunt.'

'We shall have to see what we can do. I have many friends with beautiful daughters.'

'I am not in town to find a bride, but to escort my sister,' Teddy said, shouting into her ear.

'Pshaw.' She turned to Mark. 'My lord, you are very welcome. How is my dear Jane? And little Harry? One day perhaps I shall have the pleasure of making his acquaintance. You will stay for supper, won't you? Then you can tell me all about him.'

Mark declined supper, but agreed to take tea and spent most of the time answering her ladyship's questions about Jane and their son. Sophie was impatient to know what they would be doing while she was in London and, in a break in the conversation, ventured, 'What have you planned for tomorrow, Aunt Emmeline?'

'I thought you might be a little tired after your journey, so have arranged nothing of import,' her aunt replied. 'A carriage ride in Hyde Park in the afternoon if you should care for it, provided it is not too cold, and supper at home.'

Sophie, who had expected a round of social engagements to begin as soon as she arrived, was cast down by this. It sounded as boring as being at home. Mark smiled at her. 'Never mind, Sophie, you will be all the more ready to spring yourself upon the London scene the day after when you are fully rested. I have no doubt you will take the capital by storm.'

'Storm,' her ladyship repeated. 'Oh, do not say there is to be a storm. We cannot go out in wet weather, it brings on my rheumatism.'

Mark patiently explained to the lady what he had meant while Teddy and Sophie tried not to laugh.

'Oh, I understand,' the old lady said. 'I did not perfectly hear you. To be sure Sophie will shine. My friend Mrs Malthouse has a daughter of Sophie's age. Cassandra is a dear, sweet girl and is coming out this year, too. I am sure you will be great friends. She is to have a come-out ball later in the Season and I have no doubt you will be invited. In the meantime there is to be a dancing party at the Rowlands' next week, which is a suitable occasion for a young lady not yet out to practise her steps and no doubt Augusta will procure an invitation for you if I ask her.'

This sounded more like it, and Sophie thanked her aunt prettily and began mentally deciding what she would wear.

At this point, having agreed to dine with them the following evening, Mark took his leave, and as the evening was yet young, Teddy decided he would go out. Left to the company of her aunt and Margaret Lister, her aunt's companion, Sophie decided to write to her parents and Jane, as she had promised, to tell them of her safe arrival. After that she went to bed to dream of the pleasures to come.

* * *

A few years before, the arrival of Adam Trent, Viscount Kimberley, in town would have caused a stir among the young single ladies of society and some married ones, too. He had been reputed to be the most handsome, the most well set-up young man to grace the clubs and drawing rooms of the capital for many a year. His arrival had sent all the debutantes' mamas into a twitter of anxiety and rivalry and their daughters sighing after him and dreaming of being the one finally to catch him.

'Twenty-eight and still single. How have you managed to resist wedlock so long?' his cousin Mark had asked him.

'Easily. I have never met the woman I would want to spend the rest of my days with and, besides, I'm too busy.' At that time he had recently inherited his father's title and estate at Saddleworth in Yorkshire, which had undoubtedly enhanced his attraction.

Then he had done the unpardonable thing in the eyes of the *ton* and married Anne Bamford, the daughter of a Saddleworth mill owner. Whether it was a love match or done to enhance his own wealth no one could be sure, but after that no one had much to say for him, thinking of him only as the one that got away.

His father-in-law had died soon after the wedding, leaving him in possession of Bamford Mill, and in the following year tragically his wife had died in childbirth along with his baby son, and he was once again single. To try to overcome his loss, he had thrown himself into his work, both at the mill and on his estate, which was considerable. He was rarely seen in London.

On this evening, he was striding down South Audley Street towards Piccadilly when he encountered his cousin. 'Mark, by all that's wonderful! Fancy meeting you.'

Mark, who had been negotiating a muddy puddle, looked up at the sound of his name. 'Adam, good heavens! What are you doing in town?'

'Urgent business or I would not have bothered.'

'I was sorry to hear of your wife's passing.'

'Yes, a very sad time. The only way I could go on was to throw myself into work.' This was a gross understatement of how he had felt, but he was not one to display emotion. It was easier to pretend he did not feel at all.

'All work and no play is not good, you know. And you are no longer in mourning.'

'Mourning is not something you can put a time limit on, Mark.'

'No, of course not, clumsy of me. I beg your pardon.'

'Granted. I was on my way to White's. Do you care to join me?'

Mark agreed and they were soon seated over supper in that well-known establishment. 'How is married life?' Adam asked his cousin. 'I am sorry I could not attend your wedding, but at the time I had only recently taken over the running of Bamford Mill and there was a great deal of resentment that had to be overcome. There was, and is, much unrest and I needed to persuade my people not to join the Blanketeers' march.'

The march to London from the industrial north, which had been organised by the Lancashire weavers two years before, had been for the purpose of petitioning the Prince Regent over the desperate state of the textile industry and to protest over the suspension of the Habeas Corpus Act, which meant any so-called troublemakers could be imprisoned without charge. They had carried blankets, not only as a sign of their trade, but because they expected to be several days on the march. It had been broken up by the militia and its leaders imprisoned. None of the marchers had reached his goal and the petition was never presented.

'Did you succeed?'

'Unfortunately, no. I am afraid nothing will really satisfy them but having a say in their own destiny. I fear some dreadful calamity if they are not listened to.'

'Surely not your people? You have the reputation of being a benign employer.'

'I do my best, but that will not stop some of the hotheads persuading the rest that to stand apart will bring down retribution on their heads.'

'What can you do to prevent it?'

'I don't know. I pay them more than the usual wage for the work they do and provide them with a good dinner, but that has brought censure from my peers that I am setting a bad example and will ruin all our businesses. I am in a cleft stick, but hoping to avert trouble by other means.'

'Militia?'

'No, that is a last resort. Innocent people are apt to get hurt when soldiers are let loose. I intend to speak in the Lords in the hope that the government will listen to reason and grant at least some of their demands.'

'Do you think they will?'

'I doubt it, but I must try. If I can rally enough men of good sense on my side, I might achieve something. Times are changing, Mark, and we must change, too, or go under. Ever since I inherited the mill, I have tried to put myself in the shoes of my workers. I have cut the hours of work of the children by half and have set aside a room as a schoolroom and employed a teacher, so the other half of their day is gainfully employed getting an education. Even that does not always go down well—some parents accuse me of giving their children ideas above their station. I answered that by trying to educate the adults, too. It incensed the other mill owners who fear giving the workers an education will make them even more rebellious.'

'I would have thought that a man who can read and write would be a better and more efficient worker because of it.'

'My argument exactly. Everyone should be able to better themselves.' He paused. 'But I believe you have been doing something similar.'

'Ours is a home for orphans, but we have a schoolroom, too, and good teachers. It is my wife's project more than mine, but I help out when I can. We started with only a handful of children, but there are so many of them now and more in need, we have to expand. I am in town to hire an architect for the project and to try to drum up more funds. Everything has become so dear, it is hard work to keep it all afloat.'

'You are not wanting in the necessary, surely? I understood Broadacres to be a thriving estate.'

'So it is, but Jane is determined to make the Hadlea Home stand on its own, and I indulge her wishes and help out in a roundabout way. Besides, it is incumbent on me to keep the estate prosperous for my son's sake and laying out blunt for the orphans, which seems never-ending, will not help to achieve that.'

'You are a father now, I collect.'

'Yes, Harry is ten months old and the darling of his mother's eye.'

'And yours, too, I've no doubt. I lost my child, you know.'

'Yes, I did know and I am sorry for you, but you will marry again and there will be other children.'

'I doubt it. There can only be one Anne.'

'That is true. We are all unique in our own way, loving and loved for different reasons. It doesn't preclude a second wife.'

'When she died, so painfully and so cruelly, I swore not to let it happen again.' He paused, unwilling to dwell on his loss, which no one who had not experienced it could possibly understand, and wondering how to change the subject. 'Shall we have a hand or two of whist?'

'Not tonight, cousin. I brought my wife's sister to London to stay with her aunt in Mount Street and have not yet been home to Wyndham House. The servants will be expecting me. Where do you stay?'

'At Grillon's. I have never felt the need of a town house when I am so rarely in town.'

'Then stay at Wyndham House. You may come and go as you please while there.'

To have congenial company and a more-than-respectable address while doing what he had come to town to do would serve him very well, Adam decided. 'Thank you. I shall be pleased to do so,' he said.

They left the club, Mark to go home and alert

his servants that a guest was expected and Adam to go to Grillon's, settle his account and arrange for his manservant, Alfred Farley, to take his luggage to Wyndham House.

Chapter Two

Sophie woke the next day to find the sun was shining, though it was still cold. Bessie was busy about the room, finding warm clothes for her to wear. 'Such weather for May,' she said. 'You would think it was winter, not the beginning of summer. Do you think you will be able to go out today?'

'Yes, I am determined on it. If Aunt Emmeline cries off, I shall ask Teddy to take me. I did not come to London to sit about indoors.'

On Bessie's insistence she put on a fine wool gown in a soft blue that was warmer than the figured muslin she had hoped to wear and went down to the breakfast room, where she ate a boiled egg with some bread and butter and drank a dish of hot chocolate in solitary splendour. Lady Cartrose was never an early riser, and when Sophie enquired of a servant if Mr Cavenhurst was up and about, she was told that

he had not come back to the house until nearly
dawn and was still abed. She was obliged to
shift for herself.

After breakfast she wandered about the downstairs rooms getting in the way of the servants
who were busy with housework that had to be
done before their mistress put in an appearance.
This inactivity was making her impatient and
cross and she went up to her room to don a full-
length pelisse, a velvet bonnet, walking shoes
and a muff and went out into the garden. It was
not a very big garden and she had soon seen all
she wanted of it. The wider world beckoned.

There was a small gate at the end of the garden that led to the mews where her ladyship's
horses and carriage were kept and her groom
lived. She walked past the stables and presently
came out on to Park Lane. It was still early in
the day, but the road was already very busy. Carriages and carts rumbled by, riders trotted towards the gate into the Park, walkers hurried
about their business and children made their way
to school accompanied by nursemaids. Three
soldiers, colourful in their red jackets, gave her a
lascivious look as they passed her on the way to
their barracks. One even went so far as to sweep
off his hat and bow to her. Haughtily, she put her
chin in the air to pass him, and that was her un-
doing. She slipped on a patch of ice on a puddle

and found herself flat on her back with her skirts up to her knees, displaying a well-turned ankle and several inches of shapely calf.

They immediately rushed to her aid. Despite her protests that she was unhurt and could rise unaided, one of them came behind her, bent to put his arms about her under her shoulders and heaved her to her feet.

She stood shaking, not so much with hurt or shock, but indignation that he could have man-handled her in such a way and seemed in no hurry to relinquish his hold of her. 'Let me go,' she said.

'But you will fall again if you are not sup-ported.'

'Indeed, I will not. I am perfectly able to stand. I insist you release me.'

They might have let her go, but her hau-teur made them want to have a game with her. 'There's gratitude for you,' one of them said. 'Did your mother never teach you manners?'

She did not answer, but repeated, 'Let me go. I shall call the constable.'

'Constable? I see no constable, do you, Jamie?'

'Never a one,' his companion concurred, pick-ing up her bonnet from the road where it had fallen, putting it on his own head and prancing about in it. They had attracted quite a crowd, none of whom seemed inclined to interfere. Most were laughing.

'You do realise that your fall broke the ice and your fine coat is wet and dirty. What will your mama say to that, I wonder?' This from the one who held her firmly in his grasp.

She was well aware of the state of her coat; the cold and damp were penetrating through to her body. 'Let me go, you great oaf.' She struggled ineffectually to free herself. It only made him hold her more firmly.

'Dear, dear, such language, but I take no offence at it, though I fear that if I let go, you would take another tumble and then, as you disdain my assistance, I should feel obliged to leave you sitting in the puddle. On the other hand, if you were to ask me prettily and give me a kiss as a reward, that might be a different matter.'

'Certainly not.' Her pride had given way to fear, though she endeavoured not to show it. No one had warned her of the perils of going out without an escort, or if they had, she had not listened, confident of being able to take care of herself. In Hadlea she thought nothing of walking about the village on her own, and no one would have dreamed of molesting her. The onlookers did nothing to help, being too busy laughing at the soldier who was wearing her bonnet and curtsying to them, pretending to hold out imaginary skirts.

She was fighting back angry tears when a gentleman pushed his way through and grabbed the soldier who held her and flung him aside. 'Off with you, or your commanding officer will hear of this.'

Recognising the voice of authority when they heard it, they flung her bonnet down and fled, leaving Sophie to fall into the arms of her rescuer. He held her a moment to steady her before releasing her. His face had a weather-worn look of someone used to being out of doors and there were fine lines at the corners of his brown eyes, above which were well-defined brows. His hair, under a tall hat, was light brown and curled a little into the nape of his neck. He was stylishly but not extravagantly dressed, but none of that counted with her because he was endeavouring not to laugh, and that annoyed her. She felt obliged to thank him, but it was done in such a superior way, he could have no reason to think his assistance was any more than her due as a lady.

He picked up her bonnet and attempted to brush the mud off it, but it was ruined, and he simply handed it to her. 'Have you far to go?'

'Only to Mount Street.'

'I will escort you there.'

'That will not be necessary. I bid you good day.' She walked away, her only purpose at that moment to return to the safety of her aunt's garden and make up her mind how to explain the state of her clothing.

* * *

Thankfully her aunt and brother were still abed, so she was able to creep up to her room unseen. Bessie was there, unpacking the things from her trunk that had not been taken out the night before. 'Mercy me, Miss Sophie, whatever happened to you?' she asked, seeing the state of her young charge.

'I slipped on the ice and fell into a puddle.'

'Are you hurt?'

'No, except my pride.'

'You had better take off those wet things before you catch cold.' Bessie bustled about fetching clean clothes for her. 'Where did this happen?'

'On the way to the park. I had seen all there was to see of the garden, so I thought I would take a walk.'

'Miss Sophie,' Bessie said while busy helping Sophie out of her clothes, 'you cannot, indeed you must not, go out on your own.' The maid had been with the family so long, she felt at liberty to speak her mind to the young lady she had known since the day she was born. 'This is London, not Hadlea. Anything could have happened. Did anyone see you?'

'Only the people walking in the street, but I soon got up again and came home.'

'No harm done, I suppose, but you should

have come indoors and asked me to go with you, if there was no one else.'

'I didn't think of it. I have never had to do it before.'

'Isn't that just what I have been saying? What is permissible in Hadlea is not permissible or wise in London.'

'You won't tell my aunt, will you? It is too mortifying.'

'No, of course I will not, but you must not do anything like it again. You could have twisted your ankle or broken your arm. It is fortunate that you did not.'

'It was more humiliating than painful.' Just how humiliating she was not prepared to divulge.

Her aunt came downstairs at noon to find her niece in the morning parlour with a novel by Miss Jane Austen in her lap, although she was not reading it but daydreaming. Not even Miss Austen's elegant prose could hold her attention. She had never expected to be so bored. It was worse than being in Hadlea, where at least she could go out walking or riding or visit her sister.

'When we have had nuncheon, we will go out in the carriage,' her aunt said. 'I must go to the library and change my book.' She nodded towards the volume Sophie was holding. 'Unless you want to read it.'

'No, Aunt, I have already read it.'

'Then to the library we will go and then we will call on my friend Mrs Malthouse in Hanover Square. Mr and Mrs Malthouse are very wealthy, but it makes no matter for I have often spoken of you and dear Jane and Issie and their husbands and how well up in the stirrups they are, so you do not need to feel in any way inferior.'

Sophie did not see why she should feel inferior and was tempted to say, 'I do not', but held her tongue.

Mrs Malthouse was even rounder than Aunt Emmeline, but in spite of that wore fussy clothes with a great many lace flounces and ribbons. Her daughter, Cassandra, was nothing like her mother, being tall and slim, with dark brown hair arranged in ringlets and a merry smile.

'You remember me speaking of my sister's family, do you not?' Lady Cartrose explained to her friend. 'Sophie is staying with me, but as you know, I seldom venture out in the evenings nowadays. Her brother is also with us and will escort her to whatever function has been arranged for her to attend. Everyone knows I do not go out so very often these days and I am wanting in invitations. I am come to appeal to you to help me out. I know Cassandra is engaged to attend the Rowlands' dancing party and wondered if you might ask them to include Sophie in the invitation.'

Sophie disliked the way her aunt was begging on her behalf and would as lief forgo the dance as to be invited out of charity. 'Aunt, we should not put Mrs Malthouse to the inconvenience,' she said. 'Doubtless there will be other invitations.'

'It is a public subscription dance,' Cassandra put in. 'It is only being held at the Rowlands' because they have a large ballroom. You have only to buy a ticket. I think it costs five guineas.'

'That is a prodigious amount,' Emmeline said.

'It is so high as to keep out the undesirables,' Mrs Malthouse put in. 'And because it is to raise money for a suitable gift for the new princess. She is to be christened Alexandrina Victoria, though I believe she is to be known as Princess Victoria.'

'In that case I shall naturally obtain tickets for Teddy and Sophie,' Emmeline said. 'I shall not go.'

'If Sophie is in need of company,' Mrs Malthouse added, 'then she and her brother are welcome to join our party.'

'Thank you, Augusta. I knew you would help,' Emmeline said.

Sophie added her gratitude while wondering who was to pay for the tickets. The pin money she had been given would not stretch to it. Her aunt seemed unconcerned, so perhaps she expected Mark to put his hand in his pocket yet again, but Mark might judge ten guineas for two tickets a monstrous imposition and refuse to pay. It would be a bitter disappointment if she could not go.

'Shall we take a turn in the garden?' Cassandra suggested to Sophie. 'We can leave Mama and Lady Cartrose to their gossip.'

She readily agreed and the two young ladies left the house by the conservatory. The sun had come out and chased off the frost, and the garden was secluded and sheltered. It was pleasant strolling about an immaculately tended garden and talking. 'Have you been to London before?' Cassandra asked her.

'No, never, though my sisters have. They are older than me and both married. Jane is married to Lord Wyndham, and Isabel to Sir Andrew Ashton, who owns a fast clipper and takes her all over the world on it. My brother is in town with me. He is older than Issie and younger than Jane.'

'Yes, I have heard Lady Cartrose talk of your sisters. Your father has a substantial estate in Norfolk, I believe.'

'It is fairly extensive. It is mostly arable land and grazing. I have often heard Papa say the land is very fertile, but I know nothing of agriculture so cannot vouch for it.'

'We don't have a country estate. It is not that we could not afford it, but that Papa's business as a top lawyer in constant demand keeps him in town all the year round and we would hardly ever use it. Sometimes I go and stay with my uncle and aunt in the country, but I miss the entertainments and the shops and meeting my friends, so I am always thankful to come back home.'

'I can quite see that. I should, too, I am sure.'

'You are very pretty and I do admire your dress,' Cassandra said, looking at Sophie's yellow sarcenet gown with its high waist and puffed sleeves, over which she was wearing a matching silk shawl. 'It must have been made by the finest mantua maker.'

'Indeed it was,' Sophie said. 'Just because I live in the country does not mean I am ignorant of fashion, or unable to procure the best.' This was all dreadfully boastful and not exactly accurate, but she couldn't bear to be thought of as a country yokel. Besides, Jane's needlework was up to anything a London mantua maker could produce.

'I am so pleased to hear it, Miss Cavenhurst. I can think of nothing worse than having to stint. We are fortunate not to have to think of it.'

Sophie had only intended to praise Jane's work, but her aunt had already told everyone she was well connected and she felt she could not contradict her, so she let it go. 'If we are to be friends, please call me Sophie.'

'Of course we shall be friends, so Sophie it shall be. You may call me Cassie. Everyone does except Mama and Papa and my grandparents.'

'Cassie, do you have a beau?'

'No, Mama would never tolerate it before I come out, but this year I hope to find a husband. What about you? Do you expect to find one while you are in town?'

'That is the idea of a Season, is it not?'

'Indeed it is. Have you anyone in mind?'

'No one. My brother says I am too particular, but I will not marry just for the sake of it. I have already turned down three offers.'

'Three!' exclaimed Cassandra. 'You cannot mean it.'

'Indeed, I do.'

'Were they all handsome and rich? Did they have titles?'

'One was handsome and tolerably rich, one was a baronet and one a lord, but none combined all the attributes I am looking for. The lord was a widower with two children. I have no wish to be a second wife. I had no difficulty in rejecting them.' She was boasting again, although she had said nothing that was not true and was amused by the expression on Cassandra's face, a mixture of shock and incredulity.

'What manner of man are you looking for?'

'The same as every other young lady, I expect. Handsome, rich and titled, but he must be kind, considerate and care about the things I care about, and he must of all things be wildly in love with me, as I must be with him.'

'You and I think alike, Sophie. Let us hope we are not both vying for the same man, if such a man can be found who is single and looking for a wife.'

'Tell me about the dance.' Sophie felt they had exhausted the topic of future husbands and she was feeling a little guilty over her boastfulness. It was not at all how she felt inside. 'What shall you wear?'

'Mama will not allow colours until after I have my come-out later in the Season, so white it will have to be, but I can have a coloured sash and coloured ribbons in my hair. Which colour would suit me, do you think?'

Sophie stopped walking to turn towards her. 'Green,' she said. 'Definitely green, it will enhance the colour of your eyes. And green slippers, of course.'

Cassandra clapped her hands. 'Yes, I am sure Mama will allow that. What about you? You are very fair and have blue eyes, so perhaps blue for you. Or maybe pink. Do you like pink?'

'It depends on the shade, but I like blue best. I have a lovely blue ball gown in my luggage and a rose-pink gauze evening gown.'

'You mean the whole dress is coloured, not white?'

'I hate white. It may look delightful on you, but it makes me look insipid.'

'Will your aunt allow it?'

'I don't see why not.'

'But you will be defying convention.'

'Pooh to convention.'

Cassandra laughed. 'Oh, I can see you are going to set the *ton* by the ears.'

Sophie joined in the laughter. 'That is the whole idea.' She paused. 'The gowns shall be a secret until the night I wear them, so do not say anything of them to your mama.'

'I won't. Shall we go back indoors? Lady Cartrose will be taking her leave by now.'

They returned to the drawing room to find that Cassandra's brother, Vincent, had arrived and their departure was delayed while Sophie was introduced to him.

He was very like Cassandra in looks, half a head taller than she was and rather too thin to be called handsome. He was dressed in a dark grey coat and lighter grey pantaloons. His neckcloth was extravagantly tied and his shirt points starched to a board. They certainly made him keep his head up. His dark hair was cut short and curled towards his face. He bowed to her and took her hand. 'How do you do, Miss Cavenhurst. I am told that you will be gracing the Rowlands' dance with us. I shall look forward to that.'

She withdrew her hand and smiled at him. 'You are too kind.'

'Come, Sophie,' Emmeline said. 'We have time for a turn around the park before going home. Lord Wyndham is to dine with us, so we shall have a little company this evening.'

They took their leave and, once they were seated in the barouche and trotting along Brook Street towards Park Lane, her aunt asked her what she thought of Cassandra.

'I think we shall deal very well together,' Sophie said, speaking very loudly into her aunt's ear. 'She already thinks of me as her friend.'

'Good. That means you will have a companion for outings when I cannot go with you. What did you think of Vincent?'

'I really did not think of him at all, Aunt. We met so briefly.'

'He is an admirable young man, and though he does not have a title, he will come into a considerable fortune when he inherits. In the meantime he is employed in his father's law firm.'

'If he is anything like Teddy, he doesn't do much work there.' She was obliged to repeat this twice before her aunt comprehended.

'You are unkind to your brother, Sophie. I collect he worked very hard when he was in India, for he made a fortune there, enough to get himself and your papa out of dun country by all accounts.'

'Oh, yes, I will give him that, but as for law work, he hated being behind a desk all day. Now he helps Papa on the estate. Mr Malthouse has no estate.'

'That is true. But Mr Vincent Malthouse is only the first of many young men you will meet in the course of the next few weeks. I am persuaded you will be able to choose whomever you please.'

Sophie was not so sure about that, considering she had so far only been engaged for a subscription dance. She needed more than that. She needed something happening every day and she needed to make an impression at every one of them.

They turned in at the park and followed a parade of carriages passing others going in the opposite direction. Lady Cartrose knew so many people and they were continually stopping for her to gossip and introduce Sophie. Sophie bowed her head and said, 'How do you do?' and answered politely when they enquired if she was enjoying her stay in London, but she doubted she would remember all their names. One rider she would not forget, though he did not stop. He simply rode slowly past them on the other side of the rail, and she concluded he was not known to her aunt, for which she was thankful. She was not sure whether he had seen and recognised her, but turned her head away to talk to Lady Cartrose.

'It is lovely to see the trees bursting into leaf,' she said. 'It makes me think of summer.'

'And let us hope it is better than last summer,' her aunt answered, unaware of Sophie's agitation.

'There,' the old lady said, as they turned out of the gate to go home. 'Everyone knows you are in town now, and if they do not they very soon will.'

Mark arrived at six that evening to dine with them as promised. He was in a cheerful mood and listened attentively to Lady Cartrose's recital of their afternoon. 'There is to be a subscription ball to honour the new princess,' she told him. 'You have no objection to Sophie attending with Mr and Mrs Malthouse and their daughter, Cassandra, have you? They are very respectable people, well up in the *ton*. I know she should not be attending balls before her come-out, but this is not a formal ball and it is in a good cause.'

'My lady, I can have no say in the matter, I am merely a bystander. It is for you and Sophie's brother to say what she may and may not do.'

Lady Cartrose turned to Teddy. 'Edward, what do you think? Shall you allow it?'

'Don't see why not,' he said lazily. 'What's it all about, this ball?'

He had not been attending the conversation, and her ladyship was obliged to repeat what she had said to Mark. 'It will be a very select dancing party,' she explained. 'The tickets are five guineas.'

'Five guineas! Whoever heard of having to pay for an invitation to a dance? Sounds rummy to me.'

'It is to raise money to buy the new royal baby a present,' Sophie explained.

'What does she want a present for? She'll not be short of the dibs.'

'Oh, Teddy, don't be difficult,' Sophie said. 'I want to go. After all, it is why I came to London.'

'To go to subscription dances?'

'You know what I mean. You're not going to deny me, are you?'

'No, sis, we'll go to your dance and I'll buy the tickets. Will that satisfy you?'

The look that Mark shot her brother might have puzzled her if she had noticed it, but as she was turning a beaming smile on her sibling, she did not see it. 'Oh, you are the best of brothers. Thank you. Thank you.'

'Talking of raising money,' Mark said, 'I have been busy today finalising the arrangements for a concert to raise funds for the Hadlea Home extension. I hope you will all attend. It is to be at Wyndham House next Saturday. I have hired some excellent musicians.'

'Do we have to pay to come to that, too?' Teddy asked with a grin.

'Donations are voluntary, of course,' Mark said. 'But since you seem to be in funds, I hope to see a contribution from you.'

This remark was so pointed, Sophie looked from one to the other. 'What is going on?'

'Nothing,' Teddy said. 'I do not always have pockets to let, you know.'

'I know that,' she said. 'I believe Papa gave you some money to top up my pin money should I need it.'

'Quite right,' he said, visibly relieved.

After they finished their meal, the two men did not linger long in the dining room, but joined Sophie and her aunt in the drawing room for tea, where the conversation centred around who might be present at the Rowlands' dance. Mark pointed out that perhaps the elite might not wish to attend an event in which anyone could be present, but he supposed the high price of the tickets would keep out the riff-raff. He hoped the princess's parents appreciated what was being done for their offspring.

'How far down the line is she?' Sophie asked.

'Well, there's the Prince Regent, then his brothers, all six of them,' Mark said. 'The new princess is presently the only legitimate child of any of them, but who is to say that won't change, especially if the prince manages to divorce his wife and produce another child of his own.'

'Who would want to marry him?' Sophie said, with a shudder.

'Almost anyone, I should think,' Teddy said. 'To be Queen of England must surely be a great lure.'

'Well, I shouldn't be lured by it.'

'You are hardly likely to be given the opportunity,' Teddy said. 'You will have to satisfy yourself with a lesser title or perhaps none at all.'

'It is not the title I'm concerned with, but the man.'

'Well said, Sophie.' Mark laughed. 'Now I must take my leave. I have a cousin staying with me at Wyndham House and I have been shamefully neglecting him.' He rose, bowed to Lady Cartrose and thanked her for her hospitality, kissed Sophie's hand and was gone. This seemed to be the signal for Lady Cartrose to retire and left brother and sister to amuse themselves.

'Which cousin can Mark mean?' Sophie asked. 'I collect there were several at his father's funeral and at the wedding. I do not recall their names.'

'No doubt we will find out when we go to the concert.'

'Teddy,' she said, 'am I to rely on a concert that will be boring and attended by old people and dull married couples for some excitement?'

'There is the Rowlands' dance.'

'But that's a whole week away.'

'What do you want me to do about it? I cannot conjure up excitement for you.'

'You can take me riding. I do miss my daily rides in Hadlea. We could go to Hyde Park. That is where everyone goes, is it not?'

'And what do we do for mounts?'

'You can hire them. Jane made me a splendid habit in forest-green grosgrain taffeta and I can't show it off if you will not take me riding, can I? You cannot expect Aunt Emmeline to do so.'

He laughed. 'No, it would break the poor beast's back, even supposing she could be got up on it.'

'Then you will? Tomorrow morning early. You haven't anything more pressing to do, have you?'

'Oh, very well. But I had better go now and see about mounts, otherwise the good ones will be gone and we will be left with the rejects.' He rose to leave her. 'Don't wait up for me.'

Left alone, she picked up her aunt's latest library book, but it was not one that interested her and she decided to go early to bed so as to be up betimes the following morning.

Bessie had been unable to see anything improper about Sophie going riding with her brother and so she woke her early as instructed, bringing her breakfast on a tray. Afterwards she helped her into the riding habit. It had a very full

skirt and a fitted jacket in military style with ep-
aulettes and frogging. A white silk shirt, frilled
at the neck and the wrist, and a black beaver with
a curled brim and a tiny veil completed the en-
semble. 'There, Miss Sophie, you look a picture,'
she said. 'But I hope you will ride sedately and
not attempt to gallop.'

'Oh, no, Bessie. I want to be seen at my best
and that won't happen if I dash off at a gallop,
will it?'

She sat to put on her boots, then picked up her
crop and went downstairs, expecting her brother
to be already there. But he was not. Vexed with
him, she sent a servant to wake him.

He came down half an hour later, dressed for
riding.

'Teddy, you are too bad. I have been waiting
this age and you not even out of your bed.'

He yawned. 'Sorry, sis, overslept.'

'Why? What time did you go to bed?'

'I disremember. Some time after midnight.'

'Well, you are here now. Are you ready to go?'

'Not until I've had some breakfast. You
wouldn't want a fellow to ride on an empty stomach, would you?'

She had to rein in her impatience while he
ate, but she did think of sending a manservant
to the mews to bring the horses round so that
they might set off the minute Teddy had finished eating.

* * *

An hour and a half later than she had intended, they were riding through the gates of the park. It was too early for ladies in carriages, but the Row was full of riders, most of them men, but some were ladies riding with their escorts as she was doing. She was so pleased with life she beamed at everyone, turning now and again to speak excitedly to her brother. 'Oh, this is capital. The sun is shining, the birds are singing and everyone is smiling.'

'Of course everyone is smiling,' he said. 'You cut a very fine figure in that rig, even though I shouldn't say it for making you more conceited than you are already.'

'I am not conceited.'

'Then stop grinning like a Cheshire cat. You are putting me to the blush. A little cool modesty, if you please.'

'Oh, very well.' She assumed a serious expression that was so comical it only served to make him laugh.

They were attracting the amused attention of other riders, one in particular. As they drew abreast, he bowed slightly towards her. She recognised him easily from the upright way he carried himself, the curl of his light brown hair, his brown eyes and strong mouth, twitching a little in amusement. She felt the colour flare in her face, but quickly brought herself under control and put her chin in the air and gathered up her reins to ride at a trot.

'Who was that?' Teddy asked, catching up with her after her unexpected burst of speed. 'Someone you know?'

She slowed down again. 'Who?'

'The fellow on the bay. A magnificent creature.'

'You call him a magnificent creature?'

'The horse, silly, not the man, though I own he looks top of the trees to me. Who is he?'

'I have no idea.'

'But you smiled at him.'

'I certainly did not. Whatever gave you that idea?'

'He smiled back and bowed, as if he knew you. Is that why you wanted to come riding today, so that you might meet him?'

'Certainly not. I have no idea who he is.'

'Oh, I knew all that preening in front of everyone would cause trouble. Strange men smiling and bowing, it is not the thing, Sophie, really it is not.'

'I couldn't help him smiling at me, could I? I didn't ask him to bow.'

'You encouraged him.'

'I did not. Why would I do that? He is conceited if he thought that, and if I ever meet him again I shall make sure he knows it. Not that I wish to meet him again,' she added hastily.

'No, of course not,' he said with heavy irony.

'Well, I don't. Let us go home and see if Aunt Emmeline is up and about. I might prevail upon her to go shopping.'

'Beats me what you ladies find to go shopping for,' he murmured following her as she turned towards the gate. 'You seem to have all the fripperies you need.'

'Much you know about it,' she said. 'But you will find out when you marry and have a wife to please.'

'Then I don't think I'll bother.'

She laughed at that, and they returned to Mount Street in good humour.

Adam, who had recognised her as the girl he had seen with the soldiers, rode on, wondering who she might be. She was unaccompanied by a duenna or a groom, probably out clandestinely, unless her parents or guardians, whoever they were, did not trouble themselves about propriety. She was lovely, and when she smiled or laughed her blue eyes sparkled. Out secretly with her swain and enjoying herself, he did not doubt, but devoid of all sense of decorum.

He had seen her the day before in a carriage with an older woman—a relation or guardian perhaps? Not a very protective one to let her out to be molested by common soldiers. He smiled at the memory; she was a feisty young lady, to be sure, and by no means cowed, even when her clothes were wet and muddy and she had lost her bonnet. He turned out of the gate and made his way back to South Audley Street. He had better put her from his mind; he had more important things to think of than a slip of a girl, however fetching. He had a speech to compose.

The foreman at the mill had warned him that Henry Hunt, known as Orator Hunt, was planning another great rally, but he had no idea where it was to be. He had a great deal of sympathy for the plight of the workers, who subsisted on very low wages that his fellow mill owners had no compunction in cutting when profits went down. Wages for a weaver, which had been as much as fifteen shillings for a six-day week in the boom year immediately after the war, had now dropped to five. Their hardship was not helped by the Corn Laws, which kept the price of wheat, and therefore bread, so high they were hard put to afford it.

Sir John Michaelson, a neighbouring mill owner, was particularly insensitive to his workers, many of whom had left him to come and work at Bamford Mill as soon as they heard he had a vacancy. It did not endear him to his neighbour, who'd come to him in high dudgeon the last time it had happened.

'Look here,' he had said. 'You can't go paying exorbitant wages. It gives the men a false value of their worth and makes them uncontrollable. You're making them soft and undermining the rest of us. A little hunger never did them any harm. Makes 'em work harder.'

'They are not just hungry, they are starving,' Adam had answered, referring to Michaelson's workforce. 'Starving men cannot work well.'

'So you feed 'em, too.'

'If I give my workers a dinner, that is my affair, not yours, Sir John.'

'If we don't stand together, we won't win,' the man said truculently.

'I have no doubt that is what the men are saying,' he had said.

'And you, no doubt, know exactly what they are saying. I am disgusted with you. You are a traitor to your heritage.'

Adam was soon back at Wyndham House and settled down in the library to write his speech. He was not a natural orator like Henry Hunt and had never made a public speech before, except to talk to his workers. He believed in keeping them informed of how the business was doing, telling them when a big contract had come their way and how long they had to fulfil it and congratulating them if they fulfilled it on time, paying them a bonus, as well. They worked the better for it. Now he had to make a speech to his peers, men who probably held the same views as

Sir John and whom he had to persuade. He had covered several sheets of paper, all of which he had screwed up and thrown aside, when Mark came in.

'You look as if you've been busy,' his cousin commented.

'All to no purpose. I can't seem to find the right words.'

'The words you used the other night sounded good to me.'

'Two or three sentences when I have to write a whole speech. And my audience will be less sympathetic than you.'

'Make your speech to me and I will act as devil's advocate.' Mark laughed. 'I will even heckle you, if you like, and see how you deal with it.'

An hour later Adam was feeling a great deal better about the ordeal.

'You are much more convincing when you speak from the heart,' Mark told him. 'You don't need to write out the whole speech. Simple notes will suffice to get you going.'

'Do you think I have a chance of swaying any of them?'

'Those who are undecided, perhaps, but the diehards will be more difficult. You might have more luck in the Commons, if you could find a sympathetic member to take up the cudgels.'

'I know neither of the members for Lancashire will do anything. They are in Sir John's pocket. Two members of parliament for a whole populous county and two for a little place like Dunwich, which has all but disappeared into the German Ocean, is ridiculous. Parliamentary reform is long overdue.'

'I agree, but you will hardly persuade the members for those rotten boroughs to give up their seats.'

'Now, if workingmen could vote, that would be different,' Adam went on. 'And if they could also stand for election, we might have a more equitable means of governing the country.'

Mark laughed. 'And that is what you advocate, is it? I advise you to take one step at a time, coz, if you don't want to sink your whole argument. Now, you have done enough. I am hungry. What do you say to repairing to the club for something to eat? Then I will tell you my plans and you can advise me.'

Chapter Three

Sophie decided she needed some ribbon for the evening gown she intended to wear for Mark's concert. It was a rose-pink gauze worn over a white silk underdress. In her view it was too plain and needed a long ribbon tied in floating ends beneath the bust and to embellish the puffed sleeves. She had suggested as much to Jane when she was altering it, but her sister had said it was fine as it was. On the other hand, she really could not allow herself to be outshone by Cassandra. 'You never know whom I shall meet,' she said to Bessie. 'Mark might contrive to introduce me to eligibles of his acquaintance. I wonder if his cousin will be there. He is staying at Wyndham House, you know.'

'No, I did not know. Do you know the gentleman?'

'I don't know. I might have met him at my sisters' wedding.'

'He cannot have made much of an impression if you cannot remember him.'

'I might if I knew his name, but Mark did not mention it when he told us a cousin was staying with him. I wonder if he is like Mark?'

'So you are adding frippery to impress someone you do not know.'

'Certainly not. I simply want to look my best. Wyndham House is quite grand, you know, and no doubt Mark's friends are top of the trees. I know Cassandra will be showing herself off. I cannot be seen to lag behind.'

'Has Lady Cartrose ordered the carriage this morning?'

'Yes, but not for me. She is going to fulfil a long-standing engagement with some old friends and I am not required to go with her. Goodness knows where Teddy is. You will come with me, won't you? We can walk.'

'Yes, of course I will come.'

As soon as Lady Cartrose had left, Sophie and Bessie set out on foot for Bond Street. It was no longer so cold, but it had rained again and the streets were wet and muddy, and they were obliged to lift their skirts a little and watch carefully where they were putting their feet. Bessie would rather have postponed the outing, but Sophie would not hear of it. 'Don't be so poor-spirited, Bessie,' she said. 'It is not so bad.'

They were walking down the busy shopping

street when a high-perch phaeton sped past them, spraying Sophie, who was walking a little ahead of Bessie, with filthy water. 'Of all the inconsiderate muckworms,' she said, staring after it, fury on every line of her face. 'Now look at my gown. I shall have to go back and change.' She was turning to go back the way they had come when she realised the vehicle had stopped and its driver was descending with the intention of coming back to them.

Bessie pulled on her arm. 'Do not speak to him, I beg of you.'

'Why not? I mean to tell him just what I think of him.'

It was only when he turned towards her and she could see his face that she recognised Sir Reginald Swayle, one of her erstwhile suitors. 'Oh, lord, it's that dandy, Reggie,' she murmured.

He wore a double-breasted long-tailed coat in dark blue superfine, a flamboyantly tied cravat, yellow pantaloon trousers and a tall hat with a narrow brim, which he doffed on approaching her. 'A thousand pardons, Miss Cavenhurst. If I had known it was you, I would have stopped and taken you up.'

'Meaning, I suppose, that if it had been anyone else you would not have stopped at all,' she said. 'Very chivalrous of you, I am sure. It is too bad of you, sir. Driving like a lunatic down these busy streets is the height of folly and inconsiderate of pedestrians.'

'I was not driving like a lunatic. And ladies should know better than to walk down streets wet after rain.'

'Oh, so it is my fault my dress is ruined and instead of going shopping, I am now obliged to return to my aunt's to change.'

'No, I am not blaming you and I have said I am sorry. Allow me take you back to change your dress and then I will take you to buy a new one.'

'That will not be necessary.'

'Oh, but it is. Come, let me help you into my carriage.'

'There is no room for my maid.'

'She can walk.'

'Don't go, Miss Sophie, I beg of you,' Bessie said. 'If we walk quickly, we shall be back in Mount Street in no time.'

'I don't care to walk through the streets looking like a dish mop,' Sophie told her. 'It is not as if Reggie is a stranger.'

'No, indeed,' he said, offering her his arm to escort her to the carriage.

She took it, while addressing Bessie over her shoulder. 'I will see you back at Cartrose House.'

He helped her up into the extraordinary vehicle, climbed up himself and picked up the reins. 'I shall have to go a little farther along the road before I can turn round,' he said. 'But it should not cause more than a few minutes' delay.'

She was sitting almost at first-floor level and had to admit, if only to herself, that it was exciting to be so high, looking down on lesser mortals. 'When did you acquire this monstrous vehicle?' she asked.

'It is not monstrous. It is all the rage and it is fast.'

'So I observed. Too fast for city streets.'

'It cuts quite a dash in the park. I was on my way there. Should you like to try it? I cannot conveniently turn round before we reach Piccadilly and we would be almost at the park before we could turn up Park Lane. I collect your maid mentioned Mount Street.'

Unfamiliar with the side streets of the city, she accepted this explanation. 'I do not think that would be altogether proper,' she said. 'And my dress is all muddy.'

'No one can see it,' he said, turning to look at her. 'The top half is not affected. You look very fetching.'

'Is this a ploy to make me change my mind about turning down your proposal?'

'Would it succeed?'

'No. What are you doing in London? Did you hear that I was here?'

'The doings of the Cavenhursts in Hadlea are an open book, my dear, but I cannot say it was my whole reason for coming. If I cannot have you, then I must settle for second best.'

'Then I pity her. To be second best must be altogether too humiliating. If I were her, I would never agree to it.'

'Oh, she would never know.'

'Do you not think she might guess? I am sure I should.'

'Perhaps it will not become necessary.'

'No, you might fall genuinely in love.'

He laughed and manoeuvred the carriage through the park gates. 'It is as easy to drive along here as it is up Park Lane,' he said. 'We can drive out through the Grosvenor Gate.'

She was becoming slightly alarmed that he might be trying to abduct her, but shook the idea from her thoughts. He was unlikely to do anything so outrageous in Hyde Park, where there were hundreds of people to whom she could appeal. The hundreds of people were the bigger problem. Her aunt had introduced her to so many friends and acquaintances on their carriage ride, she could not remember half of them. Supposing they saw her and recognised her? Sitting so high above everyone else, she could not fail to be seen. She had no chaperone and did not even have the protection of a parasol, for there had been no sun when they set out and she had not needed one. The only thing she could do was brave it out.

'This is the most extraordinary vehicle,' she said, turning towards him so that her face was turned from the occupants of a carriage then passing them. 'I am not sure I feel altogether safe.'

'Oh, it is safe enough in expert hands,' he said. 'Though if a greenhorn were to attempt to drive it, he might come to grief.'

'And you, I collect, are an expert.'

'Yes. Shall I show you?' Instead of turning north to the next gate out into Park Lane, he turned down Rotten Row and set the horse to a trot, exposing them to yet more stares.

'Reggie, I beg of you, don't,' she said, hanging on to the side of the carriage. 'Please turn back and take me home.'

'You are not afraid I shall overturn you, are you? I never knew you to be so chicken-livered. Come, Sophie, where is your spirit of adventure?'

'It is not my spirit that is lacking,' she said. 'I am concerned that we are attracting attention.'

'Admiring glances, what is wrong with that?'

'You know perfectly well what is wrong with that, Reggie. You will quite ruin my reputation if you do not slow down to a sedate walk and turn round. Even then I fear it will not do.'

'There is no room to turn round until we reach the end.' Nevertheless he did slow the horses, though this had the effect of taking them longer to reach a turning point and longer for them to be seen and either admired or criticised. If she could have sank down on to the floor, she would have done. All she could do was pray no one would recognise her. In that she was to be disappointed and by the person she least hoped to see.

He was riding towards them on his bay and on coming level lifted his hat and bowed. He did not speak, but the amusement was evident in his brown eyes. She endeavoured to ignore him.

'Who was that?' Reggie asked as they passed him.

'I have no idea, but it seems every time I go out, I encounter him. He is the most odious man.'

'Top of the trees,' he said. 'I wonder how many cravats he ruined getting that one tied like that.'

'I do not know and care even less.'

'Tell me,' he said changing the subject abruptly, 'are you enjoying your Season? That is why you are in London, is it not?'

'Yes, and I am enjoying it excessively.'

'Ah, then, no doubt you have dozens of hopeful swains vying for your hand.'

'Dozens,' she agreed in the hope it might put him off.

He sighed as they reached a spot where he could turn round without colliding with other carriages. 'So you like being admired and set-

ting off one suitor against another. It is cruel of
you, Sophie.'

'I do not do it on purpose, Reggie.'

'My trouble,' he said regretfully, 'is that you
know me too well. I do not represent the excitement of conquest.'

'Riding in this contraption is excitement
enough, Reggie.'

They rode on in silence until they were once
again in Park Lane and turning down Mount
Street. She was never more thankful to reach
the door of Cartrose House. He jumped down
to help her out and it was then Teddy came out
of the house.

'There you are, Sophie. I was just coming to
look for you. Bessie was in such a taking, nothing would satisfy her but I come out and search
for you.' He noticed Reggie and then the high-
perch phaeton. 'Hallo, Reggie. So this is the vehicle Bessie was so upset about. What is it like
to drive?'

'Easy enough when you know how,' Reggie
answered him. 'You have to be careful not to
take too tight a turn, but it can really go with
the right cattle.'

Sophie left them talking and went indoors,
where Bessie greeted her in floods of tears.
'Where have you been, Miss Sophie? It don't
take but a few minutes to get from Bond Street

to here in a carriage and you've been gone over an hour.'

'Is it that long? Dear me, I had no idea. The high-perch phaeton needs a very wide turning circle, or so I was persuaded, and we had to drive down to Piccadilly and then to Hyde Park corner. And then Reggie decided to drive in the park.' She was mounting the stairs as she spoke, followed by her worried maid.

'Oh, Miss Sophie, how could you be so wanting in conduct as to allow that? Whatever would your mama and papa say?'

'They will never know of it, Bessie. Now I must change. I fear it is too late to go looking for ribbons today. I shall have to go tomorrow.'

'With Lady Cartrose, I hope, for I declare I could not endure another outing like today's.' She busied herself pouring water into the bowl on the nightstand for Sophie to wash her hands and face.

Sophie stripped off her muddy dress and went over to the nightstand. 'Bessie, I have mud on my face!' she exclaimed as she glanced in the mirror that hung above it. 'How mortifying.' Her thoughts went immediately to the strange, yet familiar, rider who'd had amusement written all over his face as he'd bowed to her.

'Yes, but you would go off with Sir Reginald and did not give me time to point it out to you.'

Sophie dipped a cloth in the water and

scrubbed at her cheek while Bessie rooted in the cupboard for a dress for Sophie to wear. 'What about this green muslin?'

'Yes, that will do. And, Bessie, you will not say anything to Lady Cartrose about this morning, will you?'

'You may rely on me, Miss Sophie, but what if you were seen by some of her ladyship's friends? It would not do for her to hear of it from one of those, for they will put the worst complexion on it.'

'You think I should tell her?'

'It would be best, then she will be forewarned and have her answer ready.'

'Is she home?'

'Not yet, for which I am thankful, for if she had been here while you were out, I do not know what I would have said to her. She would most likely have turned me off for allowing it.'

'She can't turn you off, Bessie. She does not employ you—my father does. And in any case, no blame can be attached to you for anything.'

'I am glad you think so.'

Once more respectably dressed, Sophie went down to the drawing room to await the return of her aunt. Teddy was waiting for her, his long legs straddling the arm of the chair in which he sat. He righted himself on her entrance. 'Racketing about on your own is not the thing, Sophie, not the thing at all. And as for accepting rides in high-perch phaetons, that is beyond anything. What can you have been thinking of?'

'I only wanted to get home quickly to change my dress. It was either ride with Reggie or walk through the streets in a soaking wet dress that was clinging to my legs. It would have been too mortifying.'

'That won't fudge, Sophie. If you had had any sense, you would have gone into the nearest dress shop and bought a dress to come home in.'

'I didn't think of that and if I had I couldn't have done it, I did not have enough money on me.'

'You could have put it on account.'

'Whose account? Yours? Aunt Emmeline's? Mark's?'

'It would have done no good naming me, but Aunt Emmeline would have stood buff and certainly Mark would.' He sighed. 'It is too late now. The damage is done. Reggie wanted to buy you a new dress, but I dissuaded him. It would not do, you know, unless you were affianced to him.'

'I am not completely devoid of sense, Teddy, and I am not affianced to him and never will be. You may rest assured I would certainly not accept a gift from him. And if no one saw me in the phaeton, then there is no damage done, is there?'

As she spoke the image of a smiling stranger with warm brown eyes flashed into her mind.

'Let us hope you are right. I have Reggie's word he will not speak of it. When Papa gave you into my care, I had no idea what an onerous task it would be. I beg you, Sophie, try not to get into any more scrapes.'

It was after dinner when Sophie and Lady Cartrose retired to the drawing room for tea that Sophie began diffidently to tell her aunt of the morning's episode. It was a tortuous business, her aunt being so deaf she had to shout what she would rather have whispered in shame, but she got through it at last and waited for her aunt's reaction.

'To be sure I have seen those high-perch phaetons about,' she said. 'They look extremely dangerous to me. It is a wonder you were not upset and killed.'

Sophie had been expecting to have a peel rung over her. This calm acceptance that all that mattered was that she was not hurt took her by surprise. 'You are not angry with me?'

'No, child. I did far worse things when I was your age and it never did me any harm, but it is to be hoped the young gentleman will not boast of it.'

'He has promised Teddy he would not. Teddy

trusts him. They have been friends since their schooldays. That's how I met him.'

'Then, there is no more to be said. Thankfully I have no more engagements to take me out without you, so I will be able to accompany you in future. Tomorrow we will take one or two afternoon calls and we will shop and buy that ribbon you are so set on. We can play a hand or two of whist in the evening. Mr and Mrs Frederick Malthouse usually come to me on a Thursday evening and Margaret makes up a four, but she will forgo it so that you may take her place.'

'But, Aunt, I do not excel at cards,' Sophie protested. 'In fact, I am the world's worst at whist. Teddy is the card player in our family.'

Teddy joined them at this point and heard Sophie's last remark. 'Not me,' he said. 'I have forsworn gambling, as Sophie well knows.'

'I am glad to hear it,' Emmeline said, giving him a beaming smile. 'But a little game among family and friends is perfectly in order. You may join us if Sophie does not care for it.'

He had a cup of tea with them and, hating the idea of spending the whole evening indoors with them struggling to converse, he made his excuses and took his leave. If Sophie wondered where he was off to, she dismissed it as none of her business, and she really had no right to haul him over the coals when her behaviour had hardly been exemplary.

* * *

'Mark, you have been closeted in this room long enough,' Adam said. 'Leave all that paper and come out and have dinner with me at White's.'

'It is this concert,' Mark said. 'You have no idea how much preparation is involved. Musicians, singers, all of them temperamental in their demands, have to be appeased, the programme decided on and the order of all the items arranged so as not to offend any of them. Refreshments and the moving of the furniture must be organised, besides deciding how the donations are to be accepted, on a tray, in a bag, during the interval or at the end. That is, if I have any. If I don't, it will all have been a dreadful waste of time and effort, not to say money, and Jane will be very disappointed.'

'Don't you have a secretary to do that sort of thing?'

'I left him behind at Broadacres. I thought he would be more useful there.'

'There is still a week to go, Mark. You can afford to take one evening off, surely? Who was it said to me, not two days ago, that all work and no play is not good for a man?'

Mark laughed and stood up. 'You are right. Let us go out.'

They could have used Mark's town carriage or hired chairs but decided to walk. The rain had gone, the night was fine and balmy and Mark said he needed some fresh air. 'How have you been amusing yourself?' he asked as they walked.

'I would hardly call it amusement. I have been endeavouring to track down Henry Hunt to find out his intentions but no one will tell me where to find him. I think he is avoiding me.'

'I am not surprised. You represent the enemy, the hated oppressors of the poor.'

'But I do not.'

'They don't know that, do they? I am sure if you were to infiltrate his meetings you would be looked on as an agent provocateur and quickly bundled out of it.'

'You are probably right. I shall have to rely on my speech. Perhaps after that, they will see I am on their side.'

'How is the speech coming along?'

'Slowly. I begin to wonder if I did right to come to London and might have fared better staying in Saddleworth.'

'Well, you are here now, so you might as well enjoy your free time.'

Adam laughed. 'And the same goes for you, cousin.'

'*Touché.*'

They turned into the club and were soon seated in the dining room, giving an order for onion soup, turbot, roast partridges, raised mutton pie, broiled mushrooms and a selection of vegetables. They followed this with sweet pastries, clotted cream and a jelly. Once replete, they adjourned to the card room for a few hands of whist.

They played well together, not too deep but enough to satisfy the two gentlemen who made up the four, one of whom was Sir Reginald Swayle, known to Mark, and the other Captain Mountworthy, of the Hussars, on leave and looking for a little diversion. The captain, not being as well up in the stirrups as the other three, broke the party up a little after midnight, having come to the end of the stake he'd allowed himself. Adam and Mark both said they fancied an early night and rose to go.

They were about to pass two gentlemen who had just arrived when Adam heard his cousin address one of them. 'Teddy, you here?'

'Yes, you cannot expect me to sit listening all evening to Sophie trying to hold a conversation with Aunt Emmeline. I should die of boredom or laugh aloud and disgrace myself.'

Mark turned to Adam. 'Adam, may I introduce my wife's brother, Mr Edward Cavenhurst. Teddy, my cousin, Adam Trent, Viscount Kimberley.'

The two men shook hands, murmured, 'How do you do?' then Teddy, indicating his companion, said, 'Do you know Captain Toby Moore?'

'I do.' Mark's voice was clipped and made Adam turn to him in surprise. There was obviously no love lost between the two men. He shrugged his shoulders and followed his cousin, leaving Teddy and Captain Moore to make their way into the club. They heard Teddy greeting Sir Reginald with great affability as they made their way out of the building.

'A young dandy,' Adam said as they walked on. 'You seemed not pleased to see him.'

'Oh, I like him well enough, but he is too fond of the gaming tables. He is in town to escort his sister, not to indulge his weakness.'

'His sister being the young lady you have recently left in the care of her aunt?'

'Yes.'

'I would have expected her parents to bring her to town.'

'Lady Cavenhurst is a very poor traveller and Sir Edward much wrapped up in his estate, which is only now recovering from a near disaster two years ago—a disaster I might add, partially brought about by that rake shame, Captain Moore. I wonder at Teddy associating with him. I fear I shall have to keep an eye on him while I am here, though what I can do to stop him, I have no idea. Besides, I shall have to go home to Hadlea after the concert.'

'You are not his keeper, Mark, and he is surely of an age to know what he is about.'

'Gambling is an addiction with him, Adam. He has the best of intentions, but they fly away at the least temptation. I wish he had not come to town, but he was the only person who could escort Sophie, and Sophie was determined.' He grinned ruefully. 'When Sophie is determined, there is no gainsaying her. Being the youngest she has always been indulged, not only by her parents but by her brother and older sisters.'

'She sounds like a spoiled filly to me.'

'No, you mistake me. She is a charming young lady, if a little headstrong, which don't signify to the young blades who crowd round her at Hadlea. Whether she will enjoy the same adoration in town, I cannot say. She will be at the concert, so you may be able to judge then.'

'I shall look forward to being introduced to her and making up my own mind,' Adam said.

He was busy in the meantime lobbying for support for the mill workers and the repeal of the Corn Laws, but found very few takers, certainly not among his peers. What he needed was support in the Commons, but even there, the rules for standing for that institution were such that very few of them could claim working-class roots. If only he could prevail upon the likes of Orator Hunt to compromise on their demands, he might have some success, but Hunt seemed to have gone to ground. He had asked Alfred Farley if he could winkle out his whereabouts.

Alfred might be a valet who looked after his clothes and brought him his shaving things of a morning, but he was more than that. He had been serving him since he had found him in a back alley in Seven Dials, half-starved and begging, four years before. Something about the man had made him take pity on him and he had learned he had once been a soldier and had served under Adam's brother, but he had been discharged when he'd taken a piece of shrapnel from a cannonball in his leg. It had healed, but his leg was scarred and he walked with a limp. He was not an ideal valet, but he was a faithful servant and could be relied on in a crisis.

Adam had had to put all that aside in order to attend Mark's concert. He could hardly fail to do so considering the house was in an uproar of preparation and Mark distracted. The house was large, airy and well furnished, if a little old-fashioned, not that such a thing would have put off his guests; the Wyndhams were known and respected in town as well as at Hadlea, and he did not for a moment share Mark's doubts that no one would turn up. All was ready on the night, and after a light repast with Mark at six o'clock, he went up to his room to change.

He had long given up the exaggerated dress

he had adopted in his youth and now favoured simplicity, but it was an elegant simplicity that set off his splendid physique and spoke volumes for his tailor, not to mention Farley, who had learned to make sure his cravats were starched to exactly the right stiffness, enough to maintain their folds, but not enough to cause him discomfort. Tonight he favoured a dark blue tailcoat in superfine that he had been assured was called midnight blue, matching pantaloons and a white brocade waistcoat with silver buttons. Never one to be fussy about his hair, which had a natural curl, he succumbed to Farley brushing it and combing into some semblance of style.

He could hear people arriving as he left his room to go down to the first floor, where he found his cousin standing sentinel at the ballroom door that had been furnished with a small stage and rows of chairs.

'How goes it?' Adam asked, standing beside him.

'Well, I think. The chairs are filling up.'

'So I should hope, considering you have the cream of the musical world to entertain everyone.'

They heard voices down in the hall as more guests arrived, and in a few moments, a party came up, led by a matronly woman in a hideous purple gown and a turban with a long feather, escorted by young Cavenhurst, but he hardly had eyes for them because they were accompanied by a young lady who caused him to catch his breath.

'Lady Cartrose, how do you do,' Mark said, while Adam endeavoured not to allow his twitching lips to become a broad grin. 'May I present my cousin, Lord Kimberley.'

Pulling himself together, Adam bowed. 'Your servant, my lady.'

'And this is my sister-in-law, Miss Sophie Cavenhurst,' Mark went on, unaware of the unspoken message going from Sophie to Adam, though that gentleman was fully cognisant of the appeal in her blue eyes.

'Miss Cavenhurst, your obedient servant,' he said, bowing.

There were more people coming up the stairs, and Mark was obliged to turn to greet them. 'Adam, will you take Lady Cartrose and Miss Cavenhurst to find good seats before they are all taken up? I will join you later.'

'With the greatest of pleasure,' he said, offering them an arm each and smiling to himself when Sophie hesitated before taking it.

They found four seats in the middle of the room, and he found himself seated between Sophie and her aunt. He had a little time to study her while she perused the programme she had found on her chair. She was lovely, there was no doubting that, with her fresh complexion, fair curls and expressive blue eyes, which he could not see because she was determined not to look in his direction. He could hardly believe she was the same girl he had rescued from the soldiers, nor the one he had seen flaunting herself in that high-perch phaeton with that coxcomb, Sir Reginald Swayle. He hadn't known his name at the time, only having been introduced to him at White's.

'Are you enjoying your stay in London?' he asked her.

'So far,' she said, without looking at him.

'Only so far?'

'Well, one never knows what is around the corner, does one?'

'No, nor whom one might meet,' he added.

'Very true, and sometimes they are not the people one would wish to meet.'

'I am sorry if that has happened to you,' he said, assuming she meant him. 'But sometimes we find ourselves in situations where it cannot be avoided.'

'Quite.'

There was a long silence after this. She was evidently not in the mood to explain herself and as the seats were filling up and the musicians tuning their instruments ready to begin, he gave up trying. Instead, he turned to Lady Cartrose, but as she could not hear what he was saying above the noise of the orchestra and people talking round them, he gave that up, too.

Mark came in to introduce the quartet that

was going to provide the opening music and everyone ceased chatting and turned towards the front.

The seats were so close together, Adam was very aware of the girl beside him; he had only to lean a little sideways and their arms and heads would touch. She appeared engrossed in the music, but there was a tension in the air around her that told him she was not unmindful of his proximity. What was she thinking? Was she wishing him anywhere but where he was? He ought to reassure her he would not speak of the episode with the soldiers, or her indiscretion in riding in the phaeton; it would not be the action of a gentleman. But perhaps it would be better to remain silent.

Refreshments were served during the intermission and Adam had perforce to escort his uncommunicative ladies to the dining room, where they were joined by Mr and Mrs Malthouse and Cassandra, and Lord and Lady Martindale with Lucinda.

It was immediately apparent that Miss Sophie Cavenhurst was not normally taciturn, because she entered into a lively exchange with Cassandra and Lucinda about the merits of the music and the audience and their dress.

'Your gown is exquisite,' Cassandra said to Sophie. 'Where did you find that lovely fabric?

That green reminds me of sage shot through with silver.'

'My sister found it for me. It might have come from India. Both my brother and brother-in-law spent some time out there. They may have brought it back.'

'And the style is so elegant. Don't you think so, my lord?'

Thus appealed to, Adam turned towards Sophie as if to study her sage-green gown, although he had already decided he had rarely seen anything so becoming. It was exquisitely made and fitted the young lady's figure beautifully. 'Most certainly,' he said. 'But your own gown, Miss Malthouse, is a match for it. It suits its wearer to perfection.'

Cassandra blushed crimson. 'You are too kind, my lord.'

'You must not leave Miss Martindale out of your praises,' Sophie said, smiling at her old friend. 'I think that pale pink is just right for her colouring.'

'I had no intention of leaving the young lady out,' he said. 'You are all three beauties of the first order. I am at a loss to choose between you and you must therefore excuse me.' He bowed to each in turn and made his escape.

He joined Mark, who was standing a little to one side, making sure everyone was being looked after, ready to send for more dishes of food as those on the table emptied.

'You haven't lost your touch, I see,' Mark said, looking towards the trio. 'Three young ladies hanging on your every word. I fancy there will be three handkerchiefs thrown down ere long.'

'I shall not stoop to pick them up, Mark. I collect I told you, I have no intention of marrying again.'

'I wonder how long he will be in town,' Cassandra mused. 'Do you think he will come to my ball if I invite him?'

'Oh, so you are going to set your cap at him, are you?' Sophie said.

'Why not? He is not unhandsome and he has a title.'

'And wealth,' Lucinda put in.

'How do you know that?' Sophie demanded.

'I asked Papa and he said he has a vast estate in Yorkshire and owns a woollen mill, as well.'

'Yorkshire. I am sure I should never want to live there,' Sophie said.

'No doubt he would bring his wife to town as often as she wanted to come,' Lucinda said.

'You, too, Lucy?' Sophie queried.

'What do you mean?'

'Both of you bowled over by a handsome face and a few compliments.'

'Oh, so you are not, I suppose,' Cassandra said.

'Of course not. Anyone can learn to pay compliments. Besides he is too old and a widower and I will not play second fiddle to a dead wife.'

'I didn't know that,' Lucinda said.

'What does it matter?' Cassandra was not to be put off. 'She can't hurt anyone, can she? I am going to ask Mama to invite him to my come-out ball. He will be duty bound to stand up with me.'

'Then, I wish you joy of him,' Sophie said.

She knew she was being silly, but Viscount Kimberley disturbed her more than she was willing to admit. Her embarrassment at finding the man who had rescued her from the soldiers was her brother-in-law's cousin was profound. She could not treat him like a stranger, could not dismiss the whole incident with a shrug of her shoulders, especially as he had afterwards seen her with Reggie in his phaeton. How much of that would he tell Mark? Mark might tell Jane and she would be fetched home in disgrace. If only tonight had been their first meeting, then she might have felt the same way as her two friends. She envied them. He was not laughing at them.

She left them to mingle with Mark's guests and talk to them about the Hadlea Home, praising the work her sister and brother-in-law were doing and holding out the velvet bag Mark had provided to contain donations. Her enthusiasm was catching, and resulted in people perhaps giving more than they intended. Adam noticed it and liked her for it. There was more to Miss Sophie Cavenhurst than met the eye.

Chapter Four

In the coming days, Sophie was half afraid to go out riding or in the carriage for fear of encountering Viscount Kimberley again. On the other hand, when she did go out and did not see him, she returned to Mount Street feeling a little jaded, though not for the world would she have admitted it had anything to do with that gentleman.

She was spared the whist, but went with her aunt to tea parties and drawing-room gatherings, and Lady Cartrose hosted some herself, which Lady Martindale and Mrs Malthouse attended, along with others of her acquaintance. Sophie, Lucinda and Cassandra made a coterie of three who talked for hours and planned their social events in meticulous detail down to the last ribbon for their gowns and how they intended to purport themselves, confiding the hopes they had of the outcome. Cassie was determined to catch the eye of Viscount Kimberley and was deciding on her strategy.

'I shall drop my fan or twist my ankle or something to make him come to my rescue,' she said one day when the girls were sitting in the garden of Cartrose House enjoying the sun. The weather had at last warmed up and they were wearing muslin dresses and wide-brimmed bonnets. 'Then I shall engage him in conversation and flirt a little.'

Sophie laughed. 'Do you know how to flirt, Cassie? I'll wager he is master of it.'

'What do you know of it?' her friend asked.

'Enough to know it is not the way to go about attracting a man like Viscount Kimberley.'

'You have a head start,' Cassie said. 'You are related to him by marriage and can be more informal with him.'

'I don't want a head start,' Sophie said. 'I have no interest in the gentleman. His superior attitude annoys me. He has a way of looking down on you as if he would like to crush you underfoot, and when he's not doing that, he is laughing at you.'

'I have never noticed that about him,' Lucy said.

'Nor I,' added Cassie. 'He has always behaved like a perfect gentleman. Perhaps you have done or said something to make him like that towards you.'

'Of course I haven't.' Sophie was adamant. 'I was only introduced to him on the same evening you were. In any case he is a widower and by all accounts adored his wife. I have no wish to be a convenient replacement, even if he offers for me, which I am sure he will not.'

'If you are not interested in him, who are you interested in?' Lucy wanted to know. 'Sir Reginald Swayle? Or Mr Fanshawe? I heard he was in town, too.'

'You know very well, Lucy, that I rejected both of them, along with Lord Gorange. I told you so at the time. If he turns up as well, I shall wonder if there is some conspiracy afoot.'

'Conspiracy?' Cassie echoed. 'What can you mean?'

'I don't know, do I? But I will swear not one of them has the least affection for me, and I certainly have none for them. Now can we drop the subject? I find it prodigiously boring.' It was easier to pretend to be bored than to admit she was worried.

They went on to talk about the subscription dance and whether they would be permitted to dance the waltz. 'I don't see why not,' Sophie said. 'I am told everyone is dancing it these days, and it is even permitted at Almack's.' The ladies who ruled the dances at Almack's were sticklers for propriety and for a long time would not sanction the dance, deeming it improper. But when other notable hostesses were allowing it, they had given in.

'Yes, but we are not yet out,' Cassie said. 'If Lady Rowland allows the orchestra to play for it, I do hope Mama won't be difficult.'

'I shall ask Papa,' Lucy said. 'He is always more indulgent than Mama.'

'Aunt Emmeline is very easy-going and so is my brother,' Sophie said. 'He has been teaching me the steps.'

'Dancing with one's brother is very different from having another man put his arm about you,' Lucy said.

'Looking down your dress and breathing in your face,' Cassie added, setting them all laughing.

'Is your brother going to be there?' Lucy asked Sophie when they recovered.

'Naturally. He is my escort.'

'I have always liked him,' her friend went on. 'Ever since we were children.'

'Oh, so he is to be preferred to Viscount Kimberley, is he?'

'At least he is easy to talk to. I shake all over when his lordship speaks to me.'

'Silly! He is only a man, flesh and blood, the same as all the others.'

'Sophie, I am persuaded you are very hard to please,' Lucy said.

'So my brother tells me, but marriage is a very

serious business. If you are to spend the rest of your life with someone, you need to know he is the right someone, don't you think?'

'Yes, but how can you be sure?' Cassie put in. 'Mama says you have to listen to your elders who know best, take their advice and then work to be a good wife. That way lies contentment.'

'Poof!' Sophie said. 'I shall listen to my heart. I want to be head over heels in love with the man I marry and to be sure he feels the same way about me.'

'How will you know that?' the other two asked in unison.

'My sister Jane says I will know when the time comes and if I have any doubts, then he is not the one for me.'

'I hope you may not be hoist on your own petard,' Cassie said as a footman approached them from the house.

'Ladies,' he said. 'Her ladyship asks that you join her in the drawing room for tea.'

They rose and followed him back indoors, where they found Vincent and Teddy had joined Mrs Malthouse and Lady Martindale.

'You have been gossiping long enough,' Lady Cartrose told the girls. 'Now greet Mr Malthouse and Mr Cavenhurst and sit down to have some tea.'

They obeyed and then seated themselves in a row on a sofa.

'Beats me what you find to talk about,' Teddy said as the young men found chairs for themselves. 'Empty-headed tittle-tattle, I've no doubt.'

'And what do you find to talk about when you spend hours at your club?' Sophie responded. 'I will wager it is not the state of the country's economy or the plight of the poor or anything of more import than the cut of your coat, the negligence of your valet or the state of your luck.'

Vincent laughed. 'She has you there, old man.'

'We will have no quarrelling,' Emmeline said. 'Edward, you should be more polite to your sister.'

'Oh, do not mind him, Aunt,' Sophie said. 'We are truly rather fond of each other, you know, and where would I be without him? Who else would I have escort me to the Rowlands' dance?'

'I would gladly be of service,' Vincent said.

Sophie looked at him in surprise. 'Why, thank you, Mr Malthouse, but you are not family and can hardly chaperone me, as Teddy does.'

'No, I realise that,' he said. 'But I hope you will save a dance for me.'

'To be sure I will,' she said, while Cassie giggled. Sophie shot her a quelling look.

The footman returned. 'Viscount Kimberley and Lord Wyndham, my lady.' He stood aside for the two men to enter.

Immediately the atmosphere in the room changed subtly; there was a tension in the air that had not been there before. Cassie smiled happily, Lucy blushed crimson and Sophie's back stiffened as if to repel an attack.

'We were passing, my lady,' Mark said, addressing Lady Cartrose, 'and decided to call. I hope we have not inconvenienced you.'

'Not at all,' her ladyship said. 'We are pleased to see you. I will order fresh tea. Do sit down. We were just discussing the Rowlands' dance. Will you be one of our party?'

'I am returning to Hadlea the day after tomorrow,' Mark said. 'It is one of the reasons I called, to ask if Sophie has any messages for Sir Edward and Lady Cavenhurst. But I am sure my cousin will be pleased to join you.'

'Will you, my lord?' Cassie turned to Adam, eyes alight.

He hesitated only a second before saying, 'I will be honoured, so long as I have no other pressing engagements.'

'It is to raise money to buy the new princess a gift,' Cassie said as a servant brought in fresh tea. 'But I shall think of it as a rehearsal for my come-out in July. Do you dance the waltz, my lord?'

'My late wife taught me the steps, but I have not danced it since she passed away.'

'Oh.' Cassie was at a loss to know what to say. 'I am sorry, I should not have mentioned it.'

'Why not?' he said. 'You were not to know, and I do not mind you speaking of her.'

He spoke lightly, but Sophie noticed the pain in his eyes and concluded he must have loved his wife very much. At that moment, her animosity towards him softened and she gave him a sympathetic smile. 'Teddy taught me the steps,' she said.

'She didn't need much teaching,' Teddy put in. 'My little sister catches on quickly.'

The moment passed and everyone drank their tea and talked of the dance and how many people they thought would be there. Sophie sent messages to her parents and sister for Mark to deliver, and then Mark and Adam took their leave.

'You old rogue,' Adam said to his cousin as they walked. 'You let me in for that very neatly, didn't you?'

'Why?' Mark feigned innocence. 'Didn't you want to go?'

'Not especially. I have a feeling I am being set up for one of the young ladies, and that appals me.'

'I am sure you can let them down gently, cousin. And an evening out will do you no harm. Chasing about town looking for someone who clearly does not want to be found must be very frustrating. Give it a rest.'

He sighed. 'It seems I must. Do you have to go back to Hadlea so soon?'

'Yes, I must, but you are welcome to stay on at Wyndham House.'

'Thank you.'

'But there is something that is bothering me. I fear Teddy is slipping back into his old ways, especially since he spends so much time with Toby Moore, and I shall not be here to keep an eye on him.'

'You mentioned Captain Moore before, Mark. What is the story behind that?'

'Captain Moore was in a card-sharping partnership with Lord Bolsover and together they made a great deal of money. They were very clever. No one was able to prove they connived to cheat. They swindled Teddy out of several thousand pounds, which he could not pay, and Lord Bolsover nearly ruined Sir Edward by buying up all his debts and then demanding payment with sky-high interest. Teddy went out to India to escape and made enough money to save the estate. Bolsover was eventually discredited and had to retire to the country, his face badly scarred by fire, which happened when he tried to abduct Jane…'

'Your wife?'

'Yes, but we were not married at that time. Moore is blaming the Cavenhursts for severing a lucrative partnership. I have no doubt he is intent on revenge. How he has won Teddy over, I have no idea, but most of the trouble with Bolsover happened after he had gone to India, and he may not have known of the captain's involvement.'

'That is quite a tale. Have you warned Cavenhurst?'

'Yes, but he chooses not to listen.' He paused. 'I would deem it a favour if you could watch out for him and let me know if anything happens that requires me to intervene. I'll come back at once if you send for me.'

'Mark, it is hardly your responsibility, and it is certainly not mine, to oversee what your brother-in-law does.'

'I know, but for Jane's sake and his parents', too, I would like to keep him out of trouble if I can. He is supposed to be looking out for Sophie, and if he falls by the wayside, goodness knows what she will do. She is not one to sit about meekly doing nothing. You will do this for me, won't you?'

Adam could easily imagine the lively Miss Cavenhurst getting into mischief if not carefully watched. The way she had been seen riding unchaperoned in Sir Reginald's phaeton was an instance of it, but he did not know what he could do to stop her, short of squiring her himself and acting *in loco parentis*. He did not think she would stand for that, and he did not feel a bit like a parent. After all there were not so many years between them—ten at the most. On the other hand, Mark had been generous to him, letting him stay at Wyndham House, and Captain Moore sounded like a real villain. 'I will do what I can, but I shall have to go back to Yorkshire myself before too long,' he said. 'George Harcourt, my mill manager, is very competent, but what he will do if there is trouble, I do not know.'

'You won't go without coming to Hadlea to meet my wife and son, will you? After all, you may be worrying for nothing and there will be no uprising.'

'I hope you are right. Will you come and hear me speak in the Lords tomorrow? Perhaps that will persuade Hunt that I am not against him and he will come out of hiding.'

'I wouldn't miss it.'

The House of Lords was packed to hear the debate. Peers who had not attended in years arrived to listen and perhaps speak. Adam, not normally a nervous man, felt his whole *raison d'être* was on trial and, when called to make his speech, felt his notes fluttering in his hand. He knew what he wanted to say and abandoned them. 'My lords,' he began as the murmur of voices stilled to listen. 'I am here to expound the cause of the workingman. Times are changing. The men who work in our mills and manufactories, who stand at their benches and looms, know that without them our businesses cannot survive. They are skilled men and hold the key to our prosperity, the prosperity of the whole nation, and they deserve to be adequately recompensed. Cutting their wages when profits are down is not the way to treat loyal workers, especially now with the price of bread so high...'

'He would have us all in Poor Street,' someone shouted.

Adam ignored him and continued, 'The Corn Laws ought to be repealed. They serve no useful purpose.'

'Rubbish!' another voice piped up.

He smiled. 'I hesitate to call a law of this country rubbish, but perhaps you are right and we should throw it out.'

One or two people smiled at this, but most were too angry to see the humour.

'We all have to live, and the world will be a better, more prosperous place, if we live in harmony,' he went on. 'To that end we must educate the men so that they understand about how business is conducted, a little of economics and how to express themselves succinctly. Educated men, interested men, well-fed men with healthy families, will work all the better for it. They will not impoverish the country. It is not in their interests to do so. They should have a say in how the country governs itself, to help decide the laws that will have a bearing on their lives...'

'He's spreading sedition.'

'Revolutionary!'

He waited silently for the booing and shouting to die down, which it did eventually when they realised he was not going to sit down. 'Men who have reached a certain standard of education ought to have the franchise, an education which we must provide for all...'

This was too much for some and there was more heckling. 'Do you want a reign of terror here in England?'

'Look what happened in France!'

'Make him sit down!'

'Arrest him!'

'Is this the way our revered parliament carries on its business?' he shouted above the din. 'Like a crowd of schoolboys deprived of their favourite toys?'

This was again too much for some, and they began throwing their papers at him. From the gallery, where a few spectators had come to listen to the debate, came rotten eggs.

Adam, with egg running down his superfine coat, sat down in despair. Others rose to have their say, but none supported him except Mark, who said it was the right of every man to be heard with courtesy, whether you agreed with him or not, but he was shouted down as having no knowledge of industrial affairs and would do better to stick to agriculture.

After everyone had calmed down, the debate moved on to how trouble could be contained if any rose among the workers. There was talk of militia and even the cavalry and a ban on all gatherings with the rope as a punishment for infringement. Adam jumped up once or twice to protest at the harsh measures being put forward, but no one listened.

'My only hope is that Hunt will read the report of the proceedings and come to me,' he told Mark as they walked back to Wyndham House.

'What will you say to him? Will you advise him not to demonstrate?'

'No. It is the only way they will be heard, but I want to be sure any demonstration is orderly and peaceful and not an armed uprising. He must give the militia no excuse to intervene.'

'God forbid!'

'Amen to that.'

Sophie, unaware of Viscount Kimberley's serious mission, had come to the conclusion he was in town to find himself a second wife. And though she told herself she had no interest in what he did, she found herself wondering what sort of lady he was looking for and if any of her acquaintances would capture him. Cassie, perhaps? It would not be for want of trying on Cassie's part, she thought with a wry smile. She did not think Mrs Malthouse would spare any money or effort promoting her daughter, and the dance afforded an opportunity. 'We shall see,' she murmured to herself when undressing for bed the night before the event.

Lady Cartrose decided to rest the following day and had no engagements. Teddy was nowhere to be found and Sophie had nothing to do. She sat in the garden to finish the library book she had been reading, then enlisted Bessie to go with her to change it.

They were walking along Bond Street when they met Teddy and Captain Moore. 'Ah, my dear little sister,' Teddy said, stopping in front of her. He was swaying slightly and his words were slurred. 'You have not met my friend, Captain Toby Moore, have you, Sophie? Allow me to present him. Toby, my sister, Miss Sophie Cavenhurst.'

The man bowed. 'How do you do, Miss Cavenhurst. Teddy speaks of you often with great affection.'

'Then, you have the advantage,' she said. 'He has never mentioned you to me.'

'No reason to,' her brother murmured.

'I believe you are going to attend the Rowlands' dance this evening,' Captain Moore went on. 'I shall look forward to seeing you there. Perhaps you will consent to stand up with me.'

'You will have to get in line,' Teddy said with

a chuckle. 'Sophie is in great demand. She has turned down three offers of marriage already, and all three disappointed suitors are in town.'

'All three?' Sophie echoed in dismay. 'I knew Sir Reginald and Mr Fanshawe were here, but not Lord Gorange.'

'I saw him myself at the club yesterday evening,' he said.

This was not good news. She could only hope his arrival was coincidental and nothing to do with her. 'What did he say?'

'I didn't speak to him. In any case he was having an argument with Fanshawe, and very heated it was. Didn't want to get involved. I should stick to Reggie, if I were you, sis. He's the best of the bunch.'

'I am not sticking to Reggie or any one of them,' she snapped.

Teddy shrugged. 'As you say. Where are you off to now?'

'Hookham's to return this.' She held up the library book.

'With no escort? Dear me, Sophie, will you never learn?'

'I do not need an escort. I have Bessie with me. You would do well to go back to Mount Street and sleep it off or you will not be fit for the dance tonight. Good day to you, Captain Moore. Come, Bessie.'

She heard her brother chuckling as she left

and then she spotted Viscount Kimberley on the opposite side of the crowded thoroughfare. He appeared to be watching them. Furious, she marched down the street, pretending not to have seen him. She dare not look back. 'Is he still there?' she asked Bessie.

'Who? Your brother?'

'No, Mark's cousin Kimberley.'

Bessie turned. 'I can't see him. The pavement is very crowded.'

'Yes, but he is a head taller than anyone else.' She risked turning round to look. 'He has gone. Let us make haste.' She began to walk very fast. Why that man should upset her equilibrium, she did not know. She had no trouble dealing with other men, could converse, jest or deliver a put-down with ease. It must, she surmised, be because he had witnessed her humiliation the day after she'd arrived in the capital. It was something she could not forget, nor the amusement in his eyes when he looked at her, as if he, too, were remembering.

In spite of the high cost of the tickets, Lord Rowland's ballroom was crowded. Some were aristocrats and members of the *ton*, but many more were the newly rich who had come to hob-nob with the nobility. Sophie, accompanied by her brother and Lady Cartrose, wore a gown of pale green gauze over a white satin slip. It had little puff sleeves and a heart-shaped neck-line. The high-waisted bodice was caught under the bosom with a posy of silk flowers. Lady Cartrose had been taken aback when Sophie had joined her in the drawing room to wait for the carriage that was to take them to the dance.

'Sophie, young ladies not yet out should not be wearing colours.'

'But, Aunt, I am not to have a come-out ball, so the fact that I am here with you, going out and about, is proof enough that I am already out, don't you think?' She spoke loudly and clearly and accompanied her words with a sweet smile. 'Besides, I have already had offers. Acting the innocent would be entirely inappropriate.'

Her ladyship laughed. 'Sophie, you seem to have an answer for everything, but do not blame me if the company frowns at you.'

They were a little late arriving, and the danc-ing had already begun. She stood looking about her to see who was there that she knew and soon spotted the Malthouse party with Cassandra in virgin white decorated with the green ribbon she had suggested. They moved over to join them and Teddy, bowing, asked Cassie to stand up with him for the country dance then in progress. Vincent claimed Sophie.

'You are in looks tonight,' he said as they danced.

'Oh, does that mean I am not usually in looks?'

'No, not at all,' he said, embarrassed. 'You always look beautiful, but especially so tonight. It is very daring of you.'

'Daring, Mr Malthouse?'

'To wear colours. For someone not yet out…'

'Oh, but I am out—well and truly out. Besides, white does not suit me. It makes me look deathly.'

'I cannot imagine that. You are always full of life. Your eyes sparkle and your smile…'

'Mr Malthouse, pray do not go on. You are putting me to the blush.'

'And a delightful blush it is.' He bent closer and whispered in her ear, 'I would like to see more of it.'

'Mr Malthouse, do concentrate on the dance. That is the second time you have taken a wrong step.'

'Sorry.' He fell silent and she was glad when the dance ended and he escorted her back to her place beside Lady Cartrose. Teddy returned with Cassie, who sat beside her. 'I don't see Viscount Kimberley,' her friend said. 'He said he would come.'

'Only if he did not have other more pressing engagements,' Sophie reminded her. 'You must not count on him.'

Sophie did not sit out a single dance before the supper interval. The gentlemen flocked to ask her to stand up with them, including Sir Reginald and Mr Richard Fanshawe, who was exquisitely attired in black and white. 'What brings you to town?' she asked him as they danced a *chaîne anglaise*.

'When England's handsomest flower is in town, that is where I want to be, too,' he said.

'You are not the only one,' she said, ignoring the flattery. 'Sir Reginald is before you.'

'Yes, I know. I have spoken to him. We have agreed to a friendly rivalry.'

'In what connection?'

'Surely, Miss Cavenhurst, you know the answer to that? Your hand is our goal.'

'Then, you are both wasting your time. There are any number of beautiful young ladies in town. Turn your attention to one of them, Miss Malthouse or Miss Martindale, for instance.'

'Ah, but they do not have your attraction, my dear.'

She was glad when the steps of the dance separated them and the subject was not resumed when they joined hands again. Those two men were likely to ruin the pleasure of her Season if she were not careful. She wanted to enjoy her time in London, to meet new people, not be bothered by those she had turned down in Hadlea. So far the only new acquaintances she had made were Vincent Malthouse, Captain Moore and Viscount Kimberley. Vincent was too silly for

words and Captain Moore was considerably
older than she was and, for some reason she
could not explain, he made her skin creep. He
smiled a lot, but it was the smile of a tiger and
she wondered what Teddy saw in him. That left
only Viscount Kimberley, but he was also older
and had been married before. In spite of her pretended indifference, she found herself wondering why he was not there.

The first dance after supper was a cotillion,
and Sophie found Captain Moore bowing in
front of her with his hand held out. 'Miss Cavenhurst, may I have the pleasure?'

She would have liked to refuse, but Teddy
said, 'Go on, sis, he won't eat you.'

Somewhat reluctantly she allowed the captain
to lead her into the dance. 'When did you meet
my brother?' she asked him.

'Oh, years ago, before he went to India, but
we lost touch. It was a great pleasure to come
upon him again this year.'

'Do you live in London?'

'No, I come every year for the Season.'

'To find a wife?'

'No, I am a bachelor and always will be. I
come simply to enjoy the entertainment on offer.'

'Like dancing?'

'Among other things.'

'Such as gambling?'

'I like a game of cards now and then. Why do you ask?'

'Because Teddy is very fond of gambling and I suspect he spends a great deal of his time at the tables. I do hope he doesn't lose too heavily.'

'On the contrary, Miss Cavenhurst, I believe he is enjoying a winning streak.'

She greeted this statement with foreboding. Winning streaks did not usually last, especially in Teddy's experience, and she wondered what their father would have to say if he knew his son had broken his promise not to gamble. She would have to have it out with him, though she doubted he would listen to her.

'I hope you do not encourage him in extravagant bets,' she said.

'Me?' he queried, feigning surprise. 'Why would I do that? A man who cannot meet his gambling debts is to be shunned. I would not want that for my friend. I am hurt that you should think it of me.'

'I am sorry. I meant no offence.'

'None taken. Tell me, are you enjoying your stay in town?'

'Yes, very much.'

'How long will you be here?'

'Until after my friend Cassandra's ball, then I return to Hadlea.'

'No come-out ball of your own?'

'No, that is not possible.'

'Oh, you never know,' he said. 'Teddy might come up trumps.'

She looked sharply at him, but his expression was bland and smiling. Why did she feel threatened?

The dance came to an end and he took her back to her place, where she discovered Viscount Kimberley had arrived and had been dancing with Cassie. Her friend was hot and flushed and fanning herself vigorously. 'I think I must have some fresh air,' she said. 'Mama, may I go on to the terrace?'

'Yes, but do not go alone. Vincent, take your sister out for a few minutes, but do not be long.' She turned to Adam. 'My daughter does not like the heat, my lord. She will be back directly.'

'I understand.' He turned to Sophie. 'Will you honour me with the next dance, Miss Cavenhurst?'

She consulted her dance card, although she knew very well that the next dance had been left blank on purpose. It was a waltz, but she would not admit she had been saving it in case the viscount should ask her.

'Do you know, it is the only vacant spot on my card,' she said. 'I will be delighted to accept.'

He held out his hand, led her onto the floor and bowed before her. She curtsied, put her right hand lightly into his left and raised her other hand to his shoulder. It was the nearest she had ever been to him, the closest she had been to any man except her father and brother. It sent a quiver of excitement running through her body and made her realise why the more strait-laced of the ladies still considered the dance improper.

He danced well and seemed able to do the steps while talking at the same time. 'I noticed all the young blades flocking round you,' he said. 'From which I surmise you are enjoying yourself.'

'Yes, but…' She stopped.

'But what? Do go on. You intrigue me.'

'Most of them are very silly.'

He laughed. 'What, even the more mature among them, like Lord Gorange and Captain Moore? Older men sometimes make better husbands.'

'Lord Gorange I have already rejected,' she said. 'How did you know about him?'

'Mark told me.'

'Oh, and what else did he tell you?'

'That you have had a string of suitors who have all been rejected. I am curious as to the reason. You must be very hard to please.'

'So my brother tells me, but I am not going to fall at the feet of the first man who offers for me…'

'Nor the third either, it seems.'

'No, I do not love any of them and they do not love me. Why they want to marry me I have no idea, but it is certainly not love.'

'And is that important to you?'

'Yes, it is. You loved your wife, didn't you?'

'Indeed I did.'

'There you are, then. You understand me.'

'I am trying. Tell me, if you had so lately turned down Sir Reginald Swayle, why did you consent to ride in his phaeton? I should like to think you were persuaded against your will.'

'I was not persuaded against my will, my lord.' It was said firmly, because it was the truth and she did not want him to think she was so easily coerced.

'Oh. That sounded like a put-down.'

'A put-down, my lord? I would never dream of trying anything like that on a superior being like yourself.'

He laughed. 'Miss Cavenhurst, I think you are bamming me.'

She laughed, too. 'That is for you to decide.'

'Then I shall decide that a superior being like yourself would not be overawed by anyone, least of all me. You decide with whom you will ride and with whom you will dance and I am flattered that you consented to waltz with me. After all, I am older than Sir Reginald and almost as old as Lord Gorange.'

'Ah, but you have not offered for me,' she said.

'True,' he murmured.

She was becoming embarrassed by the way the conversation was going. As so often happened her tongue had run away with her, and she did not know how to turn it back to safer subjects. 'Lord Gorange is a widower with two small children. I believe he is looking for a replacement wife, and that I will not be.'

Oh, dear, she was making things worse. She felt the colour flood into her face and would have stumbled if his firm grip had not held her upright.

'If it helps, then be assured I am not looking for a replacement wife,' he said. 'No one can replace Anne. Not everyone comes to town to join the marriage mart, you know.'

'No, of course not. I did not mean…I forgot…' Her voice trailed away.

He smiled. 'You are forgiven. No one could be at outs with you for long. Perhaps that is why your suitors are so persevering.'

He had deftly hauled her out of the pit into which she had fallen and for that she was grateful.

'You have disposed of your three suitors,' he went on. 'What about the others, Mr Malthouse and Captain Moore?'

'Vincent Malthouse is one of the silly ones, and as for Captain Moore, he may not be silly, but I cannot like him. I fear he is leading Teddy astray.'

'You may be right. What can you do about it?'

'Nothing. Teddy never listens to me. He grumbles that I want to spoil his fun.'

'Brothers can sometimes be pests, can they not?'

'Yes. Do you have brothers?'

'I did have one, but he was killed at the Battle of Salamanca.'

'I am so sorry. You seem to have had more than your share of bereavement.'

'Yes, but we will not speak of it.'

'I don't mind you talking about it, if you want to. I am not a tattle-monger.'

'No, I did not suppose you were. But we were talking about you.'

'Were we? Then let us change the subject. Miss Malthouse has returned and is looking this way. Are you down to have another dance with her?'

'No, I don't think so.'

'But you are going to stay in town for her come-out ball, are you not?'

'I have been invited. It is true. I assume you will be there?'

'If I do not blot my copybook any more than I have already.'

'Have you? Blotted your copybook, I mean.'

'I am sure I have. Riding with Sir Reggie, for one thing—though there was a good reason for that—going out alone and allowing myself to be accosted by common soldiers, not to mention wearing this gown. There are probably more I do not even know about.'

'What is wrong with the gown? It looks delightful to me.'

'I am told I should not be wearing colours, since I am not officially out.'

'Is that so? Do you care?'

She laughed. 'Not a bit.'

The dance came to an end, he bowed, she bent her knee and he offered his arm to escort her back to Lady Cartrose.

Only later, lying sleepless in bed, did she begin to analyse their conversation, wonder what it was all about and how it made her feel. Mortified? Happy? Sad? Uncaring? Caring too much? She wasn't at all sure.

He made her heart beat faster, even when he was teasing her, but fell short of her ideal on the grounds he was too old and a widower, but as he had never shown the slightest interest in her except to tease, she did not think she would be given the opportunity to turn him down, which, in some perverse way, made her wish for it. If anyone could rival Mark, he could. She gave herself a good talking to, thumped her pillow and lay down again, determined to put him out of her mind.

Chapter Five

Sophie went with her aunt to visit Mrs Malt-house and Cassandra the next day to mull over the dance and comment on everything that had happened. Lady Martindale and Lucinda were there ahead of them. There was plenty to gossip about, but when they tired of that they began to look to the future. Cassie's ball was still three weeks away and they needed something to fill in the time.

'We could go to Ranelagh Gardens one evening when they have fireworks,' Cassie suggested.

'Or to Astley's to see the performing animals and the wire walkers,' Lucy added.

'Bullock's Museum is interesting, too,' Lady Martindale put in. 'And there's *The Marriage of Figaro* at Covent Garden.'

'But the weather is so lovely now, I would rather be out of doors,' Sophie said.

'In that case, what about a picnic?' Mrs Malthouse said.

'A picnic!' Cassie clapped her hands. 'What a splendid idea! Where shall we go and whom shall we invite? Do you think Viscount Kimberley would come?'

'We will ask him, of course,' her mother said. 'But he may be otherwise engaged.'

'And where will we go?' Sophie asked.

'Richmond Park is always pleasant at this time of year.' Lady Cartrose was managing to keep up with the conversation by concentrating hard on whoever was speaking. 'The men could ride and the ladies go in carriages.'

'I would as soon ride,' Sophie said. 'Teddy will hire a mount for me.'

'Do you think you can keep up?' Mrs Malthouse asked Sophie. 'It is several miles, you know.'

'That is nothing. I am used to riding miles all over the countryside around Hadlea.'

'I shall ask your brother what he thinks when I see him,' her aunt said.

'Oh, Sophie will be able to keep up,' Teddy said later that day when Lady Cartrose told him about the outing and expressed her doubts about Sophie riding. 'She is a natural in the saddle, better than her sisters and the equal of many men. I have no fear for her.'

'Thank you, brother,' Sophie said, giving him a beaming smile. 'You will hire a decent mount for me, won't you?'

'Of course. And one for myself. I fancy a trip out of town.'

'That will please Lucy,' she said.

'Lucy?' he queried.

'Oh, didn't you know? She has a fancy for you. You could do worse, a lot worse.'

'There is no call to be matchmaking, Sophie. I am not ready to be leg shackled yet.'

'What a horrid expression,' Lady Cartrose said. 'So vulgar. I don't know where you young men learn such things.'

'Out and about, Aunt, out and about.'

'What you need is a wife to instil some delicacy into you.'

'All in good time,' he said, laughing. 'We will despatch Sophie first.'

The party that set off two mornings later in a cavalcade of carriages and riders including Viscount Kimberley, to Cassie's intense delight, Vincent, Sir Reginald and Mr Richard Fanshawe, to Sophie's dismay. Mr Fanshawe was a Norfolk friend of Lord and Lady Martindale, who had invited him to join them. He insisted on riding beside her, and what had been anticipated as a pleasurable ride was embarrassing and uncomfortable.

'Mr Fanshawe, I am sure you would rather ride with the gentlemen,' she said, falling back in the hope he would tire of her slow pace and leave her.

'Not at all. Your company, Miss Cavenhurst, is all I want and need.'

'I do not know why you are saying that. I made it quite clear, three months ago, that I do not wish to marry you.'

'I know you did, but that was simply done out of convention. Young ladies are taught to say no on the first time of asking.'

'I don't know where you got that idea, but in my case you are under a misapprehension. I meant what I said.'

'Why?'

'Why?' she repeated. 'I do not think I am under any obligation to say why. But if it helps you to accept it, the reason is simply that I do not love you.'

'Love! That is a greatly overrated emotion by young ladies who read too many romantic novels and think they reflect real life. I thought you to be more practical than that. It is better to be well suited and comfortable.'

'Mr Fanshawe...' she began, just as Sir Reginald rode up on her other side.

'Sophie, I cannot let Dickie monopolise you. Pray, allow me to join you.'

'Oh, Lord, give me patience,' she said and

kicked her horse into a trot. They both followed suit. Unable to shake them off, she cantered and then, in desperation, dug her heels in and galloped.

She knew galloping side-saddle on a strange horse on a busy road was a foolish thing to do, but she was angry. She managed to avoid a mail coach cantering into town to keep to its schedule and an elderly pedestrian who shook his stick at her before she noticed a side road and turned down that. Thinking she had shaken off the two men, she slowed to a trot, but she was wrong. They were not far behind her and shouting at her to stop. 'You will end up in the river if you keep going like that,' Reggie shouted.

She pulled up and turned to face them. 'I am going back to the party,' she said as haughtily as she could manage, considering she was out of breath. 'I do not expect to find either of you beside me again unless I invite you. Is that understood?'

'Perfectly,' Reggie said. 'But I was concerned for your safety and your reputation.'

'My reputation! Who was it who tricked me into riding in that monstrous vehicle of yours? You were not too concerned for my reputation then.'

'Ha!' Richard said. 'What do you say to that, Swayle?'

'I say it is none of your business, Fanshawe.'

'Miss Cavenhurst's welfare is my business.'

'And how, pray, can you say that? I have not heard of an engagement which might justify it.'

'It is only a matter of time.'

Sophie had heard enough. 'Will you both get it into your heads I am not considering either of you? I have refused your offers and will not change my mind. Now, excuse me.'

She moved past them and cantered back to the main road, but unfortunately the carriages had disappeared. All she saw was an empty road. She turned in what she considered the right direction, well aware that the two men were only yards behind her. Strangely enough she was comforted by their presence, so long as they stayed well back.

She rode on until she came to a fork in the road and then she stopped, unable to decide which way to go, and that allowed the men to catch up with her. Ignoring them, she took the left-hand fork on the assumption that she needed to head south, but kept a wary eye on them in case they chose the other route, which would mean she was wrong. Right or wrong, they followed her. Very soon she came to a wooden bridge over the river that she needed to cross and she had no money for the toll. She had left her reticule containing her purse and a few coins in Lady Cartrose's carriage. The men were beside her again and soon realised her dilemma.

'Allow me,' Mr Fanshawe said, offering the toll man the money for them all.

She was obliged to thank him, and then all three crossed the bridge together. They were still together when they caught up with the rest of the party just short of the gate to the park.

'Where have you been, Sophie?' her aunt demanded, looking tellingly at her escorts. 'We thought something bad had happened to you. And where is Edward?'

'I took a wrong turn,' she said. 'I haven't seen Teddy since we set out.'

'He and Captain Moore went back to look for you.'

'They must have missed me. Fortunately, Sir Reginald and Mr Fanshawe found me.'

'Then let us carry on, and do stay beside the carriage now. I do not know what I would say to your parents if anything dreadful happened to you.'

Sophie was happy to obey. At least it would keep her two swains off her, but she was gloomily aware of the disapproving looks of the other ladies, and more than aware of the frown on the face of Viscount Kimberley. It seemed he was always to be witness to her humiliation and he was bound to add two and two and make five. Why that mattered, she would not admit.

* * *

Mr and Mrs Malthouse were riding in their barouche; their travelling coach had been sent on ahead with the servants and the food and several bottles of wine and cordial. When the cavalcade arrived, they had already selected a good spot beneath a tree and were busy unloading the hampers and laying out the picnic on a white tablecloth spread on the grass. Everyone dismounted and wandered about, stretching their legs.

'What happened?' Cassie demanded, coming across to Sophie. 'Why did you ride off with those two?' She nodded in the direction of Reggie and Richard, who were talking to Viscount Kimberley. Sophie wondered what they were saying to him and would dearly have liked to interrupt them, but decided she was in enough trouble without inviting more.

'I did not ride off with them and nothing happened. I fell behind and took a wrong turn.'

'Fell behind!' Cassie laughed. 'Was it some strategy to be alone with your *amour*?'

'I was not alone.'

'No, there were two of them. Really, Sophie, you are shocking, you know. I should never have dared.'

'I didn't ask them to follow me. In fact, I wish for nothing more than they should leave me alone. I am more than ever convinced there is something strange going on.'

'They are after your fortune, perhaps.'

'Fortune?' Sophie repeated, mystified.

'Why, yes. You said yourself you were wealthy.'

'Did I?'

'Yes, you said you could afford the best gowns and fripperies and do not need to stint, don't you remember? And that habit you are wearing is certainly very fetching and must have cost a fortune.'

'Oh, yes. But surely that is not reason enough...'

'Of course it is. It is only men like Viscount Kimberley who are rich as Croesus who can afford not to consider it.'

She had forgotten that idle boast, but both men had been to Greystone Manor and must surely know her true circumstances. 'There are other wealthy ladies,' she said. 'You, for instance, so why me?'

'Who knows?' Cassie shrugged. 'Come, let us have some of Mama's delicious picnic.'

Sophie followed Cassie to where the picnic was laid out. The older ladies were sitting in chairs, but everyone else was sprawled on the grass. Cassie managed to find a spot right next to the viscount and, as she had a firm hold on Sophie's arm, Sophie found herself sitting on the ground uncomfortably close to him.

'I hope you are none the worse for your adventure, Miss Cavenhurst?' he said and though his tone was mild, she detected a certain measure of criticism.

'It was not an adventure, my lord. I simply fell behind and took a wrong turn.'

'And Sir Reginald and Mr Fanshawe were happily on hand to set you right.'

'Yes, they were,' she said sharply.

'Tell me,' he said, still in the same mild tone. 'Why did you elect to ride and not travel in the carriage with your aunt?'

'I wanted to ride,' she said. 'It is something I enjoy above all things, and I miss my daily rides around Hadlea.'

'I see. And where is your brother? Should he not have stayed beside you?'

'I have no idea where he is, my lord. My aunt said he had ridden back to look for me.'

'Then, surely he should have returned before now.'

'My lord,' she said crossly, 'I do not know why you are quizzing me. It is nothing to do with you what I or my brother do.'

'No, thank goodness.'

Cassie was becoming frustrated at being ignored. She picked up a plate of tiny meat pies and held them out to Adam. 'My lord, do have one of these pies, they are delicious. Our chef made them. He is a master chef, you know.'

'No, I did not know,' he said, taking one from the plate. 'Thank you.'

'How long will you be in London, my lord?' Cassie asked, fluttering her eyelashes at him.

'I am not sure, Miss Malthouse. It depends on many things, some of which I have no control over.'

'Oh, you mean how many invitations you receive?'

He smiled. 'I hadn't thought of that, but if they are as delightful as the one I received for today, than I shall have to consider them.'

'I know Mama would like you to come to my ball. It will be the last ball of the Season and will be a grand affair. Everyone of any note will be there. Say you will come. Your presence will make it even better.'

'You flatter me, Miss Malthouse.'

'Not at all. I shall be the envy of all my friends to have secured you first.'

He laughed. 'Secured me, Miss Malthouse? That sounds as if you would have me in shackles.'

'Oh, no,' she said, blushing crimson. 'I did not mean... Oh, dear... And you can stop laughing, Sophie Cavenhurst.'

'Sorry,' Sophie said, trying to keep a straight face. 'But truly you asked for that.'

Adam was trying his best not to laugh, too, but the twinkle in his eyes gave him away. 'I shall be honoured to be secured for your ball, Miss Malthouse,' he said, picking up another of the little meat pies.

'I shall go and tell Mama right away,' Cassie said, scrambling to her feet, and added as Adam prepared to rise, too, 'No, please do not get up, my lord.' Then she fled.

'I must go to her,' Sophie said. 'I am afraid our teasing has upset her, and I would not have that happen for worlds.'

'Yes, do that. Please assure her I have not taken offence.'

Cassie had not gone to her mother, but wandered off a little way. Sophie went up to her and took her arm. 'Cassie, you mustn't mind his lordship, he was only teasing you.'

'But you laughed.'

'I am sorry. It was unkind of me. Will you forgive me?'

'Yes, of course. I did not realise what I had said until he spoke. I never was so mortified in my life. Whatever must he think of me?'

'He asked me to assure you he had taken no offence. I think he is sorry he was too quick to make the quip.'

'You are so much more worldly wise than me, Sophie. You would not have made such a foolish mistake.'

'Oh, I can make foolish mistakes, Cassie. Much worse ones than that,' Sophie said, knowing how inaccurate Cassie's statement was and anxious to make amends.

Cassie brightened. 'Tell me.'

'Well, I got up into Sir Reginald's high-perch phaeton and we rode in Hyde Park.'

'Alone?'

'Yes.'

'Did anyone see you?'

'The whole world, I should think.'

'How daring of you. Are you going to marry Sir Reginald?'

'Certainly not.'

'Mr Fanshawe, then?'

'Definitely not. I wish they had not come on this picnic.'

'I thought you had invited them.'

'Never. Sir Reginald is a friend of my brother and Mr Fanshawe is a neighbour of the Martindales in Norfolk. Speaking of the Martindales, where is Lucy?'

'She is with her parents. I think she was sick in the carriage.'

'Oh, then, I must go to her.'

'I'll come, too.'

With their arms about each other they returned to the rest of the party to commiserate with their friend. Now that the motion of the carriage had stopped, Lucy was feeling much better and joined Sophie and Cassie for a stroll along the riverbank. Sophie turned over the waist of her riding skirt to shorten it and stop it trailing in the dirt, unaware that she was exposing the bottom of her breeches tucked into her riding boots.

The sun shone from a cloudless blue sky that was reflected in the water, which sparkled as it rippled on its way to the capital, where it would become dirty and smelly. There were a few pleasure crafts making their way upstream, some laden barges being towed by horses on the towpath and anglers sitting on the bank, rod in hand, but they didn't seem to be catching much.

'I hate carriage rides,' Lucy said, linking arms with the other two. 'We had to keep stopping all the way from Norfolk to London, and I would as soon not have made the journey, but Mama was adamant that I had to have a Season or I would never find a husband. She has lined up a long list of gentlemen, not one of whom matches up to Mr Cavenhurst and I did not need to come to London to meet him.'

'Not even Viscount Kimberley?' Cassie said.

'Of course not. You may rest easy, Cassie, and have the field all to yourself. If you can capture him, that is. He seems to take delight in laughing with Sophie.'

'Laughing at the faux pas I keep making,' Sophie said. 'And scolding me. He has no right to censure me.'

'I heard he has vowed never to marry again,' Lucy put in.

'Mama says to bear that no mind,' Cassie said. 'If he is sufficiently attracted he will succumb in the end.'

Sophie laughed. 'I wonder what he would say if he could hear our conversation.'

Adam watched them go, relieved to see they were friends again. Miss Sophie Cavenhurst was not as uncaring as he had imagined. The scrapes she found herself in were largely due to ignorance of acceptable behaviour rather than mischief. It did not matter in present company—she was looked on with indulgence—but it could lead her into more serious trouble. Her brother was almost useless as a protector and Lady Cartrose too easy-going to restrain her. By all accounts her ladyship had been a bit wild herself in her youth.

He did wonder what Swayle and Fanshawe were up to. He had spoken to them, but as he had no business questioning what they did he had learned nothing. Both had said they had come upon her by chance and simply escorted her back to the party. It would not have been necessary if her brother had been doing his duty. Where was that young man? He had had time to ride all the way back to town and must surely have realised he had missed her. Mark's warning about Toby Moore came to his mind. Something was afoot, and if it put Sophie in danger, then he had better keep his eyes and ears open. 'You have dropped me right in the soup, haven't you,' he murmured, addressing his absent cousin.

It was not all Mark's fault. He felt drawn to the lively girl who was bright and intelligent and did not seem to care a hoot for protocol. He suspected her apparent self-assurance masked a vulnerability she tried to hide from the world. Having two sisters who had both made excellent marriages and were making their mark in the world on their own account must be hard to emulate.

The girls turned away from the towpath and struck off across the grass and were soon lost to sight among some trees. He resisted the inclination to follow them and was surprised at how relieved he felt when he saw them returning. It was ridiculous to think anything bad could happen to her strolling in a park with friends, only yards from help if they should need it.

'My lord,' Reggie called out to him. 'We are going to play cricket. Will you join us?'

He scrambled to his feet and joined the rest of the party who had fetched out a bat and ball and some stumps and were debating the rules of the game. 'There are not enough of us for two sides,' Richard said. 'So it's one batting against the rest, winner is the one with the most runs. Agreed?'

They marked out the pitch and tossed for who

should bat first and Sir Reginald won. Adam was to bowl and the rest spread out to field, including Sophie. 'Sophie, do come and sit down,' her aunt called out to her. 'You will be hit if you stand there.'

'Not I.' She laughed. 'If the ball comes my way, I shall catch it and Reggie will be out.'

Adam grinned. She was full of surprises, that one, and apparently unaware of the disapproving looks of the ladies of the party. Or perhaps she did know and enjoyed shocking them. He ran up and delivered the first ball, which Reggie fumbled. Lord Martindale picked it up and returned it to him. He sent another one down, which Reggie hit in Sophie's direction. She ran forward and caught it neatly.

'Out!' she cried triumphantly.

Reggie handed the bat to the next man and took his place in the field. And so it went on, but most of the men avoided hitting balls towards Sophie, and though she retrieved one or two balls, she was not given the opportunity to catch another. Mr Malthouse was out trying to avoid sending the ball in her direction. Adam was relieved of the bowling and Vincent took his place. Anxious to show his mettle, he bowled very fast, and one after the other fell until Adam came to the wicket.

It was obvious he knew what he was about. He piled up the runs and it seemed he would be there for the afternoon, but Sophie, who had been studying his game, came forward and a little to one side. When a ball flew towards her, she ran and caught it, though the speed of it stung her hand.

Even the ladies clapped, and Adam gave her a rueful grin. Her reply was to take the bat from his hand. 'My turn.'

He did not argue with her, but gave the ball to Lord Martindale to bowl and she stood at the wicket, bat carefully positioned behind the mark they had made in the grass.

His lordship tossed a gentle ball down to her, which she thumped into the undergrowth and ran five runs while they searched for it. The second ball, when it was retrieved and bowled again, received the same treatment and so did a third.

Adam took over the bowling again and he did not spare her. She hit it, but was unable to direct it as she would have wished, and he ran forward and caught it himself. 'Out, my valiant one,' he said. 'Let that teach you not to play games with men.'

There was more than cricket on his mind, she realised. It was a warning. It annoyed her. 'And you should not play games with ladies,' she retorted. 'We fight back.'

He laughed, but it was not a derisive laugh, not the laughter that she had complained about to her friends. It was a laugh that told her he understood her and liked her pluck.

The exchange brought an end to the game and everyone prepared to go home. In the absence of Teddy, Adam decided to ride beside her on the way back and edged Reggie and Richard out of the way. She did not complain; his company was infinitely preferable to that of those two men.

'When did you learn to play cricket?' he asked her.

'I used to play with Teddy and his school friends when they came home in the holidays. They wanted someone to make up the numbers. Sir Reginald was one of them.'

'You have known him for some time?'

'Yes. There is no harm in him, but he cannot accept that I will not marry him.'

'Why not?'

'I do not love him.'

'That is important to you?'

'Of course it is. It is the most important thing in a marriage. Don't you agree?'

'Indeed, I do.'

They were silent for a few minutes while they pondered on this. He had loved Anne more tenderly, more lastingly, than he could ever explain. Her death had been a terrible blow and had sent him spiralling down into an abyss of despair. He had gone about his business like an automaton, trying not to think, trying not to feel. He had come out of it a harder, colder man. On the surface he functioned well, but there was still that hollow feeling inside and a terrible feeling of guilt that he was to blame.

He pulled himself together and took up the conversation again. 'You ride very well. You must have had a good teacher. Teddy again?'

He looked sideways at her with a slight upward tilt to his mouth. It was a strong mouth, she noticed, and wondered idly what it would be like to be kissed by him. 'Yes, and our groom. I was put on a small pony as soon as I was big enough to sit on one.'

'Astride, I have no doubt.'

She knew he was teasing. 'Yes, there were no side-saddles small enough in the stables and I became used to it. It is much more comfortable both for me and my mount. Galloping side-saddle is a risky business.'

'Ladies are not meant to gallop.'

'This one is.'

'What else can you do?'

She turned to look at him. Was he teasing her again? 'Well, I can read and write and add up.'

'Now you *are* bamming me.'

'You asked for it.'

'So I did. Read, write, add up, dance the waltz, play cricket, ride like the wind—is there no end to your accomplishments?'

'I can shoot and fish.'

He laughed. 'Did your brother teach you that, too?'

'Of course.'

'Did he teach you to gamble?'

'No, he did not. He knows how ruinous it can be. Why did you ask that?'

'No reason. You are very fond of him, are you not?'

'Of course I am. He always had time for me when I was growing up, especially after my sisters married. He would take me about the estate and let me join in whatever he was doing. I would not have been able to come to London if he hadn't offered to escort me.'

'Where do you think he is now?'

'I don't know. Perhaps we will meet him coming back.'

'Or perhaps he has given up looking for you and is waiting at home. After all, he must know you are safe surrounded by so many friends.'

'Why wouldn't I be safe?' she asked sharply.

'No reason that I know of,' he said lightly. 'Except you seem to attract trouble.'

'Are you trying to frighten me?'

'I think it would take more than a few words of caution to frighten you, Miss Cavenhurst.'

'What am I being cautioned against?'

'Nothing in particular, except perhaps inviting the reputation of being a hoyden.'

'I am not a hoyden! But I don't see why

women cannot enjoy some of the things men enjoy. They are too stifled by convention.'

'Convention is there to protect the weaker sex.'

'It is there to make women subordinate to men,' she retorted. 'To feed their vanity and provide a breeding machine.'

'Oh, dear, such cynicism in one so young. Do you think every man is like that?'

'No, there are exceptions. Mark and Drew, for instance.'

'Who is Drew?'

'Sir Andrew Ashley. He is my other brother-in-law. He owns a clipper and takes his wife with him on all his adventures.'

'So it is adventure you wish for?'

'It might be fun.'

'It might also be dangerous.'

'Oh, we are back to the caution, are we?'

'No, for I think I should be wasting my breath.'

She laughed. It was a happy sound. Sophie could not be serious for long. Richard and Reggie looked at each other, eyebrows raised. Their friendly rivalry did not include Viscount Kimberley, but neither was in a position to do anything about it. The viscount's horse was shoulder to shoulder with Sophie's, and her aunt's carriage was close by on the other side. Occasionally everyone had to go in single file to accommodate the traffic as they neared the city, but the viscount soon positioned himself beside Sophie again.

The two men were not the only ones dismayed by Sophie's monopolising of the viscount; Cassie, riding in the open carriage beside her mother, was fuming.

Blissfully unaware of this, Sophie continued to enjoy her banter with Adam. It was light-hearted and fun and when she steered him to talk about himself, he told her how he had come to inherit a vast estate and a mill employing hundreds of workers. 'I didn't know anything about spinning and weaving and the men were mocking me, not always behind my back.'

'I cannot imagine anyone having the temerity to mock you, my lord,' she murmured.

'I think sometimes *you* do.'

'Certainly not. I would not dream of it. You can quell with a look.'

'That would not work with these men, I assure you. But I have a good manager who has worked at Bamford Mill, man and boy, and I set to work to learn from him about spinning and weaving, using wool from my own sheep. I hadn't realised what skilful work it is, nor how hard the men have to work, but I stuck at it and gained their respect in the end, not to mention a blanket I am very proud of.'

'There is a great deal of unrest among the mill workers, is there not, my lord?'

'Yes. It is why I am in London. I am trying to gain a better deal for them among other mill owners, some of whom have never been inside a mill in their lives, just as there are coal owners who have never been down a mine.'

This was a side of the viscount she had not encountered before and it gave her food for thought. 'From what I have read it is an uphill struggle.'

'It is indeed. My own men trust me, but others do not and certainly the mill owners do not. They think my ideas will spark a rebellion. I have to win them over.'

'Then, I wish you luck.'

'Thank you. I think I shall need it.'

'There are those who are sure you are in London to find a wife.'

He laughed. 'I am not unaware of that.'

'It amuses you?'

'Why not? It adds a little lightness to a heavy day.'

'Is that all?'

'As far as I am concerned, yes.'

'I shall not reveal that to them. They would not believe me in any case.'

He noticed the light of mischief in her eye and smiled. For the first time in years he had been beguiled by a young lady, who was totally unaware of the impact she had made. He had better watch his step.

* * *

The cavalcade dispersed when they arrived at Hyde Park Corner. He remained with the Cartrose carriage until they reached the corner of Mount Street, then he bade everyone farewell and rode on to Wyndham House. The day out had been a pleasant interlude, but he must not forget why he had come to London. He had arranged to meet a member of the Commons to see if he could gain support there, and he still had not located Henry Hunt. Amusement in the comely shape of Miss Sophie Cavenhurst must be set to one side. Did she share the belief that he was here to find a wife? Had he managed to convince her he was not? If not, he would have to find a way of disillusioning her.

Teddy was not at Cartrose House when they arrived. He had not come back by nightfall and Sophie became very worried. 'Something must have happened to him,' she said to her aunt after they had dined and were sitting in the drawing room. She had been straining her ears to hear sounds out in the street to tell them he had arrived. 'He's lying in a ditch somewhere, badly hurt. He could even be...' She could not speak of a worse horror. 'While I thought he must be at home, I didn't worry, but now...'

'Don't get in a taking,' her ladyship soothed.

'If he had been waylaid on the way, we should have heard about it. There would have been talk all up and down the road. No doubt he came home and, seeing the house empty, went to his club for his supper. He will be home directly.'

They waited until half past ten. Sophie could not sit still. She kept pacing the room and then running out to open the front door and look up and down the road. There was no question of going to bed.

'He has been out until breakfast time before and you have not worried,' her aunt said. 'What is so different today?'

'He was with us and came back to look for me. Surely he would have returned to the party to tell everyone he had not found me?'

'He can be thoughtless at times,' Lady Cartrose said. 'Young men are like that. He's enjoying himself and has forgotten the time. He is not going to keep me from my bed. Nor should he you. If he has not turned up by morning, we will ask the Mr Malthouse to organise a search. No doubt Lord Martindale and the viscount will join it.'

The old lady rose and went up to her room. Bessie came to see if Sophie was going up, but she sent the maid to her bed and continued her pacing.

* * *

It was dawn and the shadows in the garden and along the street were giving way to daylight, the milkmaids were driving their cows from house to house and the servants were stirring ready for their day's work when Sophie was roused from an uneasy slumber on the sofa by the sound of someone coming in the front door.

She flew out into the hall to see her brother putting his hat on the hall table. 'Sophie, you are up early.' He was swaying on his feet, obviously the worse for drink.

'I haven't been to bed.' She began beating his chest with her fists, crying with a mixture or relief and anger. 'How could you? How could you worry me so? Where have you been?'

He grabbed her hands to stop her. 'To White's. Met a few fellows, no need to worry…'

'I am disgusted with you. It would be all the same if I had been left without an escort.'

'But you had Reggie and Richard, and Aunt Emmeline. You didn't need me.'

'That is nothing to the point. You rode off to look for me, so everyone said. Did you look for me?'

'Course I did. I rode all the way back to town without seeing you, so I supposed I must have missed you on the road. No point in going back again.'

'Oh, go to bed. I am too tired to argue.' She gave him a push towards the stairs.

He stumbled his way up and she followed. In her own room, she stripped off her gown and flung herself on her bed. Teddy was a worry. Perhaps she ought to ask him to take her home where he would not be tempted to stay out all night. What an ignominious end to her Season. No more parties, no more balls, no hope of finding a husband, and her original dilemma over Mark would not have been solved. She thumped her pillow in frustration.

Chapter Six

It was gone midday when Sophie woke. Bessie had obviously found her asleep and left her. She rang her bell and climbed out of bed to draw back the curtains. The sun was shining and the road outside was busy. What had been planned for today? She could not remember.

'You are awake at last,' Bessie said, bustling into the room with a jug of warm water. 'Whatever time did you come to bed?'

'I don't know. It was getting light.'

'Did Master Edward come home?' She emptied the water into the bowl on the nightstand.

Sophie removed her nightshift and washed herself while she talked. 'Yes. He had been at his club. He said I didn't need him because I had Sir Reginald and Mr Fanshawe to escort me.'

'That is true.'

'But I didn't want their escort. I needed him to shield me from them.'

'Surely they would not harm you?'

'No, of course not, but they won't take no for an answer. It is as if they are in competition with each other to make me change my mind and that makes me cross. While they are hanging round me, what hope have I of attracting the man I really want?'

'And who might that be?'

'I don't know. I haven't met him yet.' She said it firmly, but in her heart there was a tiny doubt. She pushed it away.

Bessie laughed. 'You are making too much of this, child. Let destiny take its course. You cannot force it.'

She sighed. 'No, I suppose not.'

'What shall you wear today? It is very warm.'

'The blue flowered gingham, I think.'

She finished dressing and went down to the breakfast room, where her aunt was sitting over a cup of coffee, reading a newspaper. 'There you are,' she said, putting the paper down. 'What time did Edward come in?'

'Nearly dawn. He had been at White's and was a little foxed.' She sat down and poured herself a cup of coffee and took a slice of bread and butter.

'What did I tell you? You worry for nothing. And is that all you are going to eat? Have some eggs. I have them sent in fresh from the farm.'

'No, thank you. What are we going to do today?'

'I think you should rest. You had a tiring day riding all that way yesterday and then sitting up half the night. I certainly intend to stay at home this afternoon. This evening we are booked to go to Ranelagh Gardens.'

'With whom?'

'Just about everyone who was at the picnic. We arranged it then. Did you not hear us discussing it?'

'No.'

'No doubt you were too busy entertaining your swains. I notice that it was Viscount Kimberley who managed to jostle the other two out of the way to ride beside you on the way home.'

'Aunt, I hope you are not reading anything into that. His lordship knew I didn't want them near me.'

'Humph. You seemed to have much to talk about.'

'We were having a perfectly ordinary conversation. Nothing more to it than that.'

'I hope you can convince Cassandra of that, because she was looking daggers at you all the way home.'

'Oh, dear, I didn't think of that. I shall have to go and see her.'

'It is my "at home" this afternoon, and she may come with her mother. You had better reassure her then, though if you have designs on the gentleman yourself, that is a different matter. You may employ whatever wiles you deem fit.'

'I do not have designs on him, Aunt Emmeline, and you make it sound as though he would have no say in the matter. I am sure he is old enough and wise enough to know his own mind. Wiles would pass him by.'

'Whereas you,' her aunt added, 'are neither old enough nor wise enough to know yours.'

Sophie remained silent while she digested this. She knew her own mind—of course she did—which was why she would reject any man who did not fit her idea of a husband. Her first meeting with the viscount had been humiliating and she could not forget that, could not forget his half-hidden smile of amusement. She was never quite sure in their subsequent conversations if he was still laughing at her and whether the things he said were meant to provoke her into a response that would amuse him still further. It made her prickly. On the other hand, when he was talking about the mill and his care of the men, he hadn't been laughing, nor even smiling. She had seen a little of the real Adam and she liked him for it.

'I hope there will not be too many callers this afternoon,' her aunt said. 'I am excessively fatigued. And the weather is so hot.'

'Can you not say you are indisposed?'

'No. I go out so little and my callers are important to me. How else am I to hear all the gossip and keep up with what is going on?'

Mrs Malthouse arrived early without Cassie. 'She is not quite the thing today,' she told them. 'I think she was out in the sun too long yesterday. One forgets that though it is cooler in an open carriage when it is moving, the sun is just as hot. And walking in the park did not help.'

'I am so sorry to hear that,' Sophie said. Her friends were evidently not as robust as she was; Lucy was carriage sick and Cassie could not tolerate the sun. Their childhoods had obviously not been spent out of doors trying to keep up with a brother. 'I must go and visit her. Is there anything she would like me to take her?'

'I should not go today,' Mrs Malthouse said. 'She is not in a mood to be sociable.'

Emmeline sent Sophie a knowing look as if to say, 'I told you so.'

'Will she be well enough to come to Ranelagh Gardens tonight?' Sophie asked. 'It will be cooler by then.'

'She says not, but I shall try to persuade her. Now is not the time to withdraw from society. Lord Kimberley is not fixed to be in town beyond the next two or three weeks and she cannot afford to waste time being ill.'

'I don't suppose she is ill on purpose, Mrs Malthouse,' Sophie said.

'No, of course not. But if she does come tonight, I hope you will not monopolise his lordship as you did yesterday. It was very unfair of you.'

'I did not ask him to ride with me and could hardly be rude to him when he did.'

'Why not? You managed to rebuff Sir Reginald and Mr Fanshawe without much trouble. Very put out they were, especially after they had rescued you when you were lost and about to ride straight into the river.'

'That is nonsense. Did they think I could not see the water, or that I was so poor a rider I would allow my horse to plunge straight in with me on its back? And I was not lost. I simply took a wrong turn. I could easily have found my way back to the party. No doubt they wanted to make themselves look like heroes.'

'Be that as it may, your riding back with the viscount was certainly noticed.'

Sophie opened her mouth to protest, but they were interrupted by the arrival of more callers and the conversation came to an abrupt end. The room was soon full of friends and acquaintances, many of who had been on the picnic and were to be part of the company that evening. Reggie and Richard arrived together and, after bowing to their hostess and acknowledging others, came straight to her side.

Fortunately she was able to excuse herself with a polite smile on the grounds that she must help her aunt, who was wilting in her chair by the open window.

'Is there anything I can get you, Aunt Emmeline? I think everyone has some cool cordial and cake, and now I can look after you.'

'Thank you, child. Do you think you can fetch my big Chinese fan? You will find it in the top drawer of the chest in my bedchamber. I need something bigger than this little chicken-skin one to move the air in here.'

'Of course.'

She was passing Mrs Malthouse when she heard her saying, 'Such an accomplished flirt for one so young, and Emmeline seems not strong enough to rein her in. I fear for Vincent.'

'I heard she had been riding in the park in Sir Reginald's high-perch phaeton, just the two of them,' her listener added. 'It can't be true, surely.'

'It is. She told Cassandra so herself. I would not have her at Cassandra's ball, but the invitation has been made and accepted and I can hardly retract it. She is Lady Cartrose's niece and Emmeline has been my friend for many years.'

Pink with mortification, Sophie went on her way. It was so unfair! She was not a flirt. It was not her fault Reggie and Richard dogged her, and as for Vincent, she had hardly spoken half a dozen words to him. She was rapidly coming to dislike London and everyone in it, but if she asked Teddy to take her home, everyone would think she was running away in shame. That she could not bear.

Putting her head in the air, she made for the stairs and her aunt's room, where she found the fan and returned to her aunt.

'Thank you, child. You are a good girl.'

'Mrs Malthouse does not think so.'

'Bear her no mind. She is simply jealous that her daughter does not attract the attention you do.'

'I wish I did not.'

'It is why you came to London, surely?'

'Not to have Sir Reginald and Mr Fanshawe on my heels all the time. Why couldn't they stay in Norfolk?'

'Because you are here, my dear.' Her aunt laughed. 'And do you know, their attention is a good thing in a way—it attracts other men to find out what they are missing.'

'There is something smoky going on, and I wish I knew what it was. I'm told Lord Gorange is in town as well, though I have not seen him.'

'It may just be coincidence.'

'I hope so, I really do.' She looked up as Teddy came into the room. He was sober and perfectly groomed. Going from one to the other of her aunt's guests, he smiled and exchanged a few words before moving on and eventually reaching her.

'Well, sis,' he said, smiling disarmingly at her, 'all present and correct. Am I forgiven?'

'Yes, if you accompany us to Ranelagh Gardens this evening and stay with us. No going off and leaving us, especially if Reggie and Richard are hovering about.'

'They only want you to change your mind.'

'Well, I'm not going to.'

'Is that a promise, sister, dear?'

'It most definitely is.'

'Good, but do not let them know that. Keep them hovering, as you so inelegantly put it.'

'Why?'

'Because it amuses me to see them squirm.' He turned towards the door as a newcomer entered. 'Ah, here is Viscount Kimberley. Now, you may encourage him as much as you like.'

'Teddy, what are you up to?'

'Nothing at all. I only have your happiness at heart.' He turned to Adam. 'Good afternoon, my lord. I believe I owe you my thanks for looking after my sister so well yesterday.'

'It was a privilege and a pleasure. Good afternoon, my lady, Miss Cavenhurst. I hope I see you well.'

'Very well, my lord,' Sophie said. 'My brother

decided not to ride back to Richmond after missing me on the road.'

'No reason to,' Teddy said. 'She had so many admirers vying for her favours, I was *de trop*.'

'I would have expected you to be extravigilant under the circumstances,' Adam said.

'Why? I have known Reggie and Richard since boyhood. They would not harm a hair of her head.'

'They were prepared to subject her to gossip.'

'Stop it!' Sophie cried. 'Please do not fall out over it. I came to no harm and I do not blame Teddy for not wanting to make that ride twice in the heat. It is over and done with and he will be escorting me to Ranelagh tonight.'

'Do you go?' Teddy asked Adam.

'I have not made up my mind.'

'Oh, please do,' Sophie said, knowing how disappointed Cassie would be if he did not go, and would no doubt blame her for frightening him off. She would have to do something helpful to bring them together, and then Cassie would realise she had no designs on the gentleman and be her friend again. She had no idea she was being manipulative and would have denied it hotly if anyone had suggested it.

'We are to meet at the Rotunda at eight o'clock for supper,' Lady Cartrose told him. 'Please join us.'

'Yes, do,' Teddy added. 'It is a fireworks

night. They are quite spectacular, you know, and these are to be especially fine to honour the new princess.'

'Very well. I will be there.' Adam bowed and left, and after that everyone left one by one.

'I am going to rest,' her ladyship said, rising. 'I suggest you do the same, Sophie. And as for you, Edward, stay at home today if you please. I want you here when the carriage comes round.'

He laughed and bowed and held out his arm to escort her upstairs, then he returned to Sophie, who was looking out of the window at the carriages, carts, horse riders and pedestrians that thronged the road. She turned when he entered. 'Teddy, what is going on? What are you up to?'

'Nothing, sis. What can I be up to? I have been remiss and been scolded and am penitent. What more do you want?'

'I want to know why Sir Reginald and Mr Fanshawe are in town and buzzing round me. I have turned them down and they know I will not change my mind.'

'Perhaps they don't.'

'Teddy, have you encouraged them to think otherwise?'

'Certainly not. It is not my fault you are so comely.'

'Fustian! And I hear Lord Gorange is here, too. It cannot be coincidence.'

'I don't know what else it is.'

'And why did you say I may encourage Viscount Kimberley?'

'Well, my dear, he is obviously a better bet than Reggie and Dick.'

'A better bet!' Her voice rose. 'Another of your gambling terms. I am not a prize to be won or lost in a game of cards, Teddy.'

'Sorry, I meant he is richer and a member of the nobility—quite a catch, in fact.'

'He is also a widower who adored his wife and is determined not to marry again.'

'How do you know that?'

'He told me so.'

'A rather intimate conversation for so slight an acquaintance, don't you think?'

'Not at all. He makes no secret of it.'

'I fancy you could make him change his mind.'

'I am not even going to try. As I told Cassie and Lucy, I have no intention of playing second fiddle to a dead wife.'

He simply laughed, chucked her under the chin and wandered from the room. Sophie decided she might as well follow her aunt and rest, ready for the evening to come.

Determined to put an end to rumours of being a hoyden and a flirt, she dressed demurely in white muslin trimmed with blue ribbon for the evening excursion. Teddy, as contrite as it was possible for someone so devoid of remorse to be, was in attendance as he had promised. When they sat down to a light supper, she sat between her aunt and brother, much to the chagrin of Sir Reginald and Mr Fanshawe. She smiled across the table at Cassie, who was sitting next to Viscount Kimberley, but Cassie ignored her and began talking very fast to Adam. He appeared very attentive and spoke quietly to her, making her blush.

It was the same after supper when they strolled about the grounds, waiting for the fireworks to begin. With such a large party, they were bound to become separated. Cassie and Lucy went off, arm in arm, escorted by Vincent and Adam. Sophie stayed close beside her aunt, whose pace was exceedingly slow. After a while her ladyship begged to sit down and they found a bench where they were joined by Lady Martindale and Mrs Malthouse.

'Do go and join your friends,' her aunt said. 'Augusta and I and her ladyship will have a comfortable coze here until the fireworks begin.'

Thus dismissed, Sophie went in search of Teddy, but could not find him. It was nearly dark and the lanterns had been lit in the trees along the main pathways but more distant walks were in deep shadow, making her shiver a little. She did not find her brother but came upon Cassan-

dra and the viscount, dogged by a determined
Vincent. She had no idea how they had managed
to lose Lucy, unless she was with Teddy. She fell
into step beside Vincent, allowing the other two
to go a little way ahead. Cassie was still talking
too much, hardly pausing for breath. Adam was
smiling indulgently and putting in a 'Quite so'
or 'Indeed?' every now and again.

'It is much cooler now, isn't it?' Sophie said
to Vincent. 'So much more comfortable.'

'Yes, thank goodness. Cassie cannot stand the
heat.' He turned towards her. 'You, on the other
hand, Miss Cavenhurst, seem to thrive on it.'

'Do I? I suppose it is because I would rather
be out of doors than in.'

'You enjoyed the picnic, then?'

'Yes, very much. Did you?'

'Oh, yes, especially the cricket. I never expected to see a young lady hitting the ball with
so much gusto and making runs.'

'Teddy taught me. Sometimes I used to dress
in his outgrown breeches to play when I was a
child. It is so much easier when one is able to
move freely.'

'Did you really? What did your parents say
to that?'

'So long as it was only in the grounds of the
estate they did not mind. Of course, it had to stop
when I grew older.' She knew she was shocking
him and was enjoying it.

'But you don't do it now?'

'Oh, no, that would be decidedly improper.'

Adam, in a pause in his one-sided conversation with Cassie, turned towards them; she could tell by his smile that he had heard her. 'I think it is time to make our way towards the fireworks,' he said. 'All the vantage points will be gone if we leave it much longer.'

They turned back and joined the throng of people standing behind the ropes waiting for the display to begin.

'What are you playing at?' Adam murmured in Sophie's ear, startling her; she hadn't realised he was so close. Cassie had been claimed by her mama a few yards away. Teddy was fussing round Aunt Emmeline. Lucy and Mrs Martindale were with them.

'Playing at, my lord?' she said sweetly. 'What can you mean?'

'You know very well what I mean. You manoeuvred Miss Malthouse to sit beside me at supper. It was so obvious I wondered others did not notice it.'

'Now, how could I, a mere slip of a girl, manoeuvre you, of all people? And why would I?'

'I do not know, but it was unkind of you. I had to endure her idle chatter throughout supper and afterwards while we walked. Listening to her is exhausting.'

'I expect she is nervous.'

'Why, for heaven's sake? I am not an ogre. I do not eat silly little girls.'

She laughed. 'I believe Cassie is a few months my senior.'

'What has that to do with it? I am persuaded you must have some motive.'

'My lord, I have been accused of being a hoyden and a flirt and Cassie is convinced that I am trying to put her out with you. I had to make her see otherwise.'

'And you wouldn't be doing anything of the sort, of course.'

'Certainly not. I should be wasting my time, would I not? Have not you not declared you are not looking for a second wife?'

'Indeed I have.'

'And I am not prepared to be one, so let us be friends.'

He laughed. 'Oh, Sophie, if anyone could make me change my mind it would be you.' But his murmured words were drowned by the noise of the first rockets being sent up into the night sky, vying with the stars in their brilliance.

He remained at her side while the display continued, lighting up the sky in red, green and yellow stars which burst upon the firmament before fading to earth again. As the last one died away, they turned to leave. It was then she saw Reggie and Richard talking to Lord Gorange and her heart sank.

'Oh, no,' she murmured.

'What do you mean? Is something wrong?'

'That is Lord Gorange.' She nodded in the direction of the three men. 'I heard he was in town.'

'Is he one of your erstwhile suitors?'

'Yes. There is something very smoky go on. Teddy denies he has anything to do with it, but why are they here and why are they at every function I attend?'

'Did you hint to any of them that you might change your mind? A word of hope perhaps, an undertaking they must complete in order to win your hand?'

'Certainly not. I am not so frivolous.'

'I am glad to hear it. Marriage is a solemn undertaking, not to be treated lightly.'

'Those are my sentiments exactly, my lord.'

They had reached the little gathering, who were saying their goodbyes before dispersing. Adam excused himself and went to speak to Cassandra and her mother. His going made her feel—she could not explain how she felt—a little empty, a little vulnerable. She shook herself out of it as Lord Gorange came over to her and bowed. 'Miss Cavenhurst, your obedient servant.'

She bent her knee. 'Lord Gorange, how do you do?'

'I am well. Who is that?' he asked, indicating Adam with a nod of his head.

'That is Viscount Kimberley of Saddleworth.'

'A viscount, eh? You wasted no time, then.'

'What do you mean by that?'

'Finding someone new. When I heard you had come to London and Reggie and Dick were here, too, I had to come to see what was afoot.'

'Nothing is afoot, my lord, nothing at all. Now, please excuse me, my aunt is ready to leave and I must not keep her waiting.'

He bowed. 'With your permission, I will call on you.'

'Why?' she demanded.

'Unfinished business, Miss Cavenhurst, unfinished business. I cannot let Swayle and Fanshawe make all the running.'

His talk, just like the others', was gambling talk, bets and wagers and running. It infuriated her. 'They and you may run as far and as fast as you like,' she said. 'You will not find me at the end of it, waiting to be claimed. Unless you have any other reason to be in London, I suggest you go home and spend some time with your daughters.'

'That I will do when I take my bride back with me.'

'Then, I wish you luck in your endeavours,' she said. 'Now, I really must go.'

She escaped to join her aunt for the carriage ride home.

* * *

Adam had not come to the gardens by carriage and he was not going back to Wyndham House. His destination was the Belle Sauvage, one of the capital's principal coaching inns from which coaches left day and night for all parts of the country. It was a fair walk and he ought to have hired a cab or a chair, but he was in no hurry. Alfred Farley had discovered that Henry Hunt would be there until late, talking with his cronies. The inn would be a convenient place from which to disappear if the need arose.

Henry Hunt was a handsome man with an enviable physique, known to be good at physical pursuits, including boxing at which he excelled. Modesty was not one of his virtues. He had a voice that commanded attention and when he raised it, he could be heard from some distance. Why a man from a prosperous farming background should become the champion of the lower orders was a mystery to Adam.

At a meeting in Spa Fields in Islington in November 1816, which attracted a crowd of thousands, he had been appointed to carry a petition to the Prince Regent, which called for parliamentary reform and help for those suffering hardship. He was twice refused access to the prince, and consequently another meeting was convened in December at which he was booked to be the principal speaker. Unfortunately he arrived too

late to prevent some hotheads from taking over
the meeting and marching on the Tower of London, looting a gun shop for weapons on the way.
The government, terrified a revolution could
happen in England as it had in France, reacted
by sending troops to put down the riot. The result was mayhem, the crowd was dispersed and
several arrests made, after which the rule of habeas corpus was suspended in what came to be
known as the Gagging Acts and added to the
popular grievances. It certainly had not silenced
them, as Adam well knew.

He walked along the Strand and Fleet Street
and thence to Ludgate Hill. Even at that time
of night the roads were busy with traffic and
the walkways were crowded. Most of those who
could afford them chose to be conveyed in carriages and chairs, and so the pedestrians tended
to be workers or beggars or ladies of the night.
If they noticed the well-dressed gentleman passing them at a brisk pace they appeared not to.
He was not deceived, his senses highly tuned
to spot trouble.

He reached the Belle Sauvage whose yard was
well lit with flambeaux and busy with coaches
and travellers arriving and departing. He went
into the waiting parlour and looked about him.
Hunt was sitting at a table in the corner with the
remains of a meal in front of him. He had his

hand on an almost empty tankard of ale. Adam strode over to him.

'Mr Hunt, I was told I would find you here. I am Adam Trent.'

'I know well who you are, Viscount Kimberley, no need to hide your rank from me.'

'May I buy you another ale?'

'Thank you, yes.'

Adam beckoned a waiter and ordered two quarts of ale and sat down opposite the orator. 'If you know who I am, then you will mayhap know why I am here.'

'You tell me.'

'I have heard rumours of another meeting...'

'There are always meetings.'

'Yes, but when Orator Hunt is to be the speaker, thousands travel from all over the country to listen to him.'

'You flatter me.'

A waiter brought the ale and the diversion served Adam to gather his thoughts. It was evident Hunt was not going to help him out. 'I have heard this meeting is to be the largest yet and that you will be calling for universal suffrage and the repeal of the Gagging Acts.'

'So?'

'I have no quarrel with your aims, in fact, I support them, but I am concerned that, as happened at Spa Fields, the crowd will become unmanageable and cause a riot. The militia will be called in and there will be violence.'

'I abhor violence. I prefer peaceful demonstration.'

'Can you guarantee this will be peaceful?'

'I cannot. No one could.'

Adam recognised the truth of that. 'So you would stand by and let it happen. If troops are called in there will be injuries, even lives lost.'

'Do you think I have not thought of that? Unfortunately, there is always a price to pay for progress. With attitudes so unbending in those who govern, is it any wonder people demonstrate?'

'It is but a short step from demonstration to riot and anarchy.'

Hunt took a swig of ale before he replied, 'I can, and will, advise my followers to be unarmed and not rise to provocation. I can do no more.'

'When and where is this meeting to be?'

'That I cannot tell you.'

'Spa Fields again?'

'I have said I cannot tell you, nor would I if I could.'

'You do not trust me?'

The man gave a grunt of a laugh. 'My lord, you are an aristocrat and a mill owner. Your interest lies elsewhere than with the workingman.'

'How can you say so? There are others, like myself, in sympathy with the plight of the workers, who would change their condition if they could.'

'Too few,' Hunt said laconically. 'And they are not listened to.'

'You heard my speech in the Lords?'

'I read the report.'

'And?'

'It changes nothing.' He paused. 'My advice, my lord, is to go home and not meddle. Do your good deeds, if you must, but leave the cause of the workingman to workingmen.'

Knowing he was making no headway, Adam took his leave. He was annoyed with Hunt for his condescending attitude, even more annoyed with himself for his failure to make an impression.

He was striding back in the direction in which he had come when he realised he was being followed. He stopped; the footsteps behind him stopped. He continued; they continued. Assuming it was a footpad, who were numerous in that area, he dodged down a side street and then another and another, until the sound of footsteps behind him ceased. He did not know exactly where he was and it was dark as pitch. The alley he was in was narrow, the buildings either side tall and for the most part shuttered and their doors opened straight onto the street, whose cobbles were slick with grime. A cat yowled, startling him.

He kept walking forward, and then he saw

lights ahead and realised he was outside the Fleet prison and had almost walked in a circle. He looked up at its bulk, imagining all the people incarcerated there, some for minor offences like stealing a loaf of bread, some for grand larceny, some for insurrection, some even for murder and awaiting the hangman's rope. He shuddered and made his way back to Fleet Street and the Strand where he was able to hire a cab to convey him the rest of the way to Wyndham House.

He had told the housekeeper not to wait up for him, but she had left a tray of bread, cheese and ham and a carafe of wine for him in case he was hungry when he came in, and he sat down to eat and drink and go over his evening.

It had been an evening of contrasts. His conversation with Henry Hunt, which had achieved nothing except a mild warning to mind his own business and an unintentional trip into the darker side of the metropolis where the poorest of its inhabitants lived and scurried about like rats. He ought to go there in daylight and learn a little more of their lives. And had his follower been a footpad? Such a one would not have followed him for so long. As soon as he turned off the main road, he would have been on to him and relieved him of his pocket watch and purse, leaving him battered in the gutter. No, this man had been anxious to know where he was going. But why? He had nothing to hide.

The contrast with the dark and sombre night was the light and cheerful evening at Ranelagh, but even here there had been undercurrents. For all she denied it, he knew Miss Cavenhurst had manoeuvred Miss Malthouse to sit next to him, forcing him to be polite to the empty-headed girl. He had only been half listening to her as he'd watched Sophie from across the table. She had been more subdued than usual, as if she had been scolded, and he wondered what about. Could it possibly have been over being called a hoyden and a flirt? She might have a little of the tomboy in her, but he didn't think she was a flirt. Only someone who felt put out by her would say that. Miss Cassandra Malthouse? He smiled. That was what it was all about, she had said as much, but if either young lady thought he would play their game, they were mistaken. Besides, it was time he paid the promised visit to Mark and then went home to Yorkshire.

Chapter Seven

Surprisingly Teddy was at the breakfast table when Sophie went down next morning. He was morosely stirring a cup of cold coffee.

'You are up betimes,' she said, helping herself from the dishes on the sideboard and taking her plate to the table to sit beside him. 'Could you not sleep?'

'No. Too much to think about.'

'Oh, that means you are in a scrape.' She poured herself a cup of coffee from the pot on the table.

'You could say that.'

'Well, out with it. I assume it is a gambling debt.'

'More than one.'

'Oh, Teddy, will you never learn?'

'I'm sorry, sis.'

She sighed. 'How much?'

'A few thousand.'

'Why do you do it, Teddy? Why put yourself and everyone who loves you through so much worry time after time? It isn't fair.'

'I don't do it on purpose. I can't seem to help myself. I tell myself I am not going to gamble, but then the opportunity for a big win comes up and I find myself taking a chance…'

'And losing.'

'I don't always lose.'

'More often than not. You promised Papa…'

'I know I did. I meant it at the time. I always mean it. I can't tell him, Sophie, I can't.'

'Are you thinking of going to India again?'

'No, it is not so easy to make a fortune that way now. Besides, I don't have the blunt to get there.'

'What are you going to do, then?'

'I don't know. I suppose I'll have to talk to Mark, but Jane will slay me.'

'And I don't blame her. Have you so easily forgotten what very nearly happened to her? She was prepared to sacrifice herself to Lord Bolsover to pull you and Papa out of the mire. If it hadn't been for Mark and Drew and that brave Portuguese gentleman it could very well have happened.'

'Drew!' he said suddenly. 'Do you know where he is?'

'No. In her last letter Issie said they were going to Singapore.'

'Oh, he won't serve, then.' He paused. 'Sophie, if you were to find a very rich husband...'

'Teddy!'

'Well, you could,' he said defensively. 'That's why you came to London, isn't it? Take Viscount Kimberley, for instance.'

'Teddy, I will not take Lord Kimberley, as you so crudely put it. He has no interest in me...'

'You could change his mind.'

'I will not even try.'

'Then you will find me in some back alley with my throat cut.'

'Do not be so melodramatic. Who would kill you because you can't pay your debts? That's not the way to recover them.'

'It's the way Toby Moore works.'

'I knew that man was a bad influence on you. Why, oh, why do you play with him?'

'For revenge, sis. He was one of those who forced me to go to India and I have not forgiven him. I was winning at first and thought I could ruin him as he ruined me...'

Her laughter was more hysterical than amused. 'Teddy, when will you realise your gambling not only ruins your own life, but the lives of all those who love you? You will break Mama's heart.'

'I know.' He was in tears. She had never seen him weep before; he was always so ebullient. It tore at her soft heart. She left her seat to go and put her arms about him.

'Don't cry, Teddy, please don't cry. We'll think of something. I don't know what, but we will. But you are never to go anywhere near a gambling club again, not even a card table at a private party. Do you hear?'

'I hear.'

'And you are not to see or speak to Captain Moore ever again.'

'He will want his money.'

'Then he will have to wait for it. I think you should go home to Hadlea.'

'But your Season...'

'What of it, Teddy? You have ruined it already.'

'Oh, Sophie...' His tears were renewed.

'If someone has to marry wealth,' she said, 'why not you?'

'Because I have as good as proposed to Lucy.'

'Good heavens! When did you propose?'

'When we were walking in Ranelagh Gardens. It was such a lovely night and she was hanging on my arm and we were alone.'

'And she accepted?'

'Yes, straight away. She doesn't know anything about this, Sophie. I couldn't tell her. She was so happy and said she would speak to her parents. No doubt I shall get a grilling from her papa and what I shall say to him I have no idea.'

'Oh, Teddy, what are we to do with you?'

'Wash your hands of me.'

'I can't do that. You are my brother, you protected me when we were children, made sure I was safe, fought anyone who bothered me, and I love you.'

'Oh, sis...'

'You had better go up to your room and make yourself presentable before Aunt Emmeline comes down. She must know nothing of this.'

He scrambled to his feet and disappeared, leaving her lost in thought and very near to tears herself. Her brother had never really grown up. Although six years older than she was, he behaved like her junior, looking to her as he had to his other sisters to pull him out of the scrapes into which he sank. But how could she? Could she sacrifice herself as Jane had been prepared to do? Even if she did, she had to be sure any husband she chose was not only rich enough, but prepared to use those riches to pay Teddy's debts. She began mentally ticking off the possibilities: Reggie, Richard, Lord Gorange, Vincent Malthouse... Mr Malthouse would not do. He would have no money until he inherited, but the others, all three well up in the stirrups, all three wanting to marry her. What she could not understand was why. She shuddered. So much for her dreams of a love match.

* * *

There was something wrong with Sophie, Adam decided, when he called later that day to tell everyone that he was leaving London. Her face was pale, her blue eyes puffy and red, her whole demeanour subdued. She had been quiet the previous evening, but nothing like this. She was behaving as if she had received a body blow. Who or what had done this to her?

'Miss Cavenhurst, are you not well?' he asked gently.

'I am perfectly well, my lord. A little tired perhaps.'

Other people came and went and Lady Cartrose received them exactly as she always did. She was not unfeeling, so he could only surmise that whatever was wrong had been kept from her. Sophie had got herself into a scrape and it must be very serious to put the light out in those lovely eyes and make her move so listlessly. He felt an unaccustomed urge to take her into his arms and comfort her, and if there had been no one else in the room he might well have done so. He forgot why he had come in his determination to find out what it was and help her if he could. To do that he needed to speak to her alone.

The polite time for an afternoon call came to an end and everyone made to leave. He hung about to be the last. 'Miss Cavenhurst,' he whispered while Lady Cartrose was bidding farewell to Mrs Malthouse. 'I must speak with you alone.'

She had been looking at the floor, but now lifted her head to look at him in surprise. 'My lord, no.'

'No? What do you mean, no?'

'It is not proper.'

In spite of himself, he chuckled. 'When have you been so concerned with what is proper? That is not the Sophie Cavenhurst I have come to know. I am not about to offer for you, if that is what you are thinking. You have made it abundantly clear you would not entertain the idea. Friends, you said. It is as a friend I wish to speak to you.'

'Oh.' Too late she realised Jane had been right when she said falling in love was not something you could order, nor could you be sure that your love would be returned. The few times he had touched her had been acts of chivalry, not an indication of any deeper feelings for her. He behaved in the same way towards other ladies, young and old. She was no different. She had found the man to equal Mark, even surpass him, but Adam's own words echoed in her brain. *'I am not about to offer for you.' 'It is as a friend I wish to speak to you.'* A friend—that was all she was to him. It was a painful revelation.

'What are you two whispering about?' Lady Cartrose demanded. Mrs Malthouse had gone and he was the only one left and her deafness had prevented her from hearing their conversation.

'I was asking Miss Cavenhurst if she would care to come riding with me tomorrow morning,' Adam told her, raising his voice a little.

'I am sure if she wishes to go I have nothing against it,' the lady said. 'No doubt Edward will accompany her.'

'Will you?' He addressed Sophie. 'In the morning before the sun becomes too hot.'

Teddy had suggested she could make him change his mind. But how could she? He seemed impervious to women's wiles, and she would not demean herself by attempting it. On the other hand it would be churlish to refuse him. 'Very well, I shall be pleased to.'

'Good. I will call about nine o'clock and will bring a mount for you.'

'Thank you.'

He picked up his hat from the hall table. 'Cheer up. It won't be half as bad as you think,' he murmured, settling the hat on his head.

She watched him striding easily down the front steps and off along the road and her heart felt fit to break.

Somehow she got through the rest of the morning, conversing with her aunt, picking at her food at nuncheon and declining to go out.

Even her aunt was worried about her. 'Are you not well, child?'

'I am tired, Aunt. I am not used to such a continuous round of engagements.'

'Oh, is that all? We will have a day at home and you shall rest.'

Rest she could not. She picked up a book and pretended to read, but her thoughts were whirring round and round in her head and going nowhere. She tried some embroidery that her aunt had started but never finished, but after a few stitches, she let it drop into her lap. Outside the sun was shining; the garden invited her. She took a parasol and ventured out to pace up and down, turning Teddy's problems over in her mind, and they became all mixed up with her own huge problem. She had fallen in love and it was a state of affairs that could have no happy ending.

Teddy would probably say that was the best thing that could have happened. He would tell her to make a push to win the man, make him change his mind about not marrying again and they would both benefit; a man like Viscount Kimberley could easily afford a few thousand to pay off his debts. Even if she could change his lordship's mind—and how did one go about that? she wondered—she would be using him. That would be dishonest and would stand in the way of any chance of happiness. Far from making it easier, it made it more difficult, impossible. Teddy would never see that it was out of the question. Where was her brother? She had not seen him since breakfast. Surely he had not gone gambling again?

The person most to blame was Captain Moore. Teddy would not ask him for more time to pay, but she could. Where could she find him? The only place she thought he might be was White's, but ladies certainly could not go there. She thought about this for some time as she paced up and down, then, making up her mind, went indoors and made her way up to Teddy's bed-chamber.

Her brother had eschewed the services of a valet. At Greystone Manor he relied on his father's valet to help him with his toilette and the servants to tidy up his clothes. In London, it was Bessie who tidied up after him. She had even been known to tie his cravat for him. Hoping her maid was not in the room, she opened the door gingerly. There was no one there. It only took a minute to extract a suit of clothes, a shirt, cravat, hose and a tall hat, and then she was speeding along to her own room to change into them.

She made a passable boy, she decided as she surveyed herself in the mirror over the night table and stuffed most of her hair up into the crown of the hat. She could not wear Teddy's shoes—they were far too big—but she put on her own riding boots and tucked the breeches into those. She opened her door carefully and peered along the landing. There was no one about.

Two minutes later she was outside and strolling along the street, apparently without a care in the world. If it were not for the fact that her errand was so serious, she would have been enjoying herself. She met no one she knew on the way to St James's Street, so her disguise was not tested, but none of the strangers who passed her gave her a second glance, so she thought it must pass muster.

St James's Street was busy. Several of the gentlemen's clubs were situated there and patrons came and went, on foot and in cabs and carriages. The only women she saw were a couple of dubious characters.

She was stopped by the doorman when she attempted to enter White's. 'Members only, young man.'

'I am looking for Captain Moore.' She tried to deepen her voice. 'I have an urgent message for him.'

She was told to wait while the captain was fetched. As she stood, wishing she had never come, several people passed her and eyed her with curiosity. From farther in the building she could hear men's voices, shouts and laughter. And then she saw the captain coming towards her and her nerve almost deserted her.

'You want me?' he queried, stopping in front of her.

'Yes.'

'I don't know you, do I? What's your name?'

'It doesn't matter what my name is. I need to speak to you in private.'

'Then, let us take a stroll.' He led the way into the street. 'Now, what is it that you have to tell me? I left a lucrative game and would return to it.'

'Is Mr Cavenhurst with you?'

'Cavenhurst? No, I have not seen him today at all.'

She breathed a sigh of relief. 'Good. I believe he owes you a considerable amount.'

'He does that. What has it to do with you?'

'I am his friend. I come to ask you to give him more time to pay.'

'He is a coward as well as a welsher, sending a stripling to plead for him.' He paused and laughed. 'Of course, you are no stripling, are you, Miss Cavenhurst?' He reached out and pulled off her hat, making her hair cascade about her shoulders. 'You make a lovely boy, my dear, but I would have to be half-blind to be deceived.'

'It was the only way I could get near you.' People were looking at them and smiling. She grabbed her hat from him and put it back on, pushing her hair up into it. It wouldn't go back as well as it had when she'd had a mirror to help her, and strands of it escaped.

'I am flattered.'

'Don't be. You knew Teddy could never resist a gamble—why did you encourage him?'

'He needed no encouragement.'

She realised this was true. 'You could have refused to play with him.'

'What, and denied myself the pleasure of taking his money?'

'He has no money.'

'Now, that is a great shame, because I really need him to pay up.'

'Give him more time.'

'Why should I?'

'It is the only way you are going to get it.'

'Is that so?' He smiled, revealing a broken tooth. 'Now, I can think of an alternative. You are really stirring up my baser instincts dressed like that. I am wondering what it would be like to have a young lad in my bed who turns out not to be a lad after all. For that pleasure I might forgo the debt.'

'You are disgusting!'

He shrugged. 'Then, Teddy must find a way of paying me. Remind him, when you see him, that I charge interest by the day.'

She fled and made her way back to Mount Street, uncaring that more of her hair was escaping and her small strides were giving her away.

Her mind was whirling. She had been right about Captain Moore when she'd first met him: he made her flesh creep. He must be depraved if he thought she would consider his suggestion. She went into the house by a side door and scuttled up to her room to change back into her own clothes. Teddy's room was exactly as she had left it. She put his clothes back where she had found them and went to her room to sit on her bed with her head in her hands. Bessie found her there when she came to help her dress for supper.

'What is the matter, Miss Sophie?'

'Nothing. Have you seen anything of Teddy?'

'Not since this morning. Why?'

'I just wondered where he was.'

'He'll be back directly, I've no doubt. You are not engaged to go out tonight, are you?'

'No, the Malthouses are coming.'

'Then what about the pink sarcenet with the silk roses?'

Bessie was evidently not worried by Teddy's absence and as far as Sophie could tell, knew nothing of the afternoon's futile escapade. She dressed and went down for supper, which she ate with her aunt and Margaret. Fortunately the two ladies had plenty to gossip about and her quietness was not noted.

'I thought Edward was going to dine with us,' Emmeline said. 'He was to make a fourth for whist.'

* * *

He had not returned when Mr and Mrs Malthouse arrived for their usual game, bringing Cassie with them. Since she had been able to have the viscount's undivided attention for most of the time at Ranelagh, for which she felt grateful to Sophie, she had forgiven her and they were friends again. Margaret made up the four for the whist, so the girls were left to amuse themselves.

Cassie was bubbling over with excitement. 'He is even more agreeable than I first thought,' she said, referring to the viscount. 'He listened with grave attention to what I had to say and concurred with me on almost everything. When I stumbled he took my arm to steady me. I am sure it will not be long before he speaks to Papa.'

Sophie had not the heart to disillusion her friend. But perhaps she was not under an illusion and the reality was that the viscount's comments about Cassie being empty-headed did not count for anything. Men did not like women who were their equal in brains, she had been told. Oh, how difficult it was to tell. And what did it matter anyway? Viscount Kimberley was not for her. But she was very careful not to hint that his lordship was going to take her riding the following morning. She looked over at her aunt, who was concentrating on her cards, and hoped she would not mention it, either.

'Cassie, I have heard you play the pianoforte beautifully,' Sophie said, anxious to end the conversation about the viscount, which was twisting the knife into an already broken heart. 'Would you play something for us now?'

'Oh, I don't know…'

'Yes, Cassandra,' her mother put in, proving that she, at least, had been listening to the girls' conversation. 'Play that piece you have been practising.'

'Oh, do,' Sophie said. 'I am quite hopeless myself. Papa said it was a waste of money paying for my lessons, so I gave up.'

Cassie went over to the instrument and sat down to play. Sophie had to admit Cassandra played well, an accomplishment that Lord Kimberley would undoubtedly appreciate. What accomplishments did she have, apart from being a hoyden and having a brother for whom gambling was an addiction? Her applause and praise when the short piece came to an end was genuine. 'Encore,' she cried.

Cassie played until the game ended and her parents prepared to leave. It was after they had gone, her aunt mentioned Viscount Kimberley. 'I notice you did not tell Cassandra that he was going to take you riding tomorrow,' she said.

'Didn't I? I must have forgot.'

Her aunt laughed. 'Very wise, my dear. But do you really think his lordship is about to offer for Cassandra or is she deluding herself?'

'I don't know what is in his lordship's mind, Aunt.'

'No, I do not think anyone does. But he would hardly take you riding if he has his sights set on someone else.'

'Perhaps he wants to tell me about it himself before it becomes official.'

'Now, why would he do that, unless he thinks you have developed a *tendre* for him and he needs to let you down lightly?'

'Oh, Aunt, that is absurd.'

'We shall see. I am going to bed. I suggest you do the same if you are to be up betimes for your ride. And do not wait up for your brother— there is no telling when he will decide to come home. I have told Cook to make him up a tray of cold food for when he comes in. Leave him a note on the tray so that he knows he is to accompany you in the morning.'

When Sophie came down next morning, dressed for riding, she found the tray and her note were untouched. She sent a footman to see if her brother was in his room, but he returned to say Teddy's bed had not been slept in. Where was he? His anguished cry that she would find him in a back alley with his throat cut flew into her mind. Had something dreadful befallen him?

She had no time to dwell on this because Adam had arrived and was being ushered into the room. He bowed. 'Good morning, Miss Cavenhurst. You are ready, I see.'

'Yes, I am ready, but I am not sure...'

'Not sure of what?'

'Teddy is not here. He should be coming with us.'

'Where is he?'

'I don't know. He did not come home last night. He is often out into the early hours, but I have never known him stay out all night.'

'Shall I ask a groom to ride behind us? Would that serve?'

'What? Oh, yes, but why bother? My reputation is already in tatters.'

He came closer and put his hand on her arm. 'You are truly worried about your brother, aren't you?'

'Yes.'

'Ten to one, there is nothing to worry about. He is probably carousing with friends or might even have found other, sweeter company.'

She knew what he meant. 'Do you think so?'

'Why not? He is young and virile—it is only natural. No doubt when we come back from our ride he will be home and contrite that he has worried you so much.'

'He is always contrite,' she said dully.

'Come, then. We ought not to keep horses standing in the street. If he has not returned by the time we come back, I will undertake to go and look for him.'

She followed him out into the street where his bay and a lovely brown mare waited for them with a street urchin holding their bridles. Adam gave him a groat and bade him buy himself a good dinner and the lad scuttled off, more than pleased with his earnings.

'What do you think of her?' Adam asked, taking the bridle of the brown mare and bringing her round for Sophie to mount. 'Her name is Swift.'

'Is she swift?'

'I don't know. That is for you to find out, but I would guess she is.' He bent and cupped his hands for her foot and then threw her up into the saddle. She picked up the reins and settled her foot in the stirrup, spreading her habit neatly about her. 'I am thinking of buying her,' he added, 'and would like your opinion.'

'My opinion, my lord? What can I tell you about horses that you don't already know?'

'You could tell me how comfortable she is to ride, how docile, how responsive she is to the reins.'

'You can surely find that out yourself.'

'Ah, but not side-saddle.'

'You are thinking of buying her for a lady?'

'I might.'

'Oh.' He was unmarried, he had no daughter, so it could only be for a mistress or a potential wife. Cassie perhaps?

He mounted his bay and they walked their horses out of Mount Street and along Park Lane to the entrance to Hyde Park. Because of the traffic they had to ride one behind the other until they were in the park, where he came up alongside her.

'From a very poor start we have had a good summer so far,' he said. 'I do not think you can have been confined indoors once since you arrived in town.'

'I don't believe I have. The only rain we have had was during one night that left puddles, but that is all.'

'We might have a good harvest. After last year it is certainly needed.'

'Yes.'

He looked sideways at her, but she was looking straight ahead over the mare's ears. 'Shall we canter?'

To do so they had to leave the Ride because other riders were only walking their horses or at the most trotting and it would have been hazardous. He led the way and they soon left the crowds behind. Reaching a group of trees, he dismounted and she did likewise.

'Now,' he said firmly as the horses began to crop the grass, 'what do you think?'

'Think about what?' Her thoughts were chasing each other round in her head. His asking her opinion of a horse he was far more qualified than she was to assess and wondering who the mare was meant for, all mixed up with her continuing worry about Teddy.

'Swift. Will she do, do you think?'

'Any lady would be pleased to have her. I cannot fault her.'

'Not lively enough for your taste, though?' he queried in an endeavour to make her smile.

'I expect she would be lively enough given open country to gallop in.'

'You are probably right.'

He let the reins of his mount trail and moved nearer to her, so that she became almost overwhelmed by his size and masculinity. She wished he would move away, because his nearness was making her heart beat uncomfortably fast.

'Now tell me what is wrong,' he said.

'Nothing. I told you I cannot fault her.'

'Not with the horse, with you.'

'Nothing is wrong, my lord. Why do you say that?'

'It is obvious there is.'

'It is nothing.'

'It is more than nothing.' He paused to look closely at her, but she refused to meet his gaze.

'It cannot be that you have had an offer of marriage, for that would not make you look so wan, so let me hazard a guess. It is your brother who brings the frown to your brow and drains the colour from your cheeks. Am I right?'

It was easier to agree than tell the truth, that it was he who disturbed her and set her emotions racing. 'He was out all night. I fear something bad has befallen him.'

'Why do you think that?'

'Because…' She stopped and then went on, 'Because there are so many thieves and cut-throats about.'

He took her shoulders in his hands so that she was obliged to face him. 'Look at me.' Slowly she lifted her eyes to his. 'Now look me in the eye and tell me the truth. I cannot bear to see you like this.'

He sounded so concerned, it gave a great leap to her heart, but then it subsided back into the despair she had been feeling ever since Teddy told her of his troubles. 'My lord, I have told you the truth.'

'Then I shall be obliged to guess again. He is in dun country and has applied to you to get him out of it.'

'He wouldn't do that. He knows I cannot.'

'He needs a horsewhip to his back.' It was spoken angrily.

'Oh, no,' she cried. 'He cannot help it. It is the way he is.'

He smiled. 'There is no end to what love can forgive, is there?'

She had no answer to that. 'Let us go back and see if he has returned,' she said. 'I cannot enjoy the ride while I am worrying about him.'

'Very well.'

He helped her to remount, then sprang into his own saddle. 'Have you seen Captain Moore lately?' he asked her.

She was so startled by this question coming so unexpectedly, her hands tightened on the reins and Swift shied. Steadying her gave her time to think of an answer. 'Not lately,' she said. 'Why do you ask?'

'Because wherever the captain is, there will your brother be.'

'Oh, no, he hasn't seen him, either.'

'But you said you hadn't seen Captain Moore lately.'

'I forgot. I met him by chance yesterday and he told me so.'

'I see.'

He didn't believe her, she knew that, but she was too ashamed of what she had done to tell the truth. He would be disgusted with her. Nor could she tell him what Teddy had suggested as a way out; it would put him in the invidious position of having to let her down gently. Nor did she want him to think she would even consider marrying him for his money, even in the unlikely event that he would agree. They rode on in silence.

When they arrived outside her aunt's house, he dismounted and held out his hands to help her down. She slid off the saddle and straight into his arms. He held her there several seconds longer than was proper. It was long enough for her to feel the warmth of him, the beating of his heart, his strength and the feeling of being safely enclosed from harm.

He let her go and smiled down at her. 'Let us go inside and see if your brother has returned.'

But he had not, and even Lady Cartrose was beginning to be concerned. 'You hear such dreadful tales of footpads and the like,' she said to Adam. 'I have sent round to Mrs Malthouse and to Lady Martindale but they have not seen him since the picnic. I cannot go to the gentlemen's clubs and I cannot think where else he could be. You haven't seen him, have you, my lord?'

'No, my lady, I am afraid I have not. But don't worry. I'll take Swift back to the stables and go in search of him. He cannot be far away.'

'Would you? Oh, that is kind of you. Isn't that kind of him, Sophie?'

Sophie had not recovered from the sensation of being held in his arms and was wishing he had never let her go, for now she felt unsteady and isolated once more. 'Oh, yes,' she managed to say. 'But we are keeping his lordship from other matters more important to him.'

'Nothing that cannot wait,' he said. 'I will locate Mr Cavenhurst and bring him home to you.'

'And if you cannot find him?' Sophie queried.

'Then I will come back and tell you so. Had you planned to go out this afternoon?'

'Only for a carriage ride and a little shopping,' her ladyship said. 'We can easily postpone that. This evening we were all going to the opera.'

'I hope to have him back with you long before then.'

Adam left them to set about his errand. Ten to one the young man was at one of the clubs getting more heavily into debt. He had had an uncle on his father's side who had the gambling fever and he knew what unbridled gambling could do to a family. They had lost their house and all their assets, and in the end the man had killed himself. Adam had been looking after his wife and daughter ever since. It was the innocent who suffered most in such circumstances. He didn't want Sophie to have to endure anything like that, though how the fever could be cured he had no idea.

Deciding he would do better on foot, he left both horses at the livery stables and made for St James's where most of the gentlemen's clubs were situated. Teddy was not at any of them. Toby Moore had not seen him and he was as anxious for him to be found as anyone. 'He owes me and I would have my money,' he told Adam.

'You've no idea where he might be?'

'No, and so I told the filly when she came here.'

'The filly?'

'His sister.'

'She came here?' He could not keep the surprise from his voice.

'Yes, dressed in her brother's clothes and her hair pushed under one of his hats. Very fetching she looked, too.'

He was shocked. Were there no lengths to which she would not go? Everyone knew that ladies—real ladies—did not go to St James's and certainly did not try to enter the clubs. Whatever had she hoped to achieve? He pulled himself together. 'She was looking for her brother, no doubt.'

'No, she came to plead with me to give him time to pay his debts.'

'I doubt you agreed.'

'On the contrary, I said I would waive them—for a consideration, of course. She declined.'

He could only guess what that consideration might be. The thought of it sent his mind in a furious whirl of frustrated anger. 'What do you take her for, Captain? She is a lady born and bred…'

'Ladies have been known to fall from grace.'

'Leave her alone. She cannot help you recover your debt.' He paused. 'How much is it, by the way?'

'Five thousand seven hundred and sixty guineas.'

'You fleeced him.'

'Yes, I did, didn't I?' He was smiling with satisfaction, which made Adam want to punch his face. Brawling was not permitted in the environs of the club or he might have given in to the urge. 'But then he deserved it. He was instrumental in severing a very lucrative partnership with my friend, Lord Bolsover. It lost me thousands, that did, and cost his lordship his good looks.'

'That has nothing to do with Miss Cavenhurst.'

'No, nor you, neither. I'll thank you not to meddle in what don't concern you.'

'It does concern me.'

'Oh-ho, that's the way the wind blows, is it? I wonder what little Miss Malthouse will say to that.'

'I will send a money order to your lodging tomorrow.' His voice was clipped in an effort to remain civil. 'Five thousand seven hundred and sixty guineas, I believe you said.'

'Yes, but tomorrow it will have gone up another ten per cent. Interest, you know.'

That was extortionate, but he was not going to argue about it. 'I will add another five hundred, but I shall require a receipt from you and an undertaking never to game with Mr Cavenhurst again. It would be better if you left town.'

'I am not the only one. Teddy will soon find someone else to play with. There's Reggie and Dick and Bertie Gorange. If you look in the betting book, you will find their wagers in there.' He was grinning mischievously as Adam called for the betting book, which was brought swiftly to him by the manager.

He opened it and read: 'Mr Edward Cavenhurst wagers one thousand guineas that Sir Reginald Swayle will not become affianced to Miss Sophie Cavenhurst before the end of July. Mr Cavenhurst undertakes not to try to influence her decision in any way.' It was dated the first of May, well before Sophie came to London. Both men had signed it. There was another one relating to Richard Fanshawe and another with Lord Gorange.

He shut the book with a snap and handed it back. 'How did that come about?' he asked the manager.

'They were playing cards and bemoaning their disappointment at being turned down. Each was sure they could make Miss Cavenhurst change her mind. They were making bets on it. It was then Mr Cavenhurst intervened to say his sister was too stubborn to change her mind and he would wager they would not succeed. They all took him up on it.'

He wondered if Sophie knew about that. 'When did you last see Mr Cavenhurst?'

'Two days ago.'

Adam spent the rest of the day in the search, but as no one who knew the young man had seen him, he concluded that Captain Moore had been right and he had gone home to Hadlea to lick his wounds.

He went back to Mount Street to tell the ladies of his failure. They were dressed for an evening at the opera. 'Perhaps he has gone home to Hadlea,' he said.

'He would not do that without telling us,' Sophie said. 'Besides, he told me he daren't tell Papa about...about...' Her voice tailed off.

'Has he friends in London with whom he might stay?'

'I can only think of Sir Reginald and Mr Fanshawe.'

'I asked them. They haven't seen him.'

'You told them he was missing?'

'I told them I was looking for him and he was not at home. They did not appear to attach any significance to it.'

'I think we should go to the opera as planned,' Lady Cartrose said. 'We cannot let the *ton* know there is anything amiss. We shall say he has been detained on business for his father. Besides, he knows we are going and may very well come to us there.' She turned to Adam. 'Do you go, my lord?'

'No, I shall continue the search. I have not exhausted all avenues yet. I will come to you tomorrow.' He had quite forgotten he had planned to leave London the next day.

Chapter Eight

Teddy's disappearance was so much on her mind that Sophie could not pay attention to the opera. When the interval came, their box was invaded by Reggie and Richard, followed soon afterwards by Lord Gorange, all vying for her favour, but she could not give her attention to any of them. And when Lord and Lady Martindale also arrived with Lucy, she felt she wanted to scream and run away.

'Where is your brother?' Lucy asked her. 'I felt sure he would be here tonight and join us for supper afterwards. He promised to speak to Papa.'

'Some business cropped up he had to deal with,' Sophie said. 'Perhaps he will join us later.'

'Did he tell you…?'

'That he had proposed, yes, he did.'

'I am so happy. I did not need to come to London to find the man of my dreams, did I?'

'So it would seem. I felicitate you.' She tried
to sound sincere and in any other circumstances
she would have been pleased for them both, but
at that moment all she could think of was that
her brother had disappeared and very soon Lucy
would have to be told.

'What about you, Sophie?' Lucy queried in
a whisper. 'Will you accept Sir Reginald or Mr
Fanshawe? I cannot think you will entertain
Lord Gorange, even though he is the richest.'

'Is he? I didn't know that.'

'So Papa says.'

They were interrupted by the arrival of Mrs
Malthouse and Cassandra and the box became
very crowded. The Martindales took their leave
and returned to their own seats to make room
for the newcomers.

Cassie dragged Sophie into a corner. 'What
have you done with Viscount Kimberley?' she
demanded.

'Done with him, Cassie? Whatever do you
mean?'

'You are scheming to take him away from me.
You said you had no interest in him and yet you
go riding with him for all the world to see. And
without a chaperon. It isn't fair, Sophie.'

Sophie did not see why she should justify
herself, but Cassie was obviously furious. 'He
wanted my opinion about a horse he was thinking of buying.'

Cassie laughed harshly. 'What do you know about horses that he does not?'

'Nothing, but he wanted to know if I thought it would suit a lady.'

'What lady?'

'He didn't say.'

'Oh.'

Sophie watched her friend digesting this information and saw her expression change from anger and jealousy to bright expectation. She could only hope that his lordship really did intend the mare for Cassie, otherwise there would be tears. 'What was the horse like?'

'A beautiful brown mare. I envy the lady.'

'Not you?'

'Of course not me. Cassie, I have told you…'

'I know. I'm sorry I doubted you. We are still friends, are we not?'

'Of course.'

'Where is the viscount tonight?'

'I have no idea. Were you expecting to see him?'

'I hoped he would join us in our box and have supper with us afterwards.'

'No doubt he has business to attend to. I believe his visit to London is not all pleasure.'

'You are doubtless right,' Cassandra said after a little thought. 'Everyone is returning to their seats. I must go. Will I see you tomorrow?'

'I don't know, Cassie. I will have to see what my aunt has arranged.'

Cassie left with her parents and Sophie resumed her seat to see the second half of the performance, but her mind was not on it. Her whirring thoughts went from her missing brother to Viscount Kimberley. Teddy, who in every other way was a well-balanced, sensible young man, was weak as water when it came to gambling. It was his only vice, but what a vice! Ought she to warn Lucy? Or Lord Martindale? But she knew she could not be so disloyal to her brother.

And there was Viscount Kimberley. Cassie was determined to catch him and seemed to think fluttering her eyelashes at him and talking nineteen to the dozen would win him. Sophie was sure it would not, unless the gentleman himself wanted it. Did he? Who was the mare for, if not for Cassie? Jealousy was something Sophie had never felt in her life before, but it was taking hold of her now. Her situation was hopeless, and Teddy's predicament was making it ten times worse. Could she marry without love? Could she marry for money to help her brother? If she could, then she ought to choose the richest. Lord Gorange? She shuddered at the idea, but was it any worse than Jane agreeing to marry Lord Bolsover to save Greystone Manor?

She became aware that the curtain had fallen

and everyone was applauding. Not a word or a note of the opera had made any impression on her poor, tired brain. She clapped with everyone else and watched several curtain calls before leaving with her aunt. They had arranged to have supper with the Malthouses and she had to endure more of Cassie's chatter before they could politely take their leave and go back to Mount Street.

Teddy was not there and, according to the servants, had not been back in their absence. Neither had Viscount Kimberley. It was going to be a long, long night.

Apart from the gentlemen's clubs there were coffee houses for the middling sort and even humbler gambling dens where Teddy might have gone to play and where he was not so well known. Adam spent the rest of the evening and most of the night visiting as many of them as he could. No one had heard of Edward Cavenhurst. He could have used a different name, so Adam fell to describing him. 'Young, clean shaven, fair haired, a gentleman in his attire, though I cannot tell you exactly what he was wearing,' he said. 'So tall.' He indicated Teddy's height with his hand.

'Too much the toff to come here,' they said. Or, 'I doubt he'd find the play deep enough here. Will we tell him where to find you, if he comes in?'

'Tell him his sister is worried by his absence. Send him home.'

They laughed. 'We will that.'

Some of the coffee houses were also debating societies and here the arguments could become heated. He was detained in one after the other until they paused long enough for him to ask his questions. In one he was dragged into a debate on the franchise and could not resist giving his opinion, which set them arguing again, and it was some time before he could broach the subject of Teddy. It was after he had left there and was wondering whether to go on with the search or go home to bed, that he realised he was being followed again. He deemed it wisest to seek more busy thoroughfares and go home to Wyndham House.

The next morning he called at Mount Street at the early hour of nine o'clock where he found Sophie sitting over breakfast alone. She should have called Bessie or one of the other servants to chaperone them, but they had gone beyond the need for such niceties. She bade him be seated and poured him a dish of hot chocolate. He noticed her hand was shaking and, judging by her pale looks, her brother had not come home.

'What have you discovered, my lord?'

'I regret to say nothing. I must have visited

half the clubs and coffee houses in London. No one has seen him.'

'Something dreadful has happened to him. He said something to me about being found in an alley with his throat cut.' Her voice broke on a sob.

'I can't believe it has come that.' He reached out and put his hand over hers. 'Why did he say it, especially to you?'

'He meant Captain Moore would do away with him.'

'That is nonsense, Sophie, and you know it. Captain Moore is not a murderer. Why would he be? He has nothing to gain from such a cowardly act. Your brother should never have frightened you like that. It was very unkind of him.' Her given name had slipped out without him realising it, but she didn't seem to notice. He decided not to apologise for it.

'He didn't mean to frighten me. It was just that I was less than sympathetic and I am sorry for it now.'

'Are you sure he would not go home to Hadlea?'

'I am not sure of anything anymore. But I cannot think he would leave me in London by myself. How am I to get home?'

'Do you want to go home? It will be my pleasure to take you, if you do.'

She raised tear-filled eyes to look up at him.

'My lord, I could not ask it of you. There is Cassie's come-out ball and...'

'Damn Cassie's ball.'

'My lord!'

'I beg your pardon. I should not have used such language.' He paused. 'Have you told anyone your brother is missing?'

'No. Aunt Emmeline thought it best not to say anything, but we cannot keep it a secret forever. You know how gossip gets about. And I don't suppose Captain Moore will hold his tongue.'

'Leave Captain Moore to me.'

'My lord, you have put yourself to a great deal of trouble on my behalf and I cannot let you continue.'

He smiled. 'Who else will, if I do not?'

'I shall have to look for him myself.'

'Don't be ridiculous. How can you?'

'I am not ridiculous.' She had enough spirit left to flare up at him.

'I apologise. Of course you are not ridiculous, but you are under a strain and not your usual sensible self.' He said it with a faint smile. 'But you know very well you cannot go combing London on your own. Besides, he might have left town.'

'Yes, I know. Perhaps I should send for Mark.'

'What can Mark do that I cannot?'

'I don't know.' She was in despair.

'Sophie, it will take days for a letter to reach

him and for him to arrange to come to town. I am here already and at your disposal.'

She was crying in earnest now; the tears were rolling down her cheeks. He could not bear to see her like that. He left his seat to kneel beside her chair and put his arms about her. 'Don't cry, my dear. We will find him and all will be well. And Toby Moore will not trouble him again.'

She sniffed. 'How do you know that?'

'I spoke to him.'

'What did he say?' She ought to pull away from him, stand up and move away, but she couldn't. He held her too tightly and, besides, she did not want to.

'He only wanted what he was owed. I undertook to cover it on condition he never played with your brother again.'

'You! But why?'

'I wanted to help.' He paused. 'The trouble is it will not cure your brother and he may, at this very moment, be gaming with someone else.'

'He gave me his promise he would not.' Whatever else she did, she would have to find some way to repay him. But a few thousand! How could she obtain that sort of money?

'No doubt he did.'

'You think he will not keep it?'

'I have no doubt he meant it at the time.' Gently he put her from him and resumed his seat beside her. 'Sophie, I will continue to search for him, but I think the time has come to ask for help.'

Lady Cartrose bustled in at that point. 'Good heavens, Kimberley, you here? And so early, too.'

'I came to acquaint you both with the result of my search for Edward.'

'And?' She felt the outside of the chocolate pot, but it had gone cold. Tutting, she rang the bell for a servant.

'I am afraid I was unsuccessful.'

'Well, young men can be thoughtless sometimes. It is too soon to be alarmed.' To the maid who had just entered, 'More hot chocolate, Lilly, and more bread and butter. Conserve, too, if you please.'

Sophie waited until the maid had left and then said, 'Aunt, it's been three days.'

'He's doubtless gone into the country on a repairing lease. Isn't that what young men do who have gone in over their heads?'

'How do you know he has gone in over his head?' Sophie asked.

Her aunt shrugged. 'It is the obvious conclusion. I have seen him at the gaming tables. He can sometimes be rash in his bids.'

'My lady,' Adam said, 'I have enquired at all the coaching inns hereabouts and as far as I can tell, he has not left on the stage or the mail.'

'He could have asked someone to take him.'

'True,' Adam conceded.

'Then we are at a stand,' Sophie said.

'Not quite,' he said. 'I know someone who is very good at tracking people down. He knows the ins and outs of the city and has contacts in places you would never dream of going. Will you let me ask him?'

'What manner of man is he?'

'He is an honest man who has served me well for years and he knows how to keep his tongue between his teeth.'

'Aunt, what do you think?'

'Let him try, if it means you will lose that doleful look,' her aunt answered. 'You cannot go to Cassandra's ball looking like that.'

'Cassie's ball! You surely do not expect me to attend that?'

'Why not? Augusta has put herself about for you and Cassandra is your friend. We cannot let them down.' She turned to Adam. 'You will be going, will you not, my lord?'

He looked at Sophie and smiled, knowing she was remembering his unflattering remark about the ball, and found an answering twinkle in her eye. She had not entirely lost her sense of humour. 'Unless some catastrophe occurs, I shall be there. I will leave you now to go and speak to my man.' He was still looking at Sophie. 'Try not to worry.'

* * *

'I think I will write to Jane and Mark, just in case Teddy has gone home,' Sophie said, when he had gone. 'I cannot write home directly because it would worry Mama and Papa, but Jane will tell us if he is at home and what reason he gave for leaving me here. In any case, Mark is coming to fetch us back after Cassie's ball.'

'I am sorry your stay has not been all you had hoped, child.'

'It is not your fault, Aunt, and truly I was enjoying myself until Teddy got into such a mess.' She gave a half-hearted chuckle that bordered on a sob. 'Not so long ago he was chiding me for getting into scrapes and not behaving with decorum. I would give anything for him to be here doing that again.'

'All is not lost, my dear. He will return looking sheepish, I do not doubt. There are still three days to go before the ball, and who knows what might happen before that is over?'

'I might get a proposal, you mean? I don't think that is going to happen, Aunt, unless it be from those I have already turned down.'

'Are you still determined not to change your mind about them?'

'I don't know. I might have need of a wealthy husband…'

'There is Viscount Kimberley, of course.'

'What about him?'

'Oh, Sophie, can you not see he loves you?'

Sophie stared at her. 'Whatever made you say that?'

'I see it in his eyes, in the way he looks at you, in his concern for you, in the way he flaps his arms about as if he would put them round you and knows he must not. Would a man who is not in love chase all over town at the dead of night to make you feel a little easier?'

'Oh, Aunt, you must be mistaken. He has said he will not marry again, but I think Cassie expects to change his mind for him.'

'And you have said you will not be a second wife, so what is either statement to the point when two hearts beat for each other?'

'What do you know of my heart?'

Her aunt laughed. 'You are wearing it on your sleeve.'

Was it that obvious? Had he noticed it? Had Cassie? Oh, she felt like running away and hiding, which was probably what Teddy had done. But there was nowhere to run to, except home. Oh, how she longed to be safe at Greystone Manor, safe in the bosom of her family. She went to the morning room and sat down at her aunt's escritoire to write to Jane.

The day of Cassie's ball arrived and they still had no news of Teddy. Jane had written that he was not at home and she had no idea where he might be. 'I have said nothing to Mama and Papa,' she had written. 'But if he doesn't turn up soon, they will have to be told.' She was obviously concerned and Sophie was sorry she had worried her.

Adam had called several times, only to bring disappointing news. He gave no sign that he thought of her in any way other than a friend. He continued the search because he had said he would, but he must be thoroughly tired of her and her troublesome brother by now. And Cassie, who had called the day before to discuss the last arrangements for what promised to be the event of the Season, was happily convinced that he would offer for her that very night and mark the occasion with the gift of a horse. If that happened she would have to be happy for her, but it was not going to be easy.

It was with great reluctance she went up to her room to change into her finery. Bessie was there to help her, but she could hardly rouse any enthusiasm, being almost as worried Sophie was. 'He is like a naughty schoolboy,' she told Sophie. 'Always wants his own way and sulks when he cannot have it.'

'Bessie, that is unfair. If you had seen how contrite and sorry he was…'

'Sorry butters no parsnips.'

Sophie, standing in her petticoat waiting for her blue gown to be put over her head, could not even smile at this. She had had such high hopes when she left Hadlea, as excited as a schoolgirl. She was going to have a Season, to be the belle of all the balls, to find a loving husband who fulfilled all her criteria. How foolish she had been! How much the child. She had done a great deal of growing up in the short time since she'd left home. She was no longer the child; her illusions had been shattered by reality. Love, real love, found its own way and sometimes it was not returned. Hearts could not be dictated to.

The gown slipped down over her shapely figure and fell in soft folds to her feet. It seemed an age since she had been boasting of it to Cassie. It didn't seem to matter anymore. Life was not about expensive gowns and fripperies; life was what you made of it and she had made a mull of everything. If she could go back in time to the beginning of May, would she still plead to be brought to London? If she had not come, would she still have met Viscount Kimberley? Would she now be breaking her heart over him?

'It looks lovely.' Bessie's voice broke in on her thoughts. 'Jane has done a superb job, but you really must try to look a little more cheerful. Anyone would think you were going to a funeral, not a ball.'

Sophie turned towards the mirror and studied her reflection. Her cheeks were devoid of colour and her eyes had lost their brightness. Even her hair looked dull. But the dress was lovely. It had a boat-shaped neckline and puffed sleeves. A fichu of the paler blue lace was intended to fill in the neckline that would otherwise leave her shoulders bare. The bodice fitted her exactly. The skirt, falling from a high waist, was tiered, each tier threaded with silver ribbon. The hem was looped up with more ribbon and revealed an underskirt of the same pale lace as the fichu.

'Sophie, you must pull yourself together if you are going to pull this off tonight,' Bessie said, taking a hairbrush and pulling it through Sophie's tresses.

'Pull what off?'

'Outshining the other young ladies.'

'Am I meant to do that?'

'Yes. You have to convince everyone there is nothing wrong, that you are as bright and sparkling as you have always been. For your pride's sake, if nothing else.' She finished coiling Sophie's hair into ringlets and began threading it with silver ribbon to match the dress. 'Otherwise you might as well be wearing white and hiding yourself behind your aunt, waiting for someone to take pity on you.'

'I don't want anyone's pity.' It was said with some feeling, but she remembered Jane cautioning her about too much pride. Had she brought this misery on herself, laying down her requirements for a husband? And then behaving like a hoyden because she didn't want anyone to know how unsure of herself she felt?

'No, I didn't think you did. Shall we try a little make-up, just to put some colour in your cheeks? Pinching them will not be enough.'

'Very well, but please, not too much.'

By the time Bessie had finished, Sophie was looking more her old self. 'There! That's not too much, is it?'

'No. You are very clever.'

'I have sometimes needed to help your mother in that way.'

'But you have spilled a little powder on the lace.' She pulled the fichu off and examined it. Brushing it with her hand only made it worse.

Bessie took it from her. 'Oh, dear, you should have worn a cape. I'll try to clean it off.'

'No, don't bother. If I am going to shock everyone I might as well do it properly.'

'Sophie!'

'It was you who said I had to sparkle.'

'I didn't mean... Oh, well, your necklace will fill in the neck a little, and you can pull the sleeves up onto your shoulders.'

The necklace, that was it! She touched it as Bessie fastened it round her neck. Mark would never give Jane paste jewels, so it might be worth something. She could sell it and repay the viscount and there would be no need to marry any of her erstwhile suitors. She suddenly felt much more cheerful. And if Teddy turned up safe and well, everything would come about. Except for her love for Viscount Kimberley. She would have to remove her heart from her sleeve and bury it away from sight.

She slipped into her shoes, donned a fine silk shawl and hung her reticule on her wrist. 'I am ready,' she said, and went down to join her aunt, who was clad in burgundy satin and a matching turban, to wait for the carriage to be brought round.

Mr and Mrs Malthouse, together with Cassie, stood at the head of the stairs to greet their guests as they arrived. Cassie was in a demure white silk gown embroidered with dainty pastel-coloured flowers. Ribbons of matching colours encircled the high waist and finished in a large bow at the back. She came forward to kiss Sophie when she arrived.

'You look lovely,' Sophie told her.

'And so do you. I didn't think you would dare wear that gown.'

'Why not? I said I would.'

'They are all here, you know.'

'Who?'

'Sir Reginald, Mr Fanshawe and Lord Gorange, all dressed to kill.'

'Oh, no, why did you invite them?'

'Why not? I want you to be as happy as I am tonight. You must surely choose one of them.'

'Why? I have said I will not.'

'Sophie, let us move on,' her aunt said, accepting Sophie's dance card from a footman who had a pile of them in his hand and handing it to Sophie. 'We are holding up those behind us.'

They moved into the ballroom, standing just inside to get their bearings and find a place to sit.

Mr and Mrs Malthouse had not spared any expense. The ballroom consisted of two reception rooms normally joined by an archway and wooden partitions. The partitions had been removed to make one very large room. The carpets and all the furniture, except chairs arranged round the perimeter for the chaperones, had been removed and the floor polished until it gleamed. A dais had been erected at one end on which a full orchestra played. There were swathes of glittering material hung between the long windows and stands of exotic flowers everywhere. And it seemed half the *beau monde* was there.

Sophie, not unaware of the stares of the young men and the disapproval of the matrons, stood up straight and smiled. No one, tonight, was going to guess that inside she was nursing a broken heart.

Lady Cartrose spotted Lord and Lady Martindale and swept off to join them. Sophie followed. Lucy was in a country dance set partnered by

Vincent. Sophie did not have time to sit down before her swains were upon her.

Reggie reached her first. Apart from a white shirt, he was dressed all in green, even down to his cravat. 'Miss Cavenhurst, may I have the honour of the next dance?'

Silently she handed him her dance card. He wrote his name and gave it back, then stood aside to allow Richard, in a black suit relieved by a white waistcoat and cravat, to ask for a dance and put his name on her card. They were followed by Lord Gorange, dressed in old-fashioned breeches, stockings and buckled shoes. Then all three stood beside her waiting for the dance then in progress to finish.

'Tell me, gentlemen,' she said. 'Why do you all go about together? I never see one of you but the others are in attendance.'

'Well, I for one cannot allow the other two to steal a march on me,' Reggie said. 'I was the first to ask you for your hand and...'

She laughed aloud, attracting those nearby to look round at her and make tutting noises at her behaviour. 'So it's first come first served, is it?'

'No, it is not.' Lord Gorange was the one to answer. 'There are other considerations. What I have to offer...'

'Is a dead wife's shoes and two motherless children,' she finished for him.

'That is not all, it is far from all,' he said,

miffed. 'You would want for nothing if you became the second Lady Gorange.'

'And what about you, Mr Fanshawe?' she asked sweetly.

'It goes without saying you would want for nothing. I have a town house and a country estate, both of which are in superb condition, which you would see if you would only consent to visit them. I have never been married and do not have children, at least, not that I know of. You would not be burdened by past encumbrances.'

'That is a consideration,' she murmured. 'But not the only one.'

'Dash it, Sophie, how can you say that?' Reggie put in. 'I have known you since we were children and I have always adored you. Teddy knows that.'

'What has Teddy to do with it?' she asked, looking from one to the other. They were all looking sheepish.

'Nothing,' they murmured.

She had been right when she said something smoky was going on, she decided. 'Do you know where he is?' she asked.

'No,' Reggie said. 'But it is strange that Viscount Kimberley asked the same question a few days ago. And come to think of it, I haven't seen Teddy for nearly a week.'

'He said he would keep out of it,' Richard said.

'Keep out of what?' she demanded.

'Helping you to choose between us,' Lord Gorange put in quickly. 'He did not want to influence you.'

'He wouldn't do that, in any case. I make up my own mind.'

'And have you?' Reggie asked eagerly.

'Will you not take no for an answer?'

'Not the first time, nor the second.'

'Nor the third, fourth or fifth,' Gorange put in.

'Not until the end of the month,' Richard added.

The other two looked fiercely at him, and Sophie was constrained to ask. 'Why the end of the month?'

'It is a goal I have set myself. After that...' He shrugged.

'Oh, dear—' she sighed, teasing them '—what *am* I to do?'

The dance ended and everyone began to drift back to their places on the sidelines. Vincent escorted Lucy back to her mother and, having done so, claimed a dance from Sophie, writing his name on her card twice. This prompted the others to take back the card and put their names against a second dance. She was beginning to wonder if she would have any left for Adam when he came. But perhaps it was just as well if she were to keep up the pretence of not having a care in the world. If she stood up with him, she would give herself away.

'Is Teddy not with you?' Lucy asked. 'Where is he?'

'I don't know, but I have just learned he is making himself scarce in order not to influence my admirers into persuading me to accept one of them.'

'That is silly.'

'Yes, it is. Very silly.'

'He promised me he would be here tonight. I have kept two dances for him. I would have made it more, but Mama says until our engagement is officially announced, two is the most allowed.'

'Perhaps he will turn up later.'

'I hope he does. The whole evening will be spoilt if he does not.'

The whole evening was already spoilt for Sophie, though she continued to talk and laugh and dance. She kept glancing at the door, hoping to see Adam come through it but, though others came and went, he did not appear. He had said he would come, so where was he? Surely he was not still searching for Teddy himself. He had Mr Farley doing that for him now. She wanted to tell him what Richard Fanshawe had said about why her brother was keeping out of the way. It could be true, but why hadn't Teddy told her so?

She would have assured him it was not necessary; she was not about to change her mind. He had said, 'Good' when she'd last told him that. Nothing made sense.

The supper interval came and went and Mr Malthouse made a short speech welcoming everyone and praising his daughter for being all things a good daughter should be. If he had hoped it might be a betrothal announcement, he gave no hint of it, and begged everyone to continue to enjoy themselves. Sophie found herself standing next to Cassie.

'Where is Viscount Kimberley?' her friend demanded in a whisper.

'I have no idea. I am not his keeper.'

'He promised to be here.'

'Something must have turned up to detain him. If it is any consolation, Teddy is not here either and Lucy is looking as doleful as you do. You may commiserate with each other.'

'It is all the same to you, isn't it? You have admirers in plenty and may amuse yourself playing one off against the other.'

'Yes, it is great fun, Cassie. You should try it.'

'Oh, you are impossible. I should look out, if I were you. You are fast earning a reputation as a flirt. One day, someone will really break your heart and then we shall see how you like that.'

Sophie did not answer. She had spoken out of bravado, but if that was what everyone was saying, then she might as well give them something to talk about. Vincent came to claim her for the second time, and she took his hand and went gaily on to the floor with him.

The rest of the evening went by in a blur. She laughed too much, drank too much and let the neck of her gown slip down to reveal creamy shoulders. But in the carriage going home, she burst into tears. 'There, there,' her aunt said, patting her hand to comfort her. 'It is over now. Cheer up. He did not come and there has been no announcement. I didn't think he would offer for that chit. She is too empty-headed. All is not lost, though I must say, you did rather overdo the not caring.'

'I *don't* care.' She sniffed. 'I shall go home and help Jane with her orphans.'

'You cannot go until Mark comes for you, nor before Edward is found.'

'I have been told he left London so as not to influence me in making a decision as to whom I should marry. I can't believe that's true.'

'It could be, I suppose. Now cheer up. Ten to one Viscount Kimberley has found him.'

'He would have come and told us if he had.'

'No doubt we will find out tomorrow. I'll have Bessie make up a sleeping draught for you and then you will have a good night's rest.'

'What's left of it,' she said, managing to smile.

* * *

Adam was in his room at Wyndham House, examining his face in the mirror. It looked a mess. There was a huge swelling over his right eye and the skin had split, allowing blood to run down into his eye. His lip was cut and there was a bruise on his chin. He reached up to touch it and winced as the pain in his arm reminded him it had been twisted behind his back. He could not have gone to the ball looking like that.

He poured cold water from the jug on his night table into a bowl and wetted a facecloth to clean off the blood. It did not look quite so bad when he finished, but he certainly could not go out and about until the swelling had subsided; he would frighten the life out of the ladies. He would write a letter of apology to Mrs Malthouse in the morning. He supposed he ought to write one to Sophie, too. But what could he say? 'I was set upon and beaten black and blue. As an investigator I am a complete failure. I am a failure as a champion of the poor, too. They do not believe me. Worse still, I cannot even conduct my personal affairs with any degree of assurance. I am leaving London forthwith before I forget who I am and what I am.'

He had been set upon, it was true, taken by surprise in a back street and robbed of his purse, his pocket watch, his signet ring and the cravat pin Anne had given him on their first anniversary; he was madder about that than any of the other items. As to the rest, he could not write any such thing.

The strange thing was that he was convinced the robbery was not premeditated and neither of the two ruffians had been the one who had followed him before. That man had not been interested in attacking him; he could have done so on any number of occasions. In fact, he was sure it was that he who had come to his rescue and helped him beat off his attackers.

'Who are you?' he asked after he had thanked him.

He was a big, brawny man, handy with his fists and surprisingly nimble on his feet. 'Names don't matter, sir.'

'Why have you been dogging my footsteps?'

'Has someone been dogging your footsteps?'

'Yes, and you know it.'

'Let me see you safely home, sir.'

'And you know where I lodge, I have no doubt.'

'Yes, sir.'

'I can see myself home.'

'Very well.' He'd picked up Adam's hat and handed it to him.

Adam would have liked to stride off, his head in the air, but his injuries had prevented that. He'd hobbled as best he could and known the man had not been far behind him. He had seen no point in trying to evade him and had made his way back to South Audley Street in the most direct way he knew.

It had taken him through Hanover Square. The house was lit up from top to bottom and he could hear the music of a waltz. She would have been there, dancing with her admirers, pretending all was well, perhaps even enjoying herself, safe in the knowledge that he would not let her down. But he had and he felt his failure keenly. He'd passed on and the music had faded until he could not hear it any more.

Farley was out when he'd arrived, no doubt still looking for that elusive Cavenhurst, and he had not wanted to rouse the housekeeper, so he had made his way up to his room. Without lighting a candle he'd gone to the window and looked out on the street. The man who had followed him was standing in the middle of the road, looking up at him. He'd smiled, saluted and walked away. Who was he? Why, if he meant him no harm, was he following him? He had nothing to do with Teddy Cavenhurst, because it had been happening before Teddy went missing. It had started after he'd spoken to Henry Hunt. But why would Hunt have him followed? He was desperately tired and his head ached. He would have to leave conundrums like that until the morning. He stripped off his clothes and flung himself on the bed.

He must have been asleep, though he could not be sure, when a vision floated into his mind of Sophie dancing. She was smiling up at whoever she was dancing with, her lips slightly parted, her blue eyes shining. The vision faded and he was sitting beside Anne's bed, watching her die. She was smiling, too. He groaned and thumped his pillow. 'Forgive me,' he muttered, though whether he was addressing Anne or Sophie he could not have said.

Chapter Nine

Lady Cartrose slept in even later than usual the morning following the ball, and Sophie was able to leave the house without any questions being asked. She did not even have Bessie with her. The necklace was in its box in her reticule. The inside of the box was inscribed with the name Rundell, Bridge and Rundell in Ludgate Hill, and that was where she was bound. Having no idea how to go about hiring a cab or a chair, she decided to walk. She was dressed in a green-and-yellow-striped gingham gown topped with a light shawl. Her plain straw bonnet, tied under her chin with green ribbon, had a wide brim that half concealed her face. She hoped this unremarkable attire would allow her to pass unnoticed.

It was a longish walk, and she was not certain of her way, but she knew if she asked for help she would be advised not to go and cer-

tainly not alone, so she did not ask. Consequently
she found herself lost in a part of London she
had never been in before. It was dreadfully
run-down. Washing hung across the road from
the upper windows of the crowded tenements,
ragged children played in the malodorous gutters
and a dog and cat fought with snarls and hisses
and bared teeth. Women stood in the doorways
and an old man sat on a stool beside an open
window. There were stalls along the street selling second-hand clothing, old shoes and cast-
off finery that she guessed had passed through
more than one pair of hands. She knew she was
attracting stares, but could not retreat. Instead,
she picked her way along, wishing fervently she
had never ventured so far from Mount Street
without an escort. She was not even sure she
was going in the right direction.

The road widened at last and she found herself
at a crossroads, where several roads met. Here,
thankfully, there was wheeled traffic, pedestrians and riders. She turned left and was relieved
when, after walking a few yards she recognised
the Covent Garden Opera House. If she walked
past that she would come out on to the Strand.
She had been along that way in the carriage with
her aunt and knew if she continued in an east-
erly direction she would come to Ludgate Hill.

Once there it was not difficult to find the jeweller's shop, but when she produced the necklace

and asked the young man who served her what it was worth, she was left standing while he went into the back of the shop to consult a colleague. She heard the murmur of voices, and then an older gentleman came out to speak to her. He had the necklace draped over his hand.

'Where did you get this, miss?'

'My sister gave it to me.'

'And your sister is…'

They thought she had stolen it! They would check with Jane and Jane would be hurt to think that she could even consider selling it. She snatched it back. 'I'm sorry, I've changed my mind.' She stuffed it in the pocket of her skirt and fled.

'Hey, come back.' The young man set off after her. She ran back the way she had come as fast as her feet would carry her with the young man in pursuit, shouting, 'Stop, thief!' Everyone on the pavement stood watching the chase, but no one thought to hinder her.

Her breath was almost spent and her legs feeling weak, when a carriage drew up beside her, the door opened, someone got out and bundled her into it and they were off again. It happened so quickly she did not have time to protest. She turned towards her rescuer, if that was what he was, and found herself face to face with Lord Gorange.

'Miss Cavenhurst, what happened? Who was

that young man? And what are you doing so far from Mount Street on your own?'

Sophie was still trying to get her breath back. 'I don't know who he is. I have been to Rundell, Bridge and Rundell. The clasp of my necklace was loose and I wanted to have it repaired before I lost it.'

'You think that was what he was after?'

'I expect so,' she said, grasping at the explanation he offered.

'But why did you not ask Lady Cartrose for the use of her carriage and someone to escort you?'

'I did not want to trouble her.'

'It is fortunate indeed that I was passing.'

'Yes,' she agreed. 'I thank you, my lord.'

'I should never forgive myself if anything happened to you.' He paused, apparently taking in her dishevelled appearance. 'My dear, I know you are not used to London ways, but you know, what is permissible in Hadlea is frowned upon in London. You will earn yourself a certain reputation…'

'I think I already have.'

'A good marriage would soon set that to rights.'

'Perhaps.' She knew what he was going to say next and needed to forestall him. 'My lord, have you seen anything of my brother?'

'Not for several days. I expect he is lying low somewhere.'

'Lying low?'

'Avoiding his creditors. It is common knowledge he is in dun country and Captain Moore is looking for him.'

'Captain Moore is a scoundrel.'

'My dear, I could not agree more, but gambling debts have to be paid, you know.' He paused and cleared his throat. 'I could get Toby Moore off his back, if you would only say the word. It could be part of the marriage settlement.'

'My lord, there is no need. Teddy's debts have been paid.'

'Have they?' he asked in surprise. 'Who paid them?'

'Why, Teddy did.'

'Excuse me, my dear, if I do not believe you. Everyone knows Teddy has pockets to let. My guess, it was either Reggie or Dickie, trying to steal a march on me.'

She laughed, the first genuine laugh she had managed since her brother disappeared. 'I do not understand you three gentlemen. Why do you all persist?'

'It is a matter of honour,' he said, then, before she could ask what he meant, added, 'I truly could not bear to see you married to either of the other two, good fellows though they are.'

She did not answer immediately. She had failed to sell the necklace and Viscount Kimberley had to be repaid before he, too, decided he needed recompensing for his generosity. The trouble was that it would be all too easy to give in to that particular gentleman.

'At least say you will reconsider,' he said into the silence. 'If this latest escapade becomes known, you will be ruined forever.'

It sounded very much like blackmail, but it would not be wise to accuse him of it. 'I will think about it.'

He grinned and lifted the back of her hand to his lips. 'At least, my dear, it is a step in the right direction.'

The carriage was back in Mount Street in a few minutes and drew up outside Cartrose House. He helped her out and escorted her inside. They found her aunt in the morning room, reading a newspaper. She looked up as they entered. 'There you are, Sophie. I did not know you were engaged to go out this morning, and so early, too.'

'I was out walking and Lord Gorange saw me and took me up to bring me home, Aunt.'

'Walking without me or Bessie? Tut tut, Sophie, that will not do, you know. Good morning, my lord. I thank you for rescuing her from her own folly. I trust no one saw you.'

'No, we were not observed.'

Sophie stifled a giggle at this untruth. Half of London must have seen her running so indecorously and being bundled into the carriage. She prayed none of the spectators knew who she was.

'No harm done, then,' her ladyship said.

'None whatsoever,' he said, smiling with satisfaction. 'I will take my leave of you now, but will call again in a few days, if I may. Good day, my lady. Miss Cavenhurst.'

He bowed and was gone, leaving her to be scolded by her aunt.

'My lord,' Farley said, standing before his master, who was enjoying a late breakfast in the dining room of Wyndham House and reading a letter he had just received. 'You need a physician.'

'No, I do not.' Adam's face and ribs were sore, but he said nothing of that. 'Tell me what you have discovered. Turned up that scapegrace, have you?'

'I believe he has been living in a low tavern down by the docks...'

'Ah! Did you speak to him?'

'No, my lord. He was no longer there. The tavern keeper told me he had been press-ganged.'

'Press-ganged! Are you sure about this?'

'Yes, my lord. When they came to take him he protested most strenuously...'

'Well, they all do.'

'Yes, but this young man tried to convince them he was a gentleman and gave them his name. Needless to say, they took no notice. He was, I gather, not in the best condition, having no change of raiment and in his cups. The innkeeper said he did not look like a gentleman and had asked for his cheapest room, for which he had not paid when he was taken. I recompensed the man from the money you entrusted with me. I could do nothing more because the ship had sailed.'

Adam began to laugh while Farley looked on in surprise. 'My lord?' he queried. 'Did I do wrong?'

'No, no, of course not,' he said, wiping his streaming eyes. 'Hard work and no money to gamble with will be the making of him, and Miss Cavenhurst can stop worrying about him.'

'Speaking of Miss Cavenhurst, my lord. I was on my way back when I saw the lady running down Ludgate Hill pursued by a young fellow in a black suit, shouting, "Stop, thief". I think they had just come out of the jewellers.'

'You must be mistaken.'

'I don't think so, my lord, I am sure it was she. You don't think…?'

'No, of course I don't,' he snapped. 'Did he catch up with her?'

'No. A carriage drew up beside her and she was bundled inside.'

'Whose carriage?'

'I do not know, but I fancy I have seen it somewhere before. I could not follow, being on foot. It could have been an accomplice—'

'Balderdash!'

'As you say, my lord.'

'I hope to God she has not been abducted. Heaven knows what her aunt will do if that is the case. I must go to Mount Street at once.'

'My lord, should you? Your face… And that villain may still be out there.'

'I am not hiding myself away indoors on his account, Farley. I recall I had a black eyepatch once before.'

'Aye, you did when you indulged in fisticuffs with that troublemaker at the mill. He didn't expect that.'

Adam smiled. 'He looked a whole lot worse than I did after it.'

'True. Shall I go and obtain such a patch?'

'If you please. And while I am out, you may start to pack. We are leaving.'

'Very well, my lord.'

'Then hire a chaise for tomorrow morning. We will be on the road betimes.'

'Yes, my lord. Back to Saddleworth, is it?'

'No. Hadlea in Norfolk. You can go over the route and decide where we will need a change of horses.'

If Farley was surprised at that, he did not comment, but went away to procure an eyepatch.

Sophie was seated by the window pretending to read, though her thoughts were elsewhere than on her book, and her aunt had gone back to her newspaper, unaware of her niece's seething emotions. If it had not been for Lord Gorange she could be in prison, accused of stealing her own necklace. She supposed the prison authorities would have allowed her to contact Lady Cartrose, who would have had her released. But, oh, the shame of it! She would have had to explain what she was doing in Ludgate Hill without any sort of escort. Word would have gone back to Jane and Mama and Papa, and they would be so hurt, not only by her behaviour, but Teddy's, too. As it was she had to rely on Lord Gorange not to tell anyone the real truth. To ensure that she had been forced to say she would think about his proposal.

She *was* thinking, and the more she thought, the more repugnant the prospect became. And if word got out of this latest escapade, how was she ever going to live it down? Viscount Kimberley would be disgusted with her. And somehow that mattered.

As if her thoughts had summoned him, the footman tapped at the door and entered. 'My lady, Viscount Kimberley enquires if you are at home.'

'Yes, of course, show him in,' Emmeline told him.

His lordship was right behind the servant, who stood aside to allow him to enter. He bowed to both ladies. 'I am heartily glad to see you both here,' he said. 'I hope I find you well.'

'As you see,' her ladyship answered while Sophie's heart began to beat uncomfortably fast. She really would have to discipline herself not to react in that way at the mere sight of him. And why had he said he was so pleased they were both there? Did he expect them not to be? Surely he did not know... No, he could not have. Word did not travel that quickly, not even in London.

'My lord, please be seated,' her aunt said, remembering the niceties even if Sophie could not. 'You have just missed Lord Gorange. I do declare that man is forever on our doorstep. Would you like some refreshment? Tea or coffee, perhaps?'

He flung up his tails and took a seat. 'No, thank you, my lady. I have but recently breakfasted.'

'What happened to you?' Sophie asked. She had been looking at the patch on his eye and the cut just above it. He looked as though he had been in a fight. The very thought of it made her tremble. 'You look like a pirate.'

'I had a little altercation with a door.'

Why didn't she believe him? 'Is that why you did not attend the ball last night?'

'Yes. Unfortunately I was not fit to be seen.'

'It looks painful.'

'It is nothing.'

'Miss Malthouse was very disappointed.'

'I am sorry for that. I have written to Mrs Malthouse to apologise.'

'But you came to explain to us personally.'

'Yes, but I have other news.'

'You have found Teddy.' She sat forward eagerly. 'Oh, please say you have found him.'

'I have not exactly found him, but I know where he is.'

'Oh, thank God! I have been fearing the worst. We must go to him at once. Where is he? Why did he not come home?'

He held up his hand to stop her flow of questions. 'Hold hard, Miss Cavenhurst, and I will tell you.'

'I'm sorry.' She subsided in her chair and waited for him to speak.

'He had taken refuge in an inn down by the docks. I think it was likely he was waiting to board a ship…'

'Going back to India,' she said. 'He did that once before, but when I asked him only a week ago if that was something he was considering, he said he did not have the money to get there. Perhaps he contrived to find it after all.'

'Possibly that was his intention,' he said. 'But he was unable to carry it out. He was taken by a press gang.'

'A press gang!' she exclaimed. 'In peacetime! Surely that is not possible?'

He smiled. 'If a ship is ready to sail and is short of crew, then it is possible. They will take whomever they can get, particularly if the vessel has a government cargo. Your brother was in a tavern frequented by seamen and he had earlier been drinking with some of them. They might have alerted the press gang...'

'Oh. Can we get him back?'

'Unfortunately when Farley obtained this information, the ship had already sailed.'

'Your man is sure it was Teddy?'

'Yes, your brother resisted and gave them his name in the hope they would release him. Unfortunately the name meant nothing to them and they hauled him aboard.'

'Poor, poor Teddy. Where is the ship bound?'

'I believe Australia. It is a convict ship.'

'Oh, no! I have heard such dreadful tales about those ships.'

'He is crew, not a convict, Miss Cavenhurst. Presumably he will come back on it.'

'Whatever will Papa and Mama say?'

'That brings me to another piece of news. I received a letter this morning from Cousin Mark. He is unable to fetch you as planned. He writes that he expects this good weather to break and would get the hay in before it does. Apparently he needs to be there.'

'Yes, he always likes to work with the men when he can. I think he must be a frustrated farmer at heart, but why did he not write to us directly?'

'He has asked me to take you home.'

'You, my lord?' she asked in surprise.

'Yes, me.'

The flare of pleasure at the thought was immediately stifled and replace by dismay. 'That is too much to ask. Bessie and I will manage on the stage.'

'Out of the question,' he said firmly. 'I had planned to visit Mark before going back to Yorkshire, so it is no inconvenience at all.'

Sophie looked at Lady Cartrose, half hoping she would forbid it, but she simply smiled knowingly. 'It is very kind of Viscount Kimberley, Sophie.' She turned to him. 'When do you plan to leave, my lord?'

'Tomorrow, if that is convenient for you.'

'So soon?' She sighed. 'I shall miss my dear Sophie and I am sorry you will be taking bad news back to Hadlea, but the sooner the better, I think. In any case, the Season is all but over and everyone will be retiring to the country. Sophie, how long will it take for Bessie to pack?'

'Not long if I help her, but my lord, are you sure you want to be saddled with me?'

He stood up and bowed. 'It will be my privilege and pleasure. I will call with the carriage at nine o'clock if you can be ready by then.'

'Yes,' Sophie said, rising to bid him farewell. 'I shall be ready.'

'There now,' her aunt said when he had gone. 'You will have at least two days in his company. If he has not made an offer by the end of it, I shall wonder what is the matter with him.'

'Aunt, he has said he will not marry again, and he is not a man to say what he does not mean. Besides, why would he choose me, who is always into scrapes?'

'I have no doubt he did mean it at the time he said it, but he can change his mind just as you can. All you have to do is make a little push to encourage him.' Having delivered this piece of advice, she added, 'Now, I suggest you go and start Bessie on the packing. There is no time to waste. I will send a note to Augusta to say you have been called home, you will not have time to go and say goodbye to Cassandra.'

Cassie. Whatever would she think? First his lordship does not turn up for her ball when she had been so sure he would offer for her; then he leaves town with nothing but a note of apology to her mother. Unless of course… Had he left Mount Street for Hanover Square? He could even now be making his offer and complaining that his cousin had landed him with an errand he did not want but could not refuse. He could easily return to London as soon as he had delivered her to her parents. She must be very, very careful not to let him even suspect how she felt about him. It would be too mortifying.

Bessie was taken aback when she was told they would be starting home the very next morning, and declared roundly they could not be ready in time.

'We have to be,' Sophie said. 'Mark asked Viscount Kimberley to take us and I do not think his lordship will wait on our convenience. He has hired a chaise and will be here at nine tomorrow morning.'

'But what about Master Edward? Surely you do not want to leave without knowing where he is?'

'I do know where he is.' She smiled and went on to tell Bessie what Adam had told her. 'He is safe,' she finished. 'Captain Moore cannot harm him now.'

'That is something, at least. Do you think it was Captain Moore who gave the viscount a black eye?'

'How do you know he has a black eye?'

'I saw him leave from the upstairs landing. He stood in the hall to adjust his hat at the mirror. It looked a real beauty.'

'He said he bumped into a door, though I am not sure it is the truth.'

'Well, you are going to have plenty of time to find out. Do you want me to pack your brother's things, too?'

Sophie considered this. 'No. When the ship docks on its return he will doubtless come here to my aunt. He will need a change of clothes. Leave them in the closet.'

They spent the rest of the afternoon packing. Sophie had more baggage to go back than she had brought and it took their combined efforts to close the lid of her trunk. Other small items and her overnight things would go in her portmanteau. It was almost supper time when they finished, and Sophie went down to rejoin her aunt.

They ate their evening meal with Margaret and the conversation was of general matters, for which Sophie was thankful. She did not linger long in the drawing room afterwards but went to bed so as to be fresh for her journey. But going to bed did not mean she would sleep. Her thoughts were churning.

She was going to have two days in Adam's company, two days of mental torture as she tried to keep her distance and be cool and composed, two days to watch him, to watch his changing expressions, the light in his eyes grow dark with anger or sparkle with humour, to note how he stayed in command, not only of those around him, but of himself. She could not imagine him crumbling with emotion. Had his wife seen any of that? Had he shown her a softer side?

Who had he been fighting with? Had he come off worse or was his antagonist in a worse case? Nobleman who quarrelled usually settled their differences by duelling, even though it was unlawful; honour had to be satisfied in some way. But fisticuffs? Was it anything to do with his search for Teddy or did he have enemies of his own? Was that why he wanted to leave town in a hurry and was using her as an excuse? She didn't like that idea.

She turned over and thumped her pillow. 'Stop thinking about him, find something less contentious to send you to sleep,' she muttered. But if it wasn't the viscount keeping her awake it was Teddy. He must have been at his wits' end to contemplate hiding out in a tavern and going abroad again. Now he was crewing a convict ship. How dreadful would that be? Would he have enough to eat? Would the work be too strenuous for him? He was fit and healthy, but hard physical labour had never been part of his life. Perhaps it would do him good, make him grow up. But what on earth was she going to say to Mama and Papa?

* * *

She was bleary eyed and disinclined to stir when Bessie shook her awake at seven the next morning. 'I've brought you some hot chocolate,' she said, putting a dish of it on the table by the bed. 'Drink it while I fetch a jug of hot water and lay out your clothes.' She went to the window and drew back the curtains. Sunshine flooded the room. 'Another hot day. Very different from the day we arrived...'

Sophie was hardly listening. She sat on the edge of the bed in her nightgown to gulp down the drink. Today she was going home with nothing to show for her six weeks in London, except a broken heart. Her Season had been a bitter disappointment. She would have to confess as much to her parents. Papa would undoubtedly say she was still young and there was plenty of time to find a suitable husband and she would have to pretend to agree, knowing there could be no husband because she had given her heart where it was not wanted.

Her aunt came down in a pink satin dressing gown to have breakfast with her. 'You must come back and visit me again some day,' she said, helping herself to coddled eggs and three slices of ham from the dishes on the sideboard. 'I have enjoyed our little excursions.'

Sophie looked down at the bread and butter on her own plate and didn't feel a bit like eating it. 'So have I, Aunt, and I thank you for having me. I am only sorry that Teddy has been a worry to you.'

'He is young and strong and can no doubt look after himself,' her ladyship said. 'I am more concerned for you.'

'Me? Why?'

'You are so obviously enamoured of Viscount Kimberley and he is too blind to see it. If you want him, you are going to have to fight for him.'

'Aunt, I could not do that. Even I know it is not proper for a lady to make the first move, even supposing she wishes to, which I do not.'

Her hurried addendum made her aunt smile. 'You must contrive to make him think he is doing all the running, my dear. You have a golden opportunity on the journey. I shall be very disappointed in you if he comes back to London and offers for Cassandra.'

Sophie had nothing to say to that and in any case there was no time, for the sound of the door knocker told them he had arrived.

He came, still wearing his eyepatch, doffed his hat and bowed to them both. 'Good morning, my lady. Miss Cavenhurst. I have taken the liberty of asking your man to load your trunk on to the roof. If we are to make the journey in two days, we must not delay. I have sent Farley on ahead to arrange horses and accommodation.'

There was a flurry of activity as Sophie's

trunk was heaved up and roped down beside his own, and her portmanteau and Bessie's stowed in the boot. Sophie put on her bonnet, but decided to carry her shawl because, even so early, it promised to be a hot day. She hung her reticule over her wrist and turned to embrace her aunt. 'Goodbye, dear aunt. I am truly grateful for all you have done for me and for Teddy. No doubt he will come and see you when he returns.'

'I will send him straight home when he does. Write to me when you are safely home and I hope you will have good news to tell me.'

'Aunt,' she protested, feeling the warmth flood her face.

Her aunt simply smiled and kissed her.

Sophie climbed into the carriage followed by Bessie and Adam and they were off. She looked back to see her aunt standing at the door, still in her dressing gown, waving a handkerchief. Then they turned the corner and she was lost to sight.

Sophie settled in her seat, wondering how they were going to occupy the long hours of travel. Ought she to say something, or leave him to begin a conversation? He did not seem inclined to do so. He sat in the opposite corner, trying not to let his long legs tangle with her skirts. The heat in the coach was oppressive. She was glad of the bottle of cold lemonade that her aunt had provided her with. She poured some in a cup and offered it to him. He shook his head. 'No thank you, Miss Cavenhurst. I will procure a drink when we stop for refreshments at noon.'

She offered the cup to Bessie, who drank it greedily. Sophie, taking the cup back, noticed the perspiration standing on the maid's brow and her flushed face and realised she was overcome by the heat. 'Bessie, would you like us to stop so that you can have some fresh air?'

'No, Miss Sophie. It will delay you.'

'That can't be helped. I cannot have you fainting on me.' She turned to Adam. 'Please ask the coachman to stop.'

He did so, and the vehicle drew to a stop beside the road where a tree offered a little shade. They all left the carriage and Bessie walked up and down a little way, fanning herself with the fan Sophie had handed to her.

'We ought to go on,' Adam said after a few minutes. 'We will fall behind schedule and the innkeeper might let others have our fresh horses.'

'Of course. I understand. Do you think the driver would mind if Bessie sat alongside him on the box? I will let her have my parasol to shield her from the sun. I am sure she would be cooler there.'

'Miss Sophie…' Bessie protested, but not vehemently.

'Just until we change the horses,' Sophie said. 'You will feel much better by then.'

'Very well.'

Sophie gave Bessie her parasol and Adam helped her up on to the box beside the coachman, who gave her a grin. 'I'm Joe Brandon,' he said. 'Welcome to my world.'

Sophie and Adam resumed seats in the carriage, but this time he sat beside her so that he could stretch out his legs.

Sophie had only been concerned for Bessie's comfort and had not considered the impropriety of being inside the coach alone with the viscount. She looked out of the window at the countryside through which they were passing, acutely aware of him. His broad shoulders were so close to hers, his thighs just inches from hers. He had his feet on the seat opposite and his hat tipped over his eyes. Was he pretending to sleep?

'My lord, did you manage to complete your business?' she queried when she could stand the silence no longer.

He pushed his hat back on his head and looked at her. 'My business?'

'Whatever it was that brought you to London. I hope that taking me home has not interrupted it.'

'No, not at all. There was no more I could do in town. I had planned to return to Saddleworth soon, in any case.'

'But you are going out of your way to take me home. I feel guilty about that.'

'There is no need, Miss Cavenhurst. I had

already promised Mark I would go to Hadlea before going home. I have yet to meet my cousin-in-law and the baby.'

'Harry,' she said. 'He is a sturdy little chap, all beaming smiles and wet kisses. He will be walking soon, I think. He already crawls everywhere and is full of curiosity.'

'Mark and Jane are fortunate to have him.'

'You have no children?'

'No, unfortunately. My wife died in childbirth, along with my son.'

'I am so sorry. I did not mean to make you sad.'

'Please do not apologise. So many people avoid mentioning her as if the subject is forbidden, almost as if she had never existed.'

'Would you like to tell me about her?' Why she asked she did not know; learning about his wife would not make her feel any better, but it might help her to understand him. Perhaps it would ease his pain, too.

He hesitated, and she wondered if she had overstepped the mark as she so often did, but then he seemed to gather himself to answer her. 'I met her in Saddleworth. Her father, Silas Bamford, owned a wool mill and employed about a thousand workers, some in the mill, some as outworkers. He and Anne were out in their carriage one day, returning from a morning call when they were met by a hostile crowd of workers who threatened to overturn their carriage. Mr Bamford was not one to be intimidated and tried to stand up to them, but Anne was terrified. I had charge of the local militia and had heard about the demonstration and arrived with my men just in time to rescue them. Fortunately no one was hurt, but I escorted them home safely and, well, the rest you can imagine. I was a frequent visitor to their home after that and Anne and I married in 1816. We had just a year together before she was taken from me.'

'It must have been dreadful for you,' she murmured, noticing the faraway look in his eyes, as if he were in some other time, some other place.

'It was. She was so beautiful, so full of life, so affectionate, it seemed cruel of God to take her so young. The baby was beautiful, too.'

'I cannot begin to think what that must have been like.'

'I pray you never need to.'

'You could marry again and still have children.'

He looked sharply at her as if she had gone a step too far. 'So I could, but I could not bear to go through that again.'

'Is that why you were not at Mark and Jane's wedding?'

'Yes. I was not in a fit state to rejoice at anyone else's happiness.' He smiled suddenly. 'But now I go to meet my cousin-in-law and make the acquaintance of young Harry.'

'And then you will go home to Yorkshire?'

'Yes.'

'Not back to London?'

'No, did you think I would?'

'I wondered. I thought perhaps Miss Malthouse…'

'Oh, so this is what the quizzing is about? You would divine my intentions so that you can relay them to your friend. You may tell Miss Malthouse that Adam Trent is not interested in marrying again, not to her, not to anyone.'

'No, no, you misunderstand me,' she said quickly.

'Then, please explain yourself.'

But she could not, could not tell him the real reason she wanted to know more about him, and now she felt mortified and wished she had remained silent and let him go to sleep if he wanted to. 'I was just making idle conversation.'

'Then I would hate to be the object of a real interrogation from you, Miss Cavenhurst.' He paused. 'Shall I quiz you now?'

'I am not very interesting.'

'Allow me to be the judge of that. For instance, what were you doing fleeing from a jeweller's shop with a member of that establishment after you shouting, "Stop, thief!" I am immensely interested in that.'

She gasped. 'Why ever would I do such a thing?'

'You tell me.'

'Whoever told you must be mistaken. I am not a thief.'

'I have not accused you of it. But I see you do not deny it was you. I am glad because I should not like to think you are a liar.'

She could feel the heat in her cheeks and knew she could not prevaricate with this man who seemed to witness or hear about every one of her indiscretions. He was looking closely at her now, waiting for her to explain. 'I did not know...'

'That you had been observed. I am afraid, my dear, you were.'

'By whom?'

'My man, Farley. He was on the way back from the docks after locating your brother when he saw you running and being bundled into a carriage. I feared you had been kidnapped, though it was Farley's opinion that the occupant was an accomplice.'

'That's silly.'

'I am not accustomed to being called silly, Sophie. Who was in the carriage?'

'A friend.'

'Had you arranged for him to be there?'

'Certainly not! It was pure coincidence, but I

own I was very glad to see him.' She sighed. 'I suppose I had better tell you the whole.'

'It would be best.'

'I went to Rundell, Bridge and Rundell to sell my necklace, but they started questioning me about where I had got it and I realised they thought I had stolen it, so I ran.'

'But surely you could have answered their questions?'

'Not without naming Jane, and it would have hurt her to think that I would sell her gift to me.'

'Why didn't you think about that before you went?'

'I don't know. I was so anxious...'

'I assume it was that scapegrace of a brother you were thinking of. Had he come to ask for more money to see him safely aboard a passenger ship? Were you supposed to meet him by the docks with it? Was this friend going to take you to him?'

'Certainly not! I had no idea where he was. You know that. You were looking for him for me. It is my belief you got that black eye in the course of your enquiries.'

If she had hoped to divert him from his questions with that, she was disappointed. 'Then why did you need the money? Are you a gambler, too?'

She stared at him. Did he really think that? 'My lord...'

'Come on out with it. How much do you owe and to whom?'

'I don't know the exact figure, my lord, but my debt is to you.'

'Me?' he asked, astonished.

'Yes. You paid Teddy's debts and as far as I am concerned it is only a loan.'

'It is his debt, not yours. Why do you have to burden yourself with his problems?'

'He is my brother. I love him in spite of his gambling. In every other way he is the best of brothers. We have always been very close. And I know he tries not to gamble.'

He was silent for some time. She wondered what he was thinking, but his face was inscrutable. She sighed and looked out of the window. They were deep into the country now. Fields, trees, farms, hovels, livestock went by in a flash as the horses cantered on. The carriage pulled up at the coaching inn in Epping where they were to change the horses. Adam went off to pay their dues and Sophie got out and asked Bessie if she wanted to return inside. 'If it's all the same to you, Miss Sophie, I'll stay here. It is so much cooler and Joe has been telling me all about his adventures as a coachman. I had no idea it could be so interesting.'

Farley had done his job well. Fresh horses were ready and waiting and they were soon on their way again, cantering northwards once more, this time through the forest, which made the inside of the coach cooler. Sophie was far from cool. She had been glad of the stop, wondering how much more Adam would have managed to worm out of her but for the interruption. She really must guard her tongue or before she knew it he would know exactly how she felt about him, and how much more mortifying would that be?

Chapter Ten

While the swaying coach negotiated the rough road, made rougher by tree roots making their way up through the hardened track, Adam contemplated the young lady beside him. For the first time since Anne's death he found himself drawn towards another woman. Sophie was as unlike Anne as it was possible for anyone to be—perhaps that was her attraction. Anne had come from working-class stock. Her father had worked his way up to become a mill manager and then had taken over the mill when the owner retired. He had been blunt and down to earth, at the same time bringing up his motherless daughter to be the epitome of genteel behaviour. He did this with the help of the daughter of a nobleman fallen on hard times who needed a home and a way to earn a living.

Anne had been loving, obedient, trusting and he had adored her. She would never have dreamed of behaving in the hoydenish way that Sophie Cavenhurst behaved. She would never have flouted convention, wandered about town unaccompanied, dressed in a man's garb, played cricket or ridden astride. Was that why he found Sophie so endearing? She did not try to be anything but what she was: maddening, intensely loyal and outspoken.

At nineteen she had already turned down three suitors. Was she so very hard to please? Or was she playing one against the other while she made up her mind? Did she know about that preposterous wager her brother had made? The irony of that was that Cavenhurst could not lose that one. If she married one of them and he had to pay up, he would still have collected from the other two and been a thousand pounds in pocket, although that would not have helped him much, considering what he owed Toby Moore. What infuriated Adam most was that they appeared to treat it as a game. None of the men needed money.

'What are you smiling about?' Sophie's voice was close to his left ear and startled him.

'Was I smiling?'

'Yes. Come, share the joke with me.'

'It is not fit for a lady's ears.'

'Then it is uncivil of you to think about it in a lady's company.'

'I beg your pardon. I was thinking about Bertie Gorange.'

'Lord Gorange. Why?'

'It was he who rescued you from being apprehended for a jewel thief, was it not?'

'How do you know that?'

'I collect your aunt saying something about Lord Gorange calling yesterday. I surmise he brought you home.'

'He happened to be passing near the jeweller's shop.'

'Just happened to be passing?'

'Yes, and I was grateful for it.'

'How grateful?'

'My lord, you are as bad as everyone else, thinking I am going to marry one of those three. What I cannot understand is why they persist in wanting me. I have no fortune and I am always falling into scrapes and, according to some, I am a hoyden and a flirt.'

'Flirt, Miss Cavenhurst? I have seen no evidence of it. And no doubt the gentlemen have their reasons.'

'Do you know what they might be?'

He was tempted to tell her, but decided she might be hurt by it. 'No, but you could always marry someone else. That would put a stop to it.'

She gave him a sharp look. He was still smiling. 'I would, if someone loved me as much as I loved him.'

'Are you in love?'

'No, I was speaking generally,' she said, feeling the colour mount in her cheeks. 'Shall we change the subject?'

'As you wish.'

'Tell me about the business that took you to London, if it was not to look for a wife.'

'I went to speak in the House of Lords about the problems of the workingman and what I thought should be done.'

'What do you think should be done?'

They were on safer ground now and he outlined his ideas on the subject. She listened carefully. 'Unfortunately, they were in no mood to listen and I fear the workers will take matters into their own hands,' he said.

'Riot, you mean?'

'Perhaps. They are certainly planning another large meeting.'

'And you mean to stop it?'

'I wish I could. I do not know when and where it is to be. And the hotheads will not listen, either.'

'And you are pig in the middle.'

He smiled. 'You could say that.'

'Is that how you received your injuries?'

'Injuries? You mean this?' He pointed to the eyepatch.

'Yes, and other injuries not quite so obvious. I noticed you flinch when that ostler bumped into you when we stopped to change the horses, and you wriggle in your seat as if you find it difficult to be comfortable.'

'You are very observant.'

'Teddy was always injuring himself when he was young and pretending it was nothing. I learned the signs.'

'I was set upon by thieves. I do not think it had anything to do with my mission to London.'

'I am sorry, my lord.'

'No need to be. I'll live.' He gave her a quirky smile, which made her heart flip. The more she learned about him, the more she loved him, if that were possible. He cared about people, especially those for whom he felt responsible. He was thoughtful and generous. Who else would have paid Teddy's debts? Certainly not Reggie or Richard Fanshawe, and Lord Gorange had only offered to do so on a consideration.

'You missed Cassie's come-out ball on account of it.'

'Yes, that is to be regretted. Was it a lively affair?'

'Yes. Everyone was in good spirits. The music was good and the food excellent. You were missed.'

'By you?'

'By everyone, particularly Cassie,' she said quickly.

'Then perhaps it was as well I did not go. I

would not want to raise false hopes. Miss Malthouse will no doubt soon find someone else.'

So Cassie was to be disappointed. It seemed he really meant to keep his vow not to remarry.

The horses were slowing for their next stop where they planned to have something to eat and drink. Bessie, helped down from the box by the jovial coachman, joined them for their meal and personal conversation was set aside. Less than an hour later they were on their way again, but this time Bessie rode inside.

Talk was desultory and for the most part consisted of Bessie, prompted by Sophie, telling them what she and the coachman had talked about and what she had viewed from her seat beside him. Adam showed no sign of being bored and listened with grave attention, even putting in a comment of his own now and again. Thus the journey continued, during which they stopped several times to change the horses. They reached the Cross Keys in Saffron Walden as dusk began to fall, late at that time of the year, and there Alfred Farley was waiting for them with bedchambers booked.

They all dined together, master and man, mistress and maid, and it did not seem to matter. Their coachman found convivial company elsewhere. Sophie was used to sharing with Bessie, but she was surprised that Adam was so easy with Mr Farley. He was not uncouth, but rough and ready and seemed to enjoy more than the usual rapport of master and man with the viscount. It was one more indication of his lordship's character, she decided.

As soon as the meal ended, Sophie and Bessie went up to the bedchamber they were to share and left the men enjoying tankards of ale.

'Did you have any trouble on the way, my lord?' Farley asked.

'No, everything went smoothly, thanks to you. But I did wonder if we were being followed. I could hear hoofbeats behind us on some of the harder roads. When we stopped to allow Miss Cavenhurst's maid to step down, they stopped, too, and resumed as soon as we were on our way again.'

'Did they follow you into the yard here?'

'No, I do not think so. Perhaps I imagined it.'

'Could be the cove who was dogging you in the Smoke.'

'But why?'

'I have no idea, my lord, but it seems someone is very curious to know what you are about.'

'I am not doing anything clandestine.'

'No, but he is.'

'Have you booked our change of horses for the rest of the way?'

'Yes, my lord, as far as Downham Market.

The last four cattle should take you to Hadlea, if not hurried.'

'Good. How did you find the mare? Was she up to it?'

'Yes, my lord. She is a goer, I'll give you that.'

'You did not press her too hard?'

'No, my lord. I left her at an inn for a couple of stages and hired a hack so that she could rest. I picked her up again on the way back, just as you instructed. She is in fine fettle.'

'Then follow on behind tomorrow, and if you should notice anyone taking more than a casual interest in us, come and tell me. I do not need to warn you to say nothing of our follower to the ladies, do I?'

'No, my lord, certainly not.'

'Better go to bed now. We still have a long way to go. I'll see to myself.'

'Very good, my lord.' Farley rose stiffly, evidence of his long hours in the saddle. Adam smiled as he watched him mount the stairs, hauling on the banister to help him up. He would go a long way before he found a man as willing and loyal as Alfred Farley. He was a good man to have at his side in a sticky situation.

Whether they were truly in a sticky situation, he did not know. But if there were someone following them, was it the same someone who had followed him back to Wyndham House two nights before and cheekily saluted him from the road? What on earth could he want? He didn't think it was anything to do with Teddy Cavenhurst or Sophie, but it would be good to be sure. He rose and went up to his bedroom, but before he climbed into bed, he primed his pistol and checked his ammunition.

The journey next day continued as the day before with casual conversation and frequent stops to change the horses. Sophie was amused to see that Farley was riding Swift and was keeping close behind them. Occasionally he rode off somewhere, but soon returned and took up his place behind them. Poor man, it must be very tiring for him. Adam was sitting opposite her again, his legs uncomfortably squashed.

'I see your man is riding Swift,' she said.

'Yes, it is one way to transport the animal, and he had to ride on ahead to arrange for horses to be ready. I did not want to leave it to chance.'

'It must have been uncomfortable riding all day. I noticed him walking rather stiffly when he dismounted at the last stop.'

'Yes, so did I. I will take a turn riding shortly and he can sit beside the coachman.'

At the next change of horses he took over the riding and Farley rode on the box, leaving Sophie and Bessie in possession of the interior of the carriage. The air was stifling and Sophie

could see Bessie was suffering. 'We will stop
again soon,' she said. 'And I will ask his lordship if we can spare a little time so that you may
go into the inn and have a cold drink and rest
in the shade.'

'We must not delay him,' the maid said. 'You
know how cross he was last time.'

'He can be as cross as he likes. I shall insist.'

'Oh, dear, I am sorry to be so much trouble
to you.'

'You are not half as much trouble to me as I
have been to you, Bessie, so do not think of it.'

'I wish the weather would cool down, then I
should be more comfortable.'

They had not gone much farther when her
wish was granted. The sun was blocked out by
dark clouds rolling in from the north and the
interior of the carriage became almost as dark
as night. 'It is going to rain,' Sophie said. 'That
will cool us all down.' As she spoke they saw
a flash of lightning and seconds afterwards a
rumble of thunder.

Adam, who was riding behind, called the
coachman to stop. He dismounted and tied Swift
on behind the carriage. 'Alfred, into the carriage
with you,' he said. Then to the coachman, who
was even then putting on a heavy overcoat with
several capes, 'Can you keep going?'

'Aye, my lord, though the horses might get a

bit skittish.' A sheet of lightning lit the sky as he spoke and the thunder seemed nearer. The horses moved restlessly.

'In that case find somewhere where we can shelter, an inn or a farm building. Not trees.'

'I do know better'n that,' he said, miffed.

Adam joined his servant and the ladies in the carriage, doubling himself up to leave them adequate room. Bessie was shivering now, not so much with cold but fear. She had always been terrified of thunderstorms and would always go round the house when one threatened, covering all the mirrors and making sure any cutlery was safely in drawers. There was no cutlery or mirrors in the coach, but the horses were definitely nervous. They were galloping at a cracking pace and they could hear the coachman calling out, trying to calm them. To make matters worse, rain was beating on the roof in a loud tattoo. Bessie threw her shawl over her head and even Sophie was uneasy as the carriage lurched from side to side. Suddenly they swung into a farmyard, turned into an open-sided barn and pulled to a sudden stop. Sophie was catapulted into Adam's lap.

Instinctively he grabbed her. She found her head against his chest and his arms enfolding her. She could feel the regular beat of his heart and tilted her head up to look at his face. He was smiling. 'Much as I would like to savour the moment, I fear I have to let you go,' he murmured in her ear. 'I must help with the horses.'

She scrambled inelegantly off his knees and returned to her seat, her face on fire. He left the coach followed by Farley and she decided to go, too, and help. Swift, with no one on her back, had had no trouble keeping up with the carriage, but she was shivering and her eyes were wide with terror. Sophie went to calm her, holding her head and murmuring softly in her ear, 'Easy now, my beauty. Easy. It will soon be over.' Outside the rain beat down and the farmyard was soon awash. The mare became calmer, but she still shook when thunder rolled.

Adam, aware that Sophie knew what she was doing, left Swift to her and concentrated on the carriage horses. It took the combined efforts of the three men to stop them rearing every time lightning lit up the gloom in the barn. There was a haywain piled with hay at the far end. Adam pulled a few handfuls from it to give to the horses, and Sophie filled a nosebag for Swift.

They heard a dog barking and turned as a large mongrel ran into the barn and stopped to growl, baring his teeth. He was closely followed by a stout man in fustian coat and breeches, wearing a sack over his shoulders. His broad-brimmed hat was dripping rain from the brim. 'What d'yer think you're a-doin'?' he demanded angrily.

Adam went forward. 'Good day, sir. I'd be obliged if you would call off your dog. He is frightening the horses. I fear they will lash out and do some damage.'

'They'd best not,' he said, but he called the dog to heel. It went to him obediently, but remained alert.

'Are you the owner of this barn?' Adam asked him.

'The tenant. What are you doing here? And stealing my hay, an' all. I'll hev the law on yer.'

'We will pay for it, of course. I am afraid our horses were terrified by the storm and we thought it best to seek shelter. We will move on as soon as the weather eases.'

'Tha's all very well, but if you've damaged anythin'…'

'I am sure we have not, except to bring a little mud in on the wheels. Naturally I will pay for the inconvenience.'

'And who might you be?'

'Viscount Kimberley of Saddleworth. This is…' he indicated Sophie still holding Swift's head '…my cousin, Miss Cavenhurst. We are travelling to Norfolk.'

'I doubt you will get there tonight,' the man said. 'Never seen a storm like it and the roads are awash. Shouldn't be surprised if the river hev burst its banks.'

'Until we are able to move on, do you think

you could provide us with some food and something to drink?' Adam appeared unruffled by this news. 'We had planned to stop at the Rutland Arms in Newmarket for a meal, but if you are right, we might take some time reaching there.'

'I'll go and talk to the missus.' He stomped out into the rain, followed by his dog.

'Do you think he is right?' Sophie asked Adam. 'Will the river have flooded?'

'I don't know. When the rain stops I'll go and reconnoitre.' He turned to the coachman. 'In the meantime, unharness the horses, will you, Mr Brandon? Let them have a rest. Give him a hand, Alfred, will you?'

While the two men obeyed, Adam went to the door and looked up at the leaden sky. The wind, which had blown the clouds up so rapidly, had dropped and there was not a breath to carry them away. The rain was pounding on the roof of the barn and filling up the dents and hollows in the farm yard until it looked like a pond. Thankfully the building was watertight, but he was aware of a sharp drop in the temperature and the ladies were shivering, especially Sophie because she had draped her shawl over Swift's back.

'Put your shawl back on, Miss Cavenhurst,' he told her. 'You need it more than the mare.'

'Would you address a cousin so formally?' she asked.

'You are not really my cousin.'

'But you told the farmer I was.'

'It was easier than trying to explain.'

She smiled. 'Then it had better be Sophie, don't you think?'

He laughed aloud. 'Sophie,' he said. 'But for that to be convincing I must be Adam.'

She had been thinking of him in those terms for some time, though she had never uttered his name aloud. 'Very well…Adam.'

The farmer returned, carrying a rough cloth coat and a pile of sacks. 'Will you come up to the house, my lord?' he said, handing Sophie the coat and distributing the sacks to the others. 'My Molly is making a meal for you. If you follow me, I'll lead you over the driest bits.'

As far as Sophie could see there were no dry bits. She draped the coat over her head, which was thick enough to keep off the worst of the rain. She went to step outside, knowing she would get wet feet, but before she could do so, Adam had scooped her up in his arms and was carrying her. 'My lord…'

'Adam,' he corrected her, marching behind the farmer. 'I am wearing boots, you are not, so no argument.' Joe, who was also wearing stout boots, had taken his cue from Adam and picked Bessie up and, despite her not-very-convincing protests, was right behind them.

Sophie clasped her arms about Adam's neck and leaned into him. He had a lean, hard body, broad shoulders and narrow hips. She could feel his muscles flexed beneath his clothes and wondered idly what he would look like stripped. She remembered his bruises, but either they had healed remarkably quickly or he was able to ignore the pain. 'Now who is savouring the moment,' she murmured under her breath.

He chuckled. 'I am. It is surprising how appealing a wet face and a fusty overcoat can be.'

She had not realised she had spoken loud enough for him to hear, and the glow in the core of her intensified. The warmth of his body enveloped her, the smell of him, a mixture of soap and horse and honest sweat, filled her nostrils. Her heartbeat tuned itself to his. She felt moulded to him, two bodies in one. It was such a lovely sensation she gave herself up to it. But not for long because they were at the door of the farmhouse and Adam was being ushered inside by the farmer. Adam set her down and they were two separate beings once more. He took the coat from her shoulders and handed it back to the farmer.

'Come this way, my lord,' the man said, leading the way along a narrow passage into a room that was evidently the best parlour. It felt cold and smelled musty as if it were little used. There were two stuffed winged chairs before an empty grate, a rather battered sofa, a couple of hardbacked chairs and a table. A shelf displayed cheap ornaments, and there was an embroidered text hanging from a nail above the mantel.

Bessie was shivering violently and Sophie feared she had caught a chill. She turned to the farmer. 'Mr...what is your name?'

'Brown, my lady.'

'Mr Brown,' she said, ignoring his mistake. 'I fear my maid is not very well. Do you think she could sit by your fire and warm herself? A hot drink might help, too.'

'We would all appreciate a hot drink,' Adam said. 'But look after the maid first.'

'Come, miss,' the man said, addressing Bessie.

She glanced at Sophie, who nodded. 'Go on.'

'I'll go, too,' Joe said. He went after the farmer and Bessie, leaving Adam and Sophie alone.

'Where is Mr Farley?' she asked.

'He is checking the carriage and horses are out of sight of the road. It would be a trifle inconvenient to find them gone when we want to continue our journey.'

'Who is likely to be on the road in this?' She gestured towards the window where the rain was running down in rivulets.

'If someone was on foot or on horseback, the prospect of riding in the dry might be too much of a temptation.'

'Surely it is the coachman's task to see that doesn't happen?'

'Yes, but at the moment, he seems to have his hands full with Miss Sadler.'

She laughed. 'They do seem rather keen on each other.'

'It is your fault for suggesting she ride on the box.'

'She was feeling sick and you were chafing at the delay. What else would you have me do?'

'Oh, I am not criticising you, simply pointing out a fact. And the delay of a few minutes is immaterial now. We are going to be hours behind schedule, and I am afraid even if we start out at once we will be forced to have another night on the road.'

'It is still raining, but the thunder and lightning have passed.'

'I had noticed that,' he said laconically. 'As soon as we have had something to eat, I will ride ahead on Swift and reconnoitre the ground.'

'Why not send Mr Farley?'

'Because he will want to eat and drink and warm himself.'

'You are very careful of him.'

'He is careful of me. Treat a man right and he will remain loyal.'

'You know, you are very like Mark. Not so much in looks, but in your philosophy. It must be a family trait. How close is his relationship with you?'

'Our mothers were sisters. My mother died when I was at school. She was perfectly well when I was home for the Easter break, but she had gone before I was due home for the summer.'

'I am sorry. It must have been very hard for you.'

'It was. I was particularly close to her. She taught me so much about the countryside, about her charitable work, about forgiveness and tolerance...' His voice cracked and he swallowed hard.

She put out a hand to touch his arm, but did not speak. He looked down at the hand and she withdrew it hastily. 'I must go and see how Bessie is doing.' She left him to gather himself in private. If she had stayed a moment longer, she would have put her arms about him to comfort him and that would have been completely the wrong thing to do. A proud man like he was would not have appreciated it.

Bessie was sitting close to the fender in the kitchen with a blanket round her, warming her hands on a hot tankard. The farmer's wife was working round her, stirring the contents of a large cooking pot that hung above the flames. On the rough table was a board containing bread, a dish of butter and a pile of plates.

'Mrs Brown, is there anything I can do to help?' she asked.

'Gracious me, no, my lady. Please go back to his lordship. I will bring food to you directly. I have given your maid a herbal remedy for I fear she has taken cold. The coachman has gone to fetch her bag. I will make up a bed for her in our spare room. It is used by our grandchildren when they come to stay, but they are not here now.'

It sounded as if she expected her uninvited visitors to stay overnight. Sophie went back to report the fact to Adam. 'I don't know where she is going to put us all,' she said. 'It is a fairly substantial farmhouse, but I doubt it extends to more than three bedchambers. Besides, I collect you are anxious to be on your way. If Bessie cannot travel, then you had better leave us here and go on without us. Mark will come and fetch us in due course.'

'Don't be a ninnyhammer, Sophie.'

'I am not a ninnyhammer. It is a perfectly sensible suggestion.'

'It is not. Mark entrusted me to see you safely home and that is what I intend to do. What do you take me for?'

She smiled. 'Not a ninnyhammer, at any rate.'

'I apologise for that, but you must see that I could never leave you.'

'Never?' she queried, raising her eyebrows at him.

'You know what I mean. I must go and speak to the good lady of the house.'

He strode from the room before he said something he would regret. She was really getting inside his skin with her flashes of insight interspersed with outspokenness and brave attempts to flirt with him. She was a strange mixture of naivety and wisdom and he was never quite sure how to respond to her. The last thing he wanted to do was hurt her.

He found Mrs Brown in the kitchen, putting the finishing touches to a homely meal. 'Madam,' he began. 'I asked for food, not a feast, and I fear we have put you to a great deal of trouble…'

'We have plenty of food, my lord, if not much else. You are welcome. I would not leave a dog out in this weather.' This statement was borne out by the fact that the mongrel was lying on a rough blanket under the table.

'My cousin tells me that you are going to find a bed for her maid.'

'Yes. She i'n't well. I don't think she oughta travel until she is better, begging your pardon, my lord.'

'In that case, we must all stay. My cousin will not go on without her and I will not go on without my cousin.'

'My lord…' Bessie protested. 'I shall manage.'

He turned to look at her, huddled in the corner enveloped in a blanket. Her eyes were puffy and her nose red. 'We will decide on that tomorrow. It is to be hoped your mistress does not succumb.' Turning back to their hostess, he said, 'Do you have a room for Miss Cavenhurst?'

'Yes, my lord, but...' She paused and he guessed she was weighing up the prospect of giving up her own bed to one of them.

'The men will manage in the coach,' he told her. 'Someone ought to keep an eye on it, in any case. I will do very well on the sofa.'

'Are you sure?'

'Yes, I am. And you do not need to lay up the table in the parlour. We can all eat in here. We do not want to put you to any more inconvenience than we can help.'

'Very well, my lord, I'll do as you say. It will be ready in five minutes.'

'I will go and fetch the men.'

'It's still a-rainin'. Take Mr Brown's big coat.' She nodded to where it hung on the back of the door.

He draped it over his shoulders and made his way across the flooded yard and into the barn. Alfred and the coachman were sitting in the coach talking about the dwindling prospects of going on. 'It's still rainin', but there ain't no more thunder and lightning,' Joe was saying. 'I reckon we could make it through.'

'Through what?' Adam asked.

'The flood, my lord,' Farley replied. 'I went to take a look. There's a dip in the road as it goes down to the river. It's about two feet deep. I rode Swift through it, though she wasn't keen. The bridge is an old stone one and looked sound to me and the road is passable beyond it.'

'We are not going on today,' Adam said. 'Miss Sadler has caught cold and the good farmer's wife is making up a bed for her, which means we all have to stay. There is a meal waiting for us in the farm kitchen, so let us go and have it. We will worry about tomorrow when it comes.'

'I don't reckon we ought to leave the coach unattended,' Joe said.

'Then you stay here and I'll have something sent out to you. Alfred, come with me.'

They picked their way over the muddy farm-yard. The rain was easing and the water was slowly draining away. 'I reckon it will be gone by tomorrow,' Farley said. 'Pity about Miss Sadler.'

'Yes. Did you hear the horse just after we turned into the barn?'

'Yes, my lord.' He grinned. 'Galloped right past, he did. I wonder how far he got before he twigged he'd lost us.'

Adam laughed. 'However far it was, he will have been very wet.'

'Serve him right.'

'Not a word now.'

They entered the house and made their way to the kitchen, where a substantial meal was set out on the big table. Bessie was no longer there and he assumed she had gone to bed. Mr Brown and Sophie were already seated at the table. She looked up as they entered. 'Is everything all right?' she asked.

'Yes. The coachman is staying with his vehicle. I wonder, Mrs Brown, if I might take something out to him?'

'I'll take it,' Farley said, holding out his hand for the plate their hostess was already filling.

Adam sat down next to Sophie. 'How is Miss Sadler?'

'She is feeling rather sorry for herself, but Mrs Brown gave her a herbal remedy to help her to sleep and assures me it will cure anything. I am inclined to believe her. Bessie pulled a sour face when she drank it.' She paused. 'I am sorry to be so much trouble to you…' She almost added 'my lord', but remembered in time, they were supposed to be on more familiar terms.

'It cannot be helped, Sophie. It means we will be a day or two later reaching Hadlea, that's all.' He evidently did remember. Hearing him say her name gave her a warm glow of pleasure. What a fool she was to be uplifted by such a little thing.

Chapter Eleven

Cooped up in the farmhouse with nothing to do and everyone itching to be gone did not help frayed nerves. Sophie looked after Bessie and did her best to help Mrs Brown. Joe used the time to check over every inch of the coach: the wheels and axles, though he knew they were sound, replacing leather that was even partially worn and cleaning it inside and out. By the time he had finished it looked as good as new. He groomed the horses until their coats were gleaming and combed and plaited their manes and tails, tying them with ribbons.

'Good enough for the showground,' Adam told him. 'Well done.'

Adam himself was at a loose end. He went round the fields with the farmer. 'It's going to be a poor winter,' Mr Brown muttered, looking at the wet, blackened wheat crop. 'I'll have to plough that in.'

'You harvested the barley and oats before the storm?'

'Aye, but they were only a few acres. They had a poor start on account o' the cold weather in spring, but June and July made up for it and in the end I got it in early, but it don' make up for the loss of the wheat. It were all but ready. I was goin' into town to hire some extra help this next week.' He sighed. 'I don' know what we're a-goin' to do. We'll have to rely on the livestock. Thank God, tha's healthy.'

Adam made a mental note to make sure the man was more than adequately paid for their board and lodging when they left.

On the third day, now without his eyepatch, he rode into Newmarket on Swift to obtain more provisions for Mrs Brown, to mail a letter to Mark explaining the situation and to find out if there were any strangers in the town. That turned out to be a vain exercise; the place was full of strangers come for the racing and he had no idea what the man looked like. Of course he and Alfred might have imagined the galloping horse, or it could have been a local man in a hurry to be home out of the rain.

He went back to the farm to find Sophie in the barn talking to Joe and Alfred. She was smiling. 'Bessie has recovered,' she told him. 'We are ready to go on.'

'Are you sure?' he asked, studying her. After three days of caring for her maid, she was looking tired, but she had washed her hair and put on a fresh gingham dress taken from her trunk. 'Your maid may have recovered, but what about you?'

'I am perfectly well. You must be anxious to be on your way, and I am sure Mrs Brown will be glad to see us gone. I fear we have been a sore trial to her.'

'Then we will leave tomorrow morning. Alfred, you ride on ahead and arrange for fresh horses. We will meet you at Downham Market. Give Swift a drink and her oats now and let her rest.'

'Yes, my lord.'

'Sophie, can you be ready?'

'Easily.'

They walked up to the farmhouse together. 'It has been a strange few days,' she said. 'I have learned something of what it is to be a farmer's wife. I knew it was a hard life, but I never realised before just how hard. It has made me so much more sympathetic to those not so fortunate as I am.'

'I am sure you have always been sympathetic,' he murmured. 'Mark has told me how helpful you are with his orphans.'

'They have had a dreadful life and I like to do what I can to help make their lives a little easier.

I find it rewarding.' She looked up at him. His eye still bore a faint bruise. 'I believe that is how you feel towards your workers. I read the report of your speech in the newspaper.'

'Yes, but it is not enough, Sophie. I failed to do any good.'

Calling each other by their given names seemed perfectly natural now. He had become more at ease with her. His up-and-down moods, teasing one minute, scolding the next, seemed to have vanished and they conversed like old friends, like cousins, she supposed. It wasn't what she wanted exactly, because she was as much in love with him as ever, but it would have to do. 'You have done me a lot of good,' she murmured.

He looked sharply at her, one eyebrow raised. She laughed. 'You have made me grow up, Adam.'

'You would have done that without my help.'

'Perhaps, but not so quickly and not with so much pleasure.'

'Oh, Sophie,' he said. 'Don't ever change, will you?'

She had no answer to that and they went into the farmhouse to tell Mr and Mrs Brown they were leaving the next morning.

Goodbyes said and with Mr Brown clutching more sovereigns than he had ever seen together before, they climbed in the carriage and were on their way. The floods had receded and though they had left mud on the roads and there was still water in the potholes, the weather was fine and they made good time. Alfred Farley had made sure there were fresh horses waiting for them at each stop and they reached Downham Market in the early afternoon, where they stopped for a meal while the last set of horses were harnessed.

'We should be in Hadlea before dark,' Adam told Sophie as they resumed their journey. Farley was once again riding behind them on Swift. Bessie, still sniffling a little, was sitting on the opposite seat with her feet up, wrapped in a blanket. Mrs Brown had given her another dose of her remedy to make her more comfortable for the journey and she was dozing. 'I will take you home first and then go on to Broadacres. No doubt you will be glad to be reunited with your parents.'

'Yes,' she said, but she had mixed feelings about the end of the journey. Of course she wanted to be home and see Mama and Papa again, but it would also mean saying goodbye to Adam. In the past few days they had been thrown together in more intimacy than would have been allowed under normal circumstances. She had become used to having him close, seeing him every day and all day, getting to know every nuance of his character, laughing with him, arguing with him, eating with him, doing everything but sleep together. It had served to reinforce her abiding love for him and she wished it could go on forever. She longed for him to become more intimate, but he seemed content with the way things were.

Aunt Emmeline had said she needed to make a push, but how to do it, she did not know. If she tried to flirt, he flirted back, but somehow left her feeling belittled. If she quizzed him, he answered politely or avoided answering by changing the subject. Once or twice she had caught him looking at her with an expression she could not fathom, as if she were a problem. And before the day was out, they would part.

'How long do you think you will stay at Broadacres?' she asked, clutching at straws.

'A few days.'

'And then it will be back to Saddleworth?'

'Yes.'

'No doubt you, too, will be glad to be home.'

'Yes. I have been too long away.'

'Is there someone waiting there for you?'

He looked at her sharply, wondering what had prompted the question. 'A great many people,' he said. 'Staff, workers…'

'No, I meant a lady.'

'Oh, I see, still fishing on behalf of your friend.'

'No, I am not. I am persuaded that is a lost

cause. I just wondered who the mare was meant for. You said she was for a lady.'

He laughed. 'She is. Mark asked me to buy her for Jane. It is to be a surprise birthday gift from him.'

'Jane?' she queried in surprise.

'Yes, your sister. You know her best. Do you think she will like her present?'

It was Jane's birthday on the fifteenth of July and she had all but forgotten it. 'She will love the mare,' she said. 'It is just like Mark to think of something like that. He is always surprising her with gifts. Jane might even let me ride her now and again and then I will think of you.'

'Will you?' he murmured.

'Of course. How could I forget you after... after what we have been through together?'

'It has been rather unforgettable,' he said with a smile.

'Tell me about Saddleworth,' she said. 'Then I can picture you there when you are gone.'

'Saddleworth is situated in a long valley between Yorkshire and Lancashire, and is made up of four small hamlets: Quick Mere, Lord's Mere, Shaw Mere and Friar Mere. It is famous for its woollen cloth, much of it superfine.'

'Ah, that is why you wear such well-made coats—the wool is woven in your mill.'

'Yes, and grown on my land. Friar Mere was once an estate belonging to the Black Friars, but it is part of my estate now. We grow a few crops but it is mostly sheep.'

'And the house?'

'Blackfriars sits on the hill above the valley. It was once the home of the friars. Anne started to refurbish it, but the alterations were not finished before she died, so it is half very old and draughty and half an elegant modern home.'

'You didn't go on with the work?'

'No. I saw no reason to. Besides, I was kept very busy with the estate and the mill.' He paused. 'If I can persuade Mark and Jane to come on a visit, they could bring you, too, and you would see it for yourself.'

'I should like that,' she murmured.

The countryside they were passing through was flatter than it had been, the land was criss-crossed with dykes and there were water mills everywhere. They were not cantering now because Adam had not planned to change the horses again and it was a longer-than-usual stage. They were moving at a leisurely trot, a pace that suited Sophie if only because it gave her a little longer to sit close to Adam, to feel his thigh close to hers, his arm touching hers, his warmth spreading all down that side of her, knowing it would be the last time.

And there was Hadlea, the village where she had been born and brought up, with its main street lined with cottages. There was the Fox and

Hounds, standing on its corner, there the church, and there, after a few minutes more, the gates of Greystone Manor. 'Home,' Adam said as the carriage drew to a stop outside the front door.

Joe hardly had time to jump down, open the carriage door and let down the step before Lady Cavenhurst came out to meet them. Sophie tumbled out and into her arms.

As Adam completed the last three miles of the long journey in the coach, he was conscious of an emptiness inside him, a feeling that something were missing, something he had lost that was valuable and had to be searched for. It was almost like an ache, but he was reluctant to put a name to it.

Sir Edward and Lady Cavenhurst had welcomed him, offered him supper and thanked him over and over again for bringing their daughter safely back to them. Hearing from Mark about Teddy's disappearance and that he had been the one to find out what had happened to him, he was thoroughly quizzed. 'It is to be hoped the voyage will do him good,' Sir Edward had said at the end of the tale. 'The tougher the better.'

Adam had silently agreed and said he ought not to keep the tired horses waiting about and Mark and Jane would be looking out for him, so he would take his leave. Swift was left in the Manor stables until Jane's birthday in two days' time; the mare was to be a surprise and she needed a long rest and some careful grooming after her long journey, which Sophie undertook to do. Now here he was with Alfred Farley once more beside him, feeling flat and empty and wishing he could go back to Sophie.

She had wormed her way into his head and his heart and, try as he might, he could not banish her. He had made a solemn vow never to let another woman into his life and he had certainly meant it, so what was he doing lusting after a female ten years his junior? Lust? He could satisfy that anywhere. This was nothing so vulgar as lust.

The carriage turned into the long drive to Broadacres and he was met with the sight of a stately home to rival any he had seen. It was not overlarge, but its proportions were exactly right and its windows were ablaze with light to welcome him. Farley jumped down and lifted the heavy knocker on the front door.

Sophie rejoiced to be home. She chatted away to her parents about all she had heard and seen and done in the capital, being very careful not to shock them with her escapades. She explored the house and the grounds, exclaiming with delight as if she had been away years. She looked after Swift as carefully as if the mare had been a child, but nothing could assuage the ache in her heart. Her mother noticed it.

'Sophie, dearest,' she said, the next afternoon when they were alone in the drawing room. Lady Cavenhurst had been doing some embroidery but set it aside. 'Is anything wrong?'

Sophie, who had been looking out of the window at the front drive wishing he would come, turned towards her mother to answer. 'No, Mama, what could be wrong?'

'I do not know, but I sense something is. Did you meet someone in London, a young gentleman perhaps, that you are not telling us about?'

'No, Mama. The only men I met were Sir Reginald, Mr Fanshawe and fat Lord Gorange, none of whom I was pleased to see. They hung round and spoiled everything.'

'Oh. What about Viscount Kimberley?'

'What about him?'

'Have you developed a *tendre* for him? From what I gather you were in his company frequently in London, and then to have spent nearly a week together…'

'Viscount Kimberley is a widower, Mama, and he has vowed never to marry again. He loved his wife so much, you see…'

'That does not answer my question.'

'Yes, it does.'

The sound of wheels on gravel alerted them to visitors and Sophie's heart leaped. A minute

later he was there with Mark and Jane and little
Harry and everyone was greeting everyone. Jane
hugged her, Mark kissed her cheek and Adam
bowed stiffly, called her Miss Cavenhurst and
asked her how she did.

'I am well, thank you, my lord,' she answered,
matching his formality with her own by bending
her knee and bowing her head. 'How are you?'

'I am well,' he said.

Lady Cavenhurst ordered tea and cakes, sent
a servant to find Sir Edward and bade them all
be seated. They distributed themselves on sofas
and chairs. Sophie took Harry onto her lap and
cuddled him.

'We have been showing Adam round the estate,' Jane said. 'He was interested in the Hadlea
Home, so we have been to Witherington, too.
The extensions are coming on well and we will
be able to admit more children very soon. We
decided to call here before we went home. Adam
was anxious to find out if Sophie had any ill
effects from her journey and, of course, I was
longing to hear all her news.'

Sophie glanced at Adam, who was seated
some distance from her. Whether he had done
it on purpose or that was the only chair left, she
did not know. 'What did you think of Jane's project?' she asked him.

'It is impressive. The children seem so happy
and sturdy. They are not shy, either. I found talk-

ing to them a real pleasure.' Seeing her nuzzling her face into her nephew's soft curls made him almost emotional enough for tears. If Anne had lived...

'Has it given you any ideas for your own schoolroom?'

He pulled himself out of his reverie to answer her. 'Indeed, it has.'

'Sophie, tell us all about London,' Jane put in. 'Did you meet anyone exciting?'

Sophie did not know how to answer that with Adam in the room, not without giving herself away. 'I met a great many people, but not the husband I went looking for.'

'Miss Cavenhurst had her admirers,' Adam said with a wry smile. 'But none that suited her.'

'Oh?'

'It was only Sir Reginald, Mr Fanshawe and Lord Gorange,' Sophie added. 'They would not leave me alone. I swear they came to London because I was there.'

'You mean they have not given up? None of them?'

'No, and try as I might, I could not convince them. Thank goodness they have been left behind in London.'

The refreshments were brought in as Sir Edward arrived and seated himself in a wing chair and surveyed his family. 'How pleasant it is to have you all here together,' he said.

'All except Teddy,' Sophie said.

'We will not speak of him,' he said.

'Oh, Papa!' she exclaimed. 'You know he cannot help himself.'

'I said we will not speak of him, Sophie.'

She subsided into silence, her face red with mortification.

'Adam is going to stay with us for a few days,' Jane said quickly. 'Why don't you all come over to Broadacres for supper tomorrow night? I will ask Cook to make something special. It is my birthday.'

'We had not forgotten,' Mark said, laughing. 'You have made sure of that.'

They stayed another half hour, chatting about London, Aunt Emmeline, the picnic in Richmond, the opera and the Malthouses, in which Adam took only a minimal part. When the visitors took their leave, he was as formal as he had been at the beginning and barely managed a smile. Sophie was miserable. He seemed to have gone back to the reserved, proud man he had been at the beginning of their acquaintance. Had he forgotten how they had been at the farmhouse, how easy with each other? Had it meant nothing at all to him?

She remembered with a wry smile how she had once insisted she would not marry a widower because she would not be a replacement wife. Now if she were given the opportunity, would she jump at it? Even if she knew he still loved and mourned the wife he had lost? 'Damn you, Anne Kimberley,' she muttered.

'What did you say, Sophie?' her mother asked.

'Nothing. I think I'll go for a ride.'

She took Patch, her own grey mare, not Swift. She did not think she would ever ride her again; the memories were too painful. Her ride took her over the common towards Witherington and the fen. She had played here with Teddy as a child, fighting imaginary battles with wooden swords and using a tumbledown hut as a fort. Poor Teddy; Papa was being very hard on him. And she had still found no way to repay Adam. For her pride's sake, she must do it.

She dismounted where the track petered off at the edge of the mere and stood looking down at the dark water with its long grassy weeds, swaying just below the surface. She heard the sound of horse's hooves behind her and turned to see Lord Gorange riding towards her and her heart sank. With deep water behind her there was no escape and she stood, watching him cantering closer while her fury mounted.

He stopped beside her and dismounted. 'Miss Cavenhurst, your obedient servant.'

'What are you doing here?' She was so angry she could not even be polite and greet him properly.

'Looking for you.'

'Why?'

'Silly question, Sophie…'

'I have not given you permission to use my given name.'

'Oh, come on, Sophie, let's not be coy. I remember a time when you were more than glad to see me. And you did say you would reconsider my offer.'

'I have reconsidered it, and the answer is still no.'

'You will change your mind.'

'Never.'

'Then I will, of course, have to tell your parents what happened in the coach when we were alone together.'

'Nothing happened.'

'No? Have you forgotten the intimacy we shared, an intimacy that could have only one outcome?'

'You are mad. Nothing like that happened. Find someone else to torment.' She tried to remount, but he pulled her back and into his arms. She struggled. 'Get away! Leave me alone! I shall scream.'

He looked about them at the deserted landscape. 'Who is there to hear you?'

'Let me go!'

'Just a little kiss to be going on with,' he murmured, twisting her round in his arms and trying to kiss her. She moved her head away and his wet lips connected with her ear. 'Now, that is not very kind,' he said. 'I will let you go if you give me just a little kiss.'

'And if I don't?' Anything to keep him talking and give her time to think of a way to escape.

'I shall take it anyway. Then we shall ride back to Hadlea together and you will tell your papa that I would like to speak to him.'

'What do you mean to say to him?'

'My dear, that depends entirely on you. Say yes, and it will be a discussion on a marriage settlement, including your brother's debts, or say no and it will not be just your parents who hear of your indiscretion, it will be the whole world.'

The prospect of everyone, including Adam, hearing his lies and believing them sent a shiver right through her. 'Why are you doing this to me? I cannot think you really want an unwilling wife.'

'You will not be unwilling, my dear, not in the end. And I do want a mother for my girls. They are growing up quite unmanageable. You are not so much older than they are, I am sure you will deal well together.'

'I feel sorry for them, but that does not mean I will ever agree to marry you. And that goes for Sir Reginald and Mr Fanshawe, too.'

'You do not have to worry about them,' he said with a laugh. 'They have given up the competition and gone for easier conquests. When I left the metropolis, Dickie was paying court to Miss Malthouse and Reggie had his sights set on Miss Martindale.'

'Lucy is promised to my brother,' she said, slightly diverted by this news.

'Ah, but where is he? Too far away to be of any use, I fancy. And under the circumstances I cannot see Lord Martindale entertaining his suit, can you?' He smiled. 'That leaves only me to take the prize.'

'I am not a prize.'

'Oh, but you are, my dear. Now give me that kiss and we will be friends.'

He was short and fat, and would not find it easy to mount without a block or boulder to help him, whereas she was fit and agile. She looked at his face; he was eagerly awaiting her to comply. She leaned towards him as if to let him kiss her and then lifted her knee into his groin as hard as she could. He doubled up in pain and she ran and was on Patch's back and galloping for all she was worth back to Hadlea.

Adam, strolling in the village, saw her galloping out of the Witherington turn as if the hounds of hell were after her. She could certainly ride, that one, but she had no hat and her hair down over her shoulders. Was this what she had meant when she boasted of galloping all over the village? He was about to call to her but changed his mind when he saw another rider coming down the same road and recognised Lord Gorange. The man did not go after her, but turned into the yard of the Fox and Hounds and dismounted.

What was going on? Had she lied to him about her involvement with Gorange, or was he still pestering her in an effort to win that wager? It was, as Sophie had pointed out to him, no business of his; he would be gone in a day or two and could forget her. Once he was back in familiar surroundings with evidence of Anne all about him—her books, her half-finished embroidery, her music on the pianoforte, the little china ornaments she liked to collect in the display cabinet, her clothes still in the closet because he could not bear to give them away—then he would go back to being the man he had been before he went to London. That was simply an interlude, he told himself severely, a short pause in the even tenor of his life.

He would stay for the birthday supper party because he had promised Mark and Jane he would, but the day after that he would go home. He turned into the Fox and Hounds to enquire about a stage coach going north. Gorange was in the parlour, sitting by himself with a glass of cognac. Curious, Adam went over to him. 'Afternoon, Gorange. What brings you here?'

The man left off contemplating the liquid in

his glass and looked up. 'Oh, it's you Kimberley. I might ask you the same question.'

Adam called for a glass of ale and sat down. 'I am here to enquire about coach schedules.'

'Back to the Smoke?'

'No, back to Yorkshire.'

'Given up, have you?'

'Given up?'

'On little Miss Cavenhurst. Just as well, we are to be married, you know.'

Adam stifled his gasp and kept his voice level. 'She has agreed?'

'As good as. It wants only Sir Edward's permission and I do not think he will withhold it, considering the circumstances.'

'What circumstances?'

'Why, the matter of a little overamorous encounter in a carriage. You know how it is…'

'No, I do not.'

'No? Do not tell me you spent—how many days was it?—on the road and you did not try to seduce her? You must be losing your touch, Kimberley. But I am glad of it. I should not like to find myself with damaged goods.'

Adam stood up so violently his chair fell back with a crash. The sound served to remind him where he was. He dropped his raised fist and composed himself with an effort. 'If you were not such an old lecher who is not worth fighting, I should call you out for that,' he said through gritted teeth. 'But if I ever come across you again, I shall certainly make sure you regret your words for the rest of your miserable life.'

He heard Gorange laughing behind him as he hurried from the building, forgetting the reason for entering it in the first place. After all her protestations that she would not marry any of her suitors, had Sophie succumbed? He felt like finding her and shaking her and shouting at her not to do it.

By the time he reached Broadacres, his pace had slowed and his anger had cooled. His head told him it had nothing to do with him what Sophie Cavenhurst did, so why did the rest of him—his gut, his heart, his muscle—refuse to believe it? One thing he could do was to tell Mark about Gorange and his brother-in-law's ridiculous wagers. If anything needed doing, Mark would be the one to do it.

It was her pride that made Sophie wear the blue gown to go to Broadacres. She spent a long time dressing, determined to shine. To that end she had Bessie arrange her curls in an elaborate *coiffure*. Her necklace, the one that had given her all that trouble, was fastened about her neck.

'You are not going to a ball,' Bessie said.

'I know, but it is Jane's birthday and that is special. Jane made the gown and gave me the necklace and she did not see me wearing them in London, so this seems a good opportunity to show her how well I look.'

'Oh, I see.'

Sophie knew the maid did not see at all. It was Adam's last day, he was going home tomorrow and he had not seen her in the gown either because someone had been giving him a beating at the time. She would show him what he had missed and perhaps he might be sorry. She slipped on her shoes, picked up her shawl and reticule and went down to join her parents. If her mother noticed her finery, she did not comment and led the way out to the waiting carriage.

Mark had sent his groom over to Greystone Manor that morning to fetch Swift and the animal had thrilled Jane. When they arrived Sophie handed over her own present, a new riding crop bought from the local harness maker, and received a hug in return. There were other presents to receive and exclaim over and then supper was served and they all trooped into the dining room.

The meal was a happy affair and there was no shortage of things to talk about: the latest *on dit*, the new fashions, the running of the orphanage, young Harry's latest accomplishment and Adam's speech in the Lords that had been reported in full in the *Thunderer* and resulted in a spate of letters to the editor, a few supporting him, but most condemning him. The workers he was defending were not ones to write to newspapers. No one seemed to notice that Sophie, in her gleaming gown and sparkling jewels, had little to say.

Her head was full of Lord Gorange's threat. A few words noised abroad that she was not the innocent she appeared to be and he could spoil all this and once again plunge everyone at Greystone Manor and Broadacres into scandal. How she could prevent it without marrying him she did not know.

It was when the ladies retired to the drawing room, leaving the men to their cigars and port, that her mother remarked on her unusual quietness. 'Sophie, you have hardly said a word all evening,' she said. 'You are not going to catch Bessie's cold, are you? It would not surprise me if you did.'

It was a heaven-sent opportunity to pass off her ill humour, but suddenly it seemed important to tell the truth. 'No, Mama, not a cold…'

'Oh, I see. It is Viscount Kimberley.'

'Adam?' Jane echoed.

'No, it is not.' Sophie rounded on her. 'I shall have to marry that horrid Lord Gorange and—'

'Good heavens, why?'

It tumbled out then, the whole sorry story, and at the end of it she was sobbing and spoiling her face. Her mother took her in her arms. 'Oh,

Sophie, why did you not say something sooner? There is no question of you marrying Lord Gorange if you do not want to. Let him do his worst.'

'But what will Papa say?'

'I have no doubt he will say he was right not to trust Teddy to look after you.'

'But it wasn't Teddy's fault.'

'If he were here now, I think I could cheerfully thrash him,' Jane said.

'But Teddy was against my accepting any of those three...'

'Of course he was,' Jane said. 'Mama, Adam has told us that Teddy made a wager with them that Sophie would not marry any one of them by the end of July. They were each intent on winning it.'

Sophie stared at her. 'Is that true?'

'Yes. Adam would not make it up, would he?'

'Why didn't he tell me?'

'He thought you might be hurt by it and asked us if we thought you should know. I felt you should be told because it would help you to understand.'

'That explains why Lord Gorange said something about the other two stealing a march on him, and yesterday he said they have given up and left the field to him.'

'Yesterday?' her mother queried. 'Is his lordship in Hadlea?'

'Yes, he accosted me while I was out riding, and very offensive he was.' She paused. 'Mama, I do not want to bring scandal down on everyone. I have been foolish and naive and I beg you to forgive me.'

'Oh, Sophie,' her mother said, 'there is nothing to forgive. But we will not tell your father. He is already very angry with Teddy. I do not wish to add to it.'

'Then I must marry Lord Gorange.'

'No, you will not,' her mother said. 'Leave it to me to tell your papa as much as he needs to know. He will give his lordship his rightabout on your behalf.'

'Best thing you could do,' the dowager Lady Wyndham put in suddenly, 'is marry someone else. That would put a stop to his lordship's antics.'

They had all forgotten she was there and turned to her in surprise. She chuckled. 'I know a young man not so very far away who has been mourning his dead wife long enough. He ought to marry again and set up his nursery or the line will die out. And so I have told him.'

Sophie looked at the old lady with her mouth open for several seconds, then burst into tears.

The men chose that moment to rejoin them. 'What is the matter with Sophie?' Sir Edward demanded.

'I think we should take Sophie home,' his wife told him. 'If everyone will excuse us.'

'Of course,' Mark said. 'Is she ill?'

'I think she has perhaps caught a cold from Bessie,' Lady Cavenhurst said, putting her arm round Sophie and helping her to her feet. 'She will no doubt be better after one of Cook's remedies and a good night's sleep.'

Shawls and wraps were fetched, Sir Edward, somewhat bemused, apologised to everyone for their rapid departure and Sophie was led away.

It was left to Jane to explain what had happened to Mark and Adam. 'I know exactly how poor Sophie is feeling,' she said. 'She feels as if she has no choice but to comply with Lord Gorange for the sake of the family.'

'But that is monstrous,' Adam burst out. 'Surely, to God, no one expects her to marry him?'

'What do you suggest, then?' the dowager said, smiling at him.

'She must defy him, Aunt Helen. Such a union is unthinkable.'

'Then, why don't you marry her yourself?'

There was a stunned silence. Adam stared at her. 'Aunt, I don't think—'

'Then I suggest you *do* think,' she said, cutting him short. 'You are a healthy young man with a whole life before you. Are you going to spend it becoming a crotchety old recluse with no friends and no children or grandchildren to comfort your old age? Sophie Cavenhurst will do you very well. She can be a little wild perhaps, but I see no harm in her and you could soon tame her.'

'I wouldn't dream of taming her.'

'No?' The old lady smiled. 'Then, take her as she is.'

'She would not have me.'

'Have you asked her?'

'No, of course I have not.'

'Then, I suggest you do.'

'Mama,' Mark put in because his cousin seemed lost for words, 'you are embarrassing Adam.'

'He needs a little embarrassment. And we are all family, are we not?'

'Excuse me,' Adam said, and hurriedly left the room.

He went into the garden. It was a warm, clear night with a full moon and a sky full of stars. A slight breeze ruffled the trees. A cat, its stomach almost on the ground, stalked its prey in the long grass. An owl hooted somewhere in the direction of a distant barn. In contrast with the peaceful atmosphere, his insides were churning. His aunt had gone far beyond acceptable manners in speaking as she had and made him angry. He did not need her to tell him what to do.

On the other hand, she was probably right and he would have to marry again some day. But not yet. Not now. Later, perhaps. Much later, when he was middle-aged and he could find someone steady and unremarkable with whom he could have children and who would not bother him. Safe, not wild, tactful, not outspoken. A little plain even, not so beautiful he caught his breath whenever he beheld her.

An image of Sophie in that lovely gown, her blue eyes bleak and tear filled, swam before him. Even like that she was far from plain. Her evident suffering touched his heart. But that didn't mean he had to marry her. You couldn't build a marriage on pity. Was it pity he felt or exasperation? Or was it something else altogether? He began walking up and down the garden, then set off down the drive to walk along the village lanes. Tomorrow he would go home and get on with his work. Honest toil would take care of his turmoil. Tomorrow he could forget her.

Chapter Twelve

Sophie was half expecting Lord Gorange when he arrived in the middle of the following morning. Peering over the banister at the top of his head, she heard him ask Travers if Sir Edward would see him. The servant disappeared while Gorange checked his cravat in the mirror, a satisfied smile on his face. Travers came back and conducted him into the library and shut the door. Sophie went back to her room and waited. A little later she was sent for.

'Lord Gorange has asked to speak to you,' her father told her, after she had frostily replied to his lordship's greeting. 'Do you wish to hear him?'

'No, Papa, I do not. I wish him to go away.'

Her father turned to the peer. 'Then, I am afraid, my lord, you have my daughter's answer.'

His lordship stared from one to the other. 'Miss Cavenhurst's reputation will be sullied by this refusal not to allow me even the courtesy of a hearing,' he said pompously.

'I think not. If any word of scandal reaches me, I shall be obliged to make known the vile wager you made and the tactics you have used to win it. I think it might very well be your reputation that suffers. Good day to you, my lord. I wish you a speedy journey home.'

There was nothing the man could do but take his leave. Sophie ran to hug her father. 'Oh, Papa, thank you. But how did you know about that wager? Mama said…'

'I know she did, but she didn't know that Mark and Adam had already told me about it. You did a very foolish thing, you know, going into the city alone and trying to sell your necklace. It is extremely valuable and it is no wonder Rundell wondered if you had stolen it.' He smiled. 'Now, we will have no more tears. You are home again and it is all forgotten.'

'But, Papa, Viscount Kimberley paid Teddy's debts and now I will not be able to repay him.'

'But why should you? You are not responsible for your brother's profligacy. I offered to pay him and so did Mark, but he would not hear of it. He begged us not to mention it again. He said the pleasure of seeing you smile was recompense enough.'

'Oh.'

'Run along now. I have work to do.'

She gave him another hug and left him. Lord Gorange had been ousted and for that she was grateful, and she supposed the ache in her heart would fade in time. She would content herself with helping Jane with her good works and loving her nephew.

Adam would have left by now and be on his way back to Saddleworth; it would be safe to visit Jane. She set off on foot and was passing the Fox and Hounds when she saw the stage draw into the yard, later than scheduled. Several passengers left it, others boarded it. She saw Adam standing in the yard watching his trunk being loaded and dodged down Church Lane so that he would not see her. She could not bear the pain of saying goodbye.

Mrs Caulder, the rector's wife, was in her garden. 'Sophie, you are back. How was London?'

'Very interesting, Mrs Caulder.'

'Tell me what you did. Did you meet anyone exciting?'

Sophie gave her a watered-down version of her adventures, and by the time she returned to the main road, the stage had gone and the inn yard was empty. She went on her way with a heavy heart. He had gone.

She passed through the village out onto the road to Broadacres. Her way led her past a row of cottages and the blacksmiths and then she was in the open. Immersed in her dismal thoughts, she was not paying attention to others on the road and only moved aside when she heard the horse coming up behind her. She gasped when she saw it was Lord Gorange.

He passed her and pulled his mount across the road in front of her, blocking her way. 'You thought I'd be fobbed off by that little charade, did you?' he said, smiling. 'There's more than one way to skin a cat.'

'I cannot think you are so in want of a thousand pounds that you must continue to bother me,' she said haughtily. 'Especially since Teddy is far away and you will not have to pay him.'

He laughed. 'It is not Teddy's little wager I am concerned about, but a much larger one.'

She was curious in spite of herself. 'Who with?'

'Why, Captain Moore, who else?'

'That mountebank. I cannot see what it has to do with him.'

'A wager is a wager and, win or lose, it has to be paid, and I do not choose to lose.'

'That is no concern of mine. Lord Gorange, you have had your answer, so please move aside and let me pass.'

He did not oblige, so she turned and started to walk back the way she had come. He rode round her and blocked her path again, bringing his mount so close to her she was afraid the stallion might kick out and injure her. She reached up and grabbed the reins with one hand and his foot in the stirrup with the other, yanking it upwards as hard as she could. He yelled as his foot left the stirrup and he was deposited on the ground. Astonished at how easy it had been, she stared down at him, then with a satisfied smile, flung herself up on the horse and galloped back towards the village. It was only when she was within sight of the cottages on the outskirts of the village she realised what an inelegant picture she must make and pulled up and dismounted. She led the horse back to the livery stables beside the Fox and Hounds from where it had no doubt been hired.

'I found this animal wandering down the road,' she told the ostler. 'He must have thrown his rider.'

'I will have someone look for him, Miss Cavenhurst.'

She handed the reins to him and left, passing the front of the inn.

'I fear that will not be the end of his lordship,' a voice said against her ear. 'It will have to be something more permanent than that.'

She spun round. 'Adam!'

'As you see.'

'But you left. I saw you…'

'And I saw you. You were coming this way, I am sure of it, but you suddenly went off down that lane.' He nodded in its direction. 'I could only surmise you did not want to see me. I had my trunk taken off the coach and waited, knowing the road only led to the church and the vicarage.'

'But why?'

'Curiosity, my dear. I saw you come back and walk past here without turning your head, so I followed.' He smiled. 'In my effort to remain hidden I was farther behind than I would have liked to be when I saw Gorange stop beside you. My God, you took a risk, Sophie. You could have been kicked to death.'

'But I was not.'

'No, thank goodness. It all happened so quickly and I was not near enough to intervene. I started to run towards you, but you galloped past me with your head almost on the stallion's neck and either did not hear me or chose to ignore me.'

'I thought it was Lord Gorange shouting.'

'He was in no position to shout.'

'Oh, Lord, I haven't killed him, have I?'

'I think he'll live, though he might be a little sore for a day or two.'

'Thank God.'

'Never do anything like that again, Sophie. My heart won't stand it.'

'Your heart? Do you have one?'

'Most assuredly I do.' He took her hand and

laid it upon his heart. She could feel its steady rhythm. 'Convinced?'

'Yes, but…' She looked up into his face. He was smiling and it was doing funny things to her inside. 'What were you doing following me in the first place when you should have been on that stage?'

'I changed my mind.'

'Why?'

He took her arm and led her into the cool interior of the inn. The next stage was not due for some time and it was too early in the day for locals to congregate, most of whom were working in the fields; the parlour was empty. He sat her down on a settee in a corner and seated himself beside her. 'I realised I could not leave you, Sophie. I can never leave you.' He smiled again. 'And someone has to keep you out of mischief.'

'What do you mean?'

He took her hand and rubbed the back of it absent-mindedly with his thumb. 'I mean that I want to take care of you. Always.'

She was trying to maintain some semblance of composure, but it was very hard and she was unsure exactly what he meant. 'And you decided all that between going to board the coach and seeing me?'

'No, I think it had been coming on me for some time, but I was trying to ignore it. When it came to stepping up into that coach, I found I

could not do it. My feet just would not obey me.'
He lifted her hand and put the palm to his lips.
It sent a shiver right through her, from her hand
to her arm, into her body and right down to the
very core of her.

'But what about your vow never to marry
again? I suppose it is marriage you are propos-
ing and not some other arrangement?'

'Sophie!' he exclaimed, shocked. 'You surely
did not think…? Oh, the devil take me and my
clumsiness. Of course I meant marriage.'

'And Anne?'

'I loved Anne and revere her memory, I will
not pretend otherwise, but in the past few weeks,
I have realised that if I am not careful I shall
become a bad-tempered old man whom no one
loves. And what is an even worse prospect, I
should lose you. So, my darling, I will break
my promise not to marry again if you will break
yours not to be a second wife. Sophie, will you
have me?'

Unable to take it in, she did not immediately
reply, but sat looking at their joined hands. Joy
was spreading through her; from the top of her
head to her toes, she was glowing.

'Say yes, Sophie. Please do not say I have
prevaricated too long and you prefer not to link
your life with a man who takes so long to make
up his mind.'

'It is less than two months since we met,

Adam. In terms of courtship that is a very short time, don't you think?'

'Are you saying yes?'

'I am saying yes, please.'

'Oh, my love. We will be happy together, I promise you.' He took her in his arms and kissed her soundly. The noise of people working in the inn, the sound of horses and carts on the road, the voice of the chef singing in the kitchen, faded and there was only the two of them in all the world locked in each other's arms.

'Adam,' she said, pulling herself out of his embrace at last, 'what do you think everyone will say?'

'Does it matter?'

'Not to me.'

'Me, neither.'

'When will you speak to Papa?'

'No time like the present. Is he at home?'

They looked up as someone came into the parlour. It was Lord Gorange, and he was hobbling and cradling one elbow in his other hand. His coat was covered in mud, his breeches were torn and he had lost the heel of one riding boot. They both burst out laughing.

'You may congratulate me, Gorange,' Adam called out to him. 'We are to be married.'

'Huh.' He turned on his heel and went out again, slamming the door behind him.

'Come on,' Adam said, standing up and holding a hand out to her. 'I want the next bit over with, then we can tell everyone our good news.'

They walked to Greystone Manor, not touching because there were people about, but they could not help looking at each other and smiling broadly. Anyone with eyes to see could guess what was afoot.

They found both her parents in the drawing room. Sophie, holding tight to Adam's hand, led him forward. 'Mama, Papa,' she said, eyes shining, 'Adam has asked me to marry him and I have said yes.'

Her mother gasped, then smiled. 'Oh, Sophie…'

'Sophie,' her father said, pretending severity. 'You are doing this all the wrong way about. It is for Viscount Kimberley to come to me first and obtain my permission to speak to you.'

'Oh, Papa. I know that. But you would not have withheld it, I know you would not.'

'This is very sudden,' her mother said. 'I understood Lord Kimberley was leaving us today.'

'He changed his mind.'

'Sir Edward,' Adam put in, 'I realise this is a little unconventional, but perhaps you would grant me an interview now?'

'Of course. Let us go into the library and leave the ladies to talk of weddings.'

The two men left the room and Sophie turned

to her mother. 'Oh, Mama, I am so very, very happy.'

'Then, I am pleased for you. But how did it come about?'

'I was going to see Jane and he was about to board the stage when he saw me and realised he did not want to leave me, so he came after me and missed the stage. He took me into the parlour at the Fox and Hounds and proposed.'

'The inn? Oh, Sophie, how improper.'

'Mama, I did not care where it was, so long as it happened.'

'I think he will make you a very good husband, Sophie, and I could not be more pleased for you, except...'

'Except what, Mama?'

'His home is such a long way off.'

'I know, but we shall visit often. Adam has promised me that. Of course he still has to go home tomorrow and leave me behind, but he will be back for the wedding and then he will take me back with him to Blackfriars.'

'And do you think you will mind that he has been married before?'

'He asked me that, but I said I would not attempt to make him forget Anne, but I would try to make him look forward to a new life with me. He seemed very pleased by that.'

He mother laughed. 'Sophie, sometimes I think you have never grown out of being a schoolgirl, but there are other times when I think you are wiser than your years. What has made you like that, I wonder?'

'I do not know, Mama. All the people around me, I suppose. You and Papa, Jane, Issie and Teddy. I am sad about Teddy.'

'So am I, child, but your papa is right. He has brought his troubles on himself.' She looked up as her husband and future son-in-law returned. Both were smiling.

'Is it all right?' Sophie asked Adam. 'Papa could find nothing against it?'

'Nothing at all,' Sir Edward put in. 'Now I am going to find the butler and order champagne so that we can raise a toast.'

'Then we must go and tell Jane and Mark the news,' Sophie said. 'They will not know that Adam did not go on the stage and they will have their boarder for another night.'

The next twenty-four hours passed in a blur for Sophie. Everyone was pleased for her. They hugged her and cried with her and wished her all the happiness in the world. They shook Adam by the hand and called him a lucky dog. The dowager Lady Wyndham smiled complacently, sure that it was her homily that had brought it about.

Practical arrangements were discussed, too. Adam would go home and see to his business and prepare his household staff for the arrival of a new mistress. Then he would return for the wedding in September, which would be conducted by the Reverend Caulder at Hadlea church. It would give Sophie time to send out invitations, for Jane to make her wedding gown and her mother to organise the breakfast feast.

The time to say goodbye came all too soon. Adam came to the manor and took his leave of Sir Edward and Lady Cavenhurst, then Sophie walked with him to the Fox and Hounds, her hand linked into his arm. 'You won't change your mind again?' she queried when they were almost there.

He looked down at her and smiled. 'No, my love, I will not change my mind.'

'Nor will I,' she said. 'The next six weeks is going to drag. I wish I could be coming with you now.'

'Next time, and then we will never be parted again.'

The coach was already in the yard and being loaded. He stopped and turned towards her. 'Be good, Sophie. No madcap escapades, because I will not be here to rescue you.' He looked around him, then drew her behind a tree to kiss her. She clung to him until the sound of the coachman calling, 'All aboard, who's coming aboard!' made them pull apart and make their way into the inn yard.

Alfred Farley had seen to his luggage and was already in his seat when Adam joined him. Sophie watched as the step was folded up and the door closed. Adam was looking at her through the window as they drew away. She waved and blew him a kiss. And then he was gone.

'My lord, there is a gentleman to see you,' the footman said. 'He says his name is Mr Anthony Byers. He would not state his business, but said it is important.'

'You had better send him in, then.'

Adam set aside the ledger he had been studying. Since he had arrived home three weeks before, the affairs of the mill and the estate had filled almost every waking hour. He had done little towards the wedding, although he had instructed the housekeeper to take Anne's clothes from the closet and store them in trunks in the old wing before making the room ready for a new mistress. Looking back, his time in London and especially that journey to Hadlea seemed like a dream, but Sophie's letters kept it alive for him. At the end of a busy day, he would sit down to read the day's missive and compose a reply. He wished the time would pass more quickly, so that any doubts about the wisdom of what he was undertaking could be set at rest.

Would Sophie be happy here, so far from home and in a very different environment from the one she was used to? Would she understand that he had to work and she would inevitably be left to amuse herself during the day? How would he feel taking another woman into the bed he had shared with Anne? How would she feel? She had been so adamant that she would not be a second wife—was she having doubts, too?

He looked up as the footman announced his visitor. Even though he had not seen him for over month, he recognised him immediately as the man who had been following him in London and who had saluted him in the middle of the road. He was immediately on his guard.

'Ask Mr Farley to join us,' he instructed the footman.

'My lord, I am glad to see you safely returned home,' the man said.

'Never mind that. Say what you have to say, but before you do that, you might tell me why you followed me from the capital. It was you, was it not?'

'It was. May I be seated?' At a nod from Adam he took the chair opposite the desk. 'I was asked to ascertain your integrity and how far you would be prepared to go for your philosophy, my lord.'

Alfred entered the room and Adam beckoned him to take a seat. 'We have a Mr Byers here, Mr Farley. I think we are about to learn the answer to something that has been puzzling us.'

He turned back to his visitor and repeated, 'My philosophy in respect of what? Why? On whose orders?'

'The Manchester Patriotic Union, and more specifically Mr Henry Hunt.'

'Mr Hunt doubts my integrity?'

'We have had many agents provocateur infiltrating our ranks, my lord, listening in to our plans in order to have the militia standing by ready to disrupt any meeting we might arrange.'

'And he thought I was one of those?'

'He wanted to be sure you are not.'

'And what conclusion have you drawn?'

'I cannot be certain, my lord.'

Adam laughed suddenly. 'Then, you are at a stand, Mr Byers, but tell me, why was Mr Hunt so anxious to discover that? I have not been to any of your meetings.'

'No, but you have shown a more-than-casual interest in what the union is planning, my lord, and you do command a company of militia.'

'So I do. Are you asking me to refrain from deploying them?'

'Yes, my lord. Also, not to go to the meeting. Your presence might inflame the crowd and deflect it from its true purpose.'

'Ah,' he said with a smile. 'There is to be a meeting. When and where?'

'I am not at liberty to tell you that, my lord.'

'Then, how am I to know what I must not attend?'

'No doubt you will learn of it.'

'And if I do not comply?'

'Mr Hunt hopes very much that you will, my lord.'

'You may go back to Mr Hunt and tell him I shall do what I think is right. He knows my views on the subject of suffrage and the relief of poverty. I have expounded them publicly. If he chooses not to believe me, that is up to him. I do not propose to try to prove myself.'

'Very well, my lord.' He picked up his hat from the desk where he had put it and rose to leave.

As soon as he had gone, Adam turned to Farley. 'What do you make of that, Alfred?'

'You are being warned off, my lord.'

'He has been very tenacious, don't you think? He followed me about town and was right behind us all the way to the farm, though I was not aware of him after that. He must have gone to report back to Orator Hunt when he lost us.'

'You have worried them, my lord. Do you intend to comply?'

'I shall certainly not mobilise the militia unless I am forced to, but as for the meeting, since I have no idea when and where it is to be held, there is little I can do. Besides, I shall be going back to Hadlea in less than a month for my wedding.'

'Speaking of the wedding, my lord, have you thought what you are going to wear? Time is slipping by.'

'I know that. I will speak to Mr Harcourt about cloth for a suit of clothes. My usual tailor will make it up. I will leave you to gather together shirts and cravats and whatever else I may need.'

'Very good, my lord. I will start at once.'

He hurried away, leaving Adam musing. He wanted this wedding, he told himself. His doubts were all on behalf of his bride and how she might view this home of his with its half-finished refurbishments. There was no time to complete them before he left for Hadlea, but he could do something about the bed. He rang for the housekeeper.

'Mrs Grant,' he said when she presented herself. 'Get a couple of the men and have the four-poster moved out of my bedchamber, put it in another part of the house and buy a new one. Buy new bed linen, too. And new curtains.'

'Yes, my lord.' She curtsied and went to leave the room.

Then he went to the stables, asked for his gig to be harnessed and was soon on his way down the winding road to the valley where the Bamford Mill was situated.

His arrival, though unheralded, did not surprise anyone. There were not many days when he did not go and oversee what was going on. He found George Harcourt in the office, working on the paperwork for a big order they had just received. The schedule to complete it was going to be tight, but he was confident they would fulfil it.

The man scrambled to his feet. 'Good morning, my lord.'

Adam returned his greeting. 'Everything running smoothly, George?'

'At the moment, my lord, but I have to report the men are restive. They have been listening to one of Orator Hunt's men and have informed me they intend to stop work to go to a meeting on the sixteenth.'

'Was the gentleman's name Mr Byers, by any chance?'

'Yes, my lord. Very persuasive he was, too. He had been talking to Sir John Michaelson's men and they had all agreed to attend, every man jack of them. Sir John has threatened instant dismissal if they go, but that appears to have had no effect.' He paused. 'I could threaten our workers with dismissal. They are reasonable men on the whole and they know they could not get better treatment anywhere else.'

'No, Mr Harcourt. Let them go.'

'But my lord, we will lose a day's production.'

'No matter. If we try to stop them, they will

go anyway, and dismissing them will hardly help to fulfil orders. Give them the day off.'

'Very well, my lord,' Harcourt said dubiously.

Having dealt with the problem of the workers' meeting, he turned to the matter of cloth for his wedding suit. 'A bolt of the finest we produce,' he said. 'Grey, I think.'

'Would you not prefer something a little more colourful, my lord?'

'No, George. This is my second venture into matrimony and I am not one to dress flamboyantly, as you know. A soft dove grey will suit me very well.'

'We have the very thing, my lord, so fine it feels more like silk than wool. We have only just perfected it. Your wearing it will be the best advertisement we could have.'

Adam laughed. 'Am I to go about with a placard round my neck proclaiming its wonders? I do not think my bride will be enamoured of that idea.'

'No, my lord, of course not.' Seeing his employer's broad grin, he smiled. 'It will advertise itself.' He put his head out of the door and yelled for someone, and very soon a tousle-haired youth of about thirteen arrived. 'Billy, go and fetch a bolt of that new superfine in dove grey from the warehouse. Be quick now. His lordship does not have all day.'

The boy ran off and returned a few minutes

later bowed under the weight of the cloth. He put it on the desk and fled. Adam fingered it thoughtfully. 'Beautiful,' he said. 'It will do very well. Send some up to the house. I will have my tailor call on me tomorrow to make a start on it. Knowing how meticulous he is, he will undoubtedly take an age to finish it.'

'Yes, my lord.'

Adam left and returned to the gig. Instead of going straight back to Blackfriars, he drove farther up the hill and sat almost on the peak with his back to a large boulder and surveyed the scene. Down in the valley, tall smoking chimneys and the high walls of the mills sat side by side with the humble tenements of the workers. Those of Sir John were in a poor state; as long as they were rainproof, the man did not care to spend money on them. By contrast, his own were well maintained and the tenants took a pride in keeping them spick and span. He found it hard to believe that the occupiers of those houses would rise up against him, but he could not be sure. It might be an idea to attend this meeting himself and if necessary speak from the platform. If enough of his own people were there, they might give him a hearing.

He turned to look in the other direction. Spread out before him were green fields crisscrossed with dry-stone walls and dotted with hundreds of sheep. Their wool made his cloth, their milk produced good cheese, their meat fed his people. This had been his home all his life. As children he and his brother had played in the meadows and bathed in its streams. They had learned to herd sheep and even shear them, though they were nothing like as handy at the task as the itinerant shearers who arrived each spring. He and his brother had been the fifth generation to live at Blackfriars and farm these acres. His brother had gone to his eternal rest, so it was up to him to preserve this precious heritage. Would Sophie come to think of it as her home, too? Or would she yearn for the very different landscape of the fens, Greystone Manor and her close-knit family? This waiting time was getting him down.

Sophie had not heard from Adam for several days. Ever since he returned to Saddleworth he had been writing to her almost every day. Sometimes the letters were long and full of what he had been doing; sometimes they were short notes because there was some crisis at the mill he had to deal with. He knew her parents would read them as a matter of course, so they were not effusive, not love letters, although he was always affectionate. She did not mind that; she could read between the lines and know he was impatient for them to be reunited and married. But long or short, they always arrived regularly.

The last one had been a whole week before. Her own letters went unanswered. She became listless. Nothing her mother said about the mail being held up or Adam being busy preparing for her arrival as his wife would console her. Adam had changed his mind. Back among his wife's things, he had realised he could not break that vow after all.

'Sophie, I am sure there is a perfectly reasonable explanation,' Jane said one day when she visited Broadacres.

'Has Mark heard from him?'

'No, but they were never regular correspondents.' She paused. 'Come up to the sewing room and see how I'm getting on with your wedding dress. It could do with another fitting. I am not sure about the neckline.'

'Do you think I am still going to need it?'

'Of course you are. Don't be silly. Adam would never break his word.'

'But he did, didn't he?' she said, as they climbed the stairs. 'He broke his word not to marry again. Now he regrets it.'

'Sophie, I shall box your ears if you keep talking like that.'

The gown was exquisite. Made of ivory satin covered in the fine Mechlin lace, it had a well-fitted bodice, a boat-shaped neckline and a skirt cut on the bias so that it fell from her waist to the floor in soft folds. Jane had made hundreds of little pink silk flowers and intended to sew them all over the gown, finishing with two large ones under the bust. 'Adam will fall in love with you all over again when he sees you in this,' Jane said, picking up her pincushion.

'But that's just the trouble,' Sophie wailed. 'He asked me to marry him and said he wanted to take care of me, but he never actually said he was in love with me.' She pulled the gown off before Jane could finish pinning it up. 'Take it away. I am never going to wear it.'

Jane sighed and folded the dress carefully in tissue. She would have to finish it without another fitting if Sophie continued in this mood. Sophie put her plain cambric dress on again and they went downstairs. She knew she had annoyed her sister, who had taken such pains with the dress, but her misery was making her tetchy and inclined to snap. She apologised and was forgiven and set off for home. Being in love was rollercoaster enough, but suffering from unrequited love was more than she could bear.

She looked up as Greystone Manor came into view with its solid grey walls and twisted chimney pots. She had been born there, brought up there and she supposed she would die there—of a broken heart.

'Sophie, is that you?' her mother called out

from the drawing room as she was putting her foot on the bottom stair on the way to her room.

'Yes, Mama.' She changed direction and went to the drawing room.

'There you are, Sophie. I was about to send the stable boy for you. There is a letter for you. It arrived by special messenger.' She nodded towards a letter lying on a tray on the table. Sophie grabbed it up, but it was not from Adam. She knew his loping handwriting by now. This was small and cramped. 'Well, open it, child. Don't keep me in suspense. I should like to know who is writing to you without the permission of your parents, but I would not be so particular as to open it before you.'

Sophie broke the seal and scanned the few lines it contained.

Dear Miss Cavenhurst,
My master, Viscount Kimberley, has been mortally wounded and is not expected to recover. He is asking for you. Make all haste to come.
Your obedient servant, Alfred Farley.

The paper fluttered from her hand and she fell down in a swoon.

Chapter Thirteen

'Oh, Sophie,' her mother said, after reviving her daughter with smelling salts and reading the note herself. She had sent a servant to find Sir Edward; this was something that required his presence. 'I am sorry for you and sorry for him, but I cannot see how you can go to Saddleworth.'

'I can go on the stage. Other women manage it.'

'They are not ladies.'

'Mama, I must go to Adam. If it were Papa ill and…dying…you would not hesitate, would you?'

'No, of course I would not, but I am married, Sophie, you are not.'

'What is that to the point? We would have been married in three weeks, in any case.' The thought of that made her burst into tears.

'Oh, Sophie.' Her mother put her arms about her and rocked her as she had done when Sophie was small and had hurt herself with her boisterous games. She looked up as her husband entered the room.

'What's amiss that I am required so urgently?'

His wife handed him the letter without speaking.

'This is very bad news, very bad indeed,' he said after scanning the letter.

Sophie raised her head. 'Papa, I must go to him. He is asking for me.'

'It says here that he has been wounded. If it had been an accident the man would have said *injured*, not *wounded*. It sounds as if he has been in a fight.'

'I can find out what happened when I get there,' Sophie cried. 'How can you be so calm? I must go to him. At once.'

'One person in a panic is enough, Sophie. Now go and lie down. Mama will give you something to make you feel better. I will ride over to Broadacres and see what Mark has to say. He may have heard more than this is telling us.'

'I'll come with you,' Sophie said, scrambling from her mother's arms.

He sighed. 'If you must.'

They left the room together.

They found Jane and Mark in Jane's small sitting room, discussing a problem the builders had found at the orphanage. If Jane was surprised to see her sister back so soon she did not say so. The stricken look on Sophie's face told her that it was something very serious. She stood up and opened her arms and Sophie ran into them. 'Adam is dying,' Sophie said between sobs. 'He is dying, Jane. I have to go to him and Papa says—'

'I can speak for myself,' Sir Edward put in. He turned to Mark and proffered the letter. 'This came today. Do you know anything about it?'

Mark read it and handed it to Jane. 'No, I have heard nothing. Wounded, the man says. I doubt my cousin would fight a duel unless he was uncommonly provoked.' He stopped suddenly as another thought came to him. 'Saint Peter's Fields! The rally. The papers are full of it. A massacre, they are calling it. Dozens killed and many more wounded. The militia were called in.'

'I read of it,' Sir Edward said. 'But Manchester is some way from Saddleworth. Would Viscount Kimberley be involved?'

'I think he might. When he was in London he was trying to find out about a meeting he knew was being planned. He talked to Orator Hunt about it.'

'While you are standing about debating, Adam is dying,' Sophie cried out. 'I need—I must—go to him.'

'I will take you, Sophie,' Mark said. 'If anything happens to Adam, there will be things to see to, and I am his only male relative. How soon can you be ready?'

'As soon as you are,' she said. 'Oh, Mark, thank you, thank you.'

Even in Mark's chaise and with the horses galloping whenever it was safe to do so and being changed every ten miles, it still took three days of travelling. Mark was as anxious as she was to arrive, and they made only very short stops to rest and eat. Sophie insisted she would not sleep if they took rooms at an inn and so they continued through the night. They spoke little, though Mark did tell her a little about the rally on St Peter's Fields. 'Some newspapers put the numbers at sixty thousand,' he said. 'Some said it was as many as eighty thousand. It was a sunny day and there were women and children there, treating it as a day out and bringing picnics with them.

'The local magistrates were afraid the mob would get out of hand and ordered the military to arrest Orator Hunt and others who were on the platform and intending to speak. Adam might even have been one of them. The militia were ordered to disperse the crowd. It was nigh on impossible with a gathering of that size. The cavalry charged with sabres drawn. In the mêlée fifteen people were killed and upwards of seven hundred injured.'

'That's dreadful. Do you really think Adam was there?'

'It would not surprise me.'

Sophie's tired brain conjured up images of Adam in all that carnage. But why would anyone want to hurt him? He was not one of the workers, unless they had turned on him. Her thoughts went round and round. Would they be in time? Had the letter been a mistake and she would find the man she loved, if not well, then on the road to recovery?

She was dozing fitfully in the corner of the roomy carriage when Mark put a hand on her shoulder and woke her. 'We are here, Sophie.'

She sat up with a start. The carriage had stopped before a large stone house which reminded her so much of Greystone Manor she thought she was home again. The feeling only lasted an instant before she came fully awake. Alfred Farley was standing in the open doorway. She scrambled out and hurried towards him. 'How is he? He isn't…'

'He is holding his own, Miss Cavenhurst.'

'Take me to him.'

'Would you not like to wash and have something to eat first?' Mark said, knowing he would not be able to persuade her that it was not proper for a single lady to enter a gentleman's bedroom.

'Later. After I have seen Adam. Show me the way, Mr Farley.'

Adam was lying on his back in a huge bed. His chest was swathed in bandages. His face was the colour of parchment, apart from the dark rings round his eyes. His eyes were shut. She fell on her knees beside the bed. 'Adam, I am here. I have come to be with you and make you better.' She turned to Farley, who hovered behind her. 'Can he hear me?'

The answer came from the bed, feebly, no more than a whisper. 'I can hear you.'

'Oh, Adam.' She took his hand. It was burning with fever. 'I came as soon as I received Mr Farley's letter. Mark is here, too. He will take care of everything and I will look after you.'

'My irrepressible Sophie,' he murmured.

'You must not tire yourself trying to talk,' she said. 'I will be here. I will always be here.'

Farley quietly left the room. Sophie hardly noticed his going. She continued to kneel at Adam's side, holding his hand and murmuring to him. She talked about the times they had spent in London, the dreadful *faux pas* she had made and the protracted journey to Hadlea. 'I was in love with you then,' she whispered. 'You didn't know that, did you? I will love you until the day I die.'

He did not answer, and all she heard was his laboured breathing. 'I won't tire you anymore with my chatter, but I am not going away. Go

to sleep. I will be here when you wake.' She got
up from her knees and walked stiffly to move
a chair close to the bed and sat down. His hand
moved towards her. She grasped it and sat watching his chest rise and fall, though occasionally it
stuttered as if it hurt him to breathe. So long as
it continued to do that, he was still living.

Mark came and dragged her away two hours
later. 'Sophie, you must come and have something to eat and then go to bed for a few hours.
Mrs Grant, the housekeeper, has had a room
made ready for you.'

'I cannot leave him.'

'Someone will watch over him while you are
away. You will be fetched immediately if there
is any change.'

She stood up and bent to kiss Adam's brow.
'I'll be back, my love.' She followed Mark from
the room, passing the nurse who was to take
her place.

She was so tired she did not notice what the
house was like as she followed Mark to a small
dining room. The table was laid with cold meats
and dishes of vegetables. 'Sit and eat,' he said.

She obeyed and put a little of the food onto her
plate and began to eat slowly, without appetite.
'Mr Farley told me a little of what happened,'
he said, sitting down beside her. 'Adam was, as
I surmised, at St Peter's Fields. They are dub-

bing it Peterloo, after the Battle of Waterloo. His account is more horrifying than the newspaper reports. It was complete mayhem. Adam went disguised in workman's clothes to hear what the speakers had to say and speak himself if the opportunity arose. He had it in mind to try to calm the more hot-headed who were demanding violent action.

'There was no sign that was likely to happen, but the magistrates panicked and ordered the cavalry in. They charged indiscriminately, slashing this way and that, uncaring that it was women and children they were hurting. Adam grabbed a child from the path of a galloping horse and took a deep sabre cut to the side of his chest as a consequence. It fractured his ribs. The doctor is afraid one of them may have punctured his lung.'

'Isn't it just like Adam not to think of his own safety?' she said dully. 'He is going to die because he tried to save a child.'

'He did save him, Sophie, and Adam is not dead yet. There is still hope.'

After she had eaten all she could, the housekeeper conducted her to a room next to Adam's. 'This was prepared for you as a dressing room when you became Lady Kimberley,' Mrs Grant told her. 'I hope it is acceptable. You will be able to hear if his lordship needs you.'

Sophie thanked her and stretched out on the

chaise longue without taking off her clothes. She did not think she would sleep, but she did.

The day of their wedding came and went and still Adam clung to life. Sophie could not make up her mind if he was getting better or worse. Some days his breathing did seem easier; other days it seemed every breath he took added to his pain and his face would reflect it. She watched over him devotedly, giving him sips of water and small spoonfuls of broth, persuading him to take the pain-killing medicine the doctor had prescribed and constantly wiping his brow with cold cloths in an effort to bring down the fever. She even helped Farley to change his night-shirt, though she left the shaving and washing the more intimate parts of his body to the valet.

It did not cross her mind that she should not be doing it. The only women in the house were Mrs Grant and a couple of chambermaids. If they were shocked by her behaviour they would not have dared say so. Mark had made a small re-monstrance at the beginning, to which she had retorted, 'There is no one else to do it, and I would not trust them if there were.'

There was one particular night when he was more than usually restless. His body seemed on fire, his face burning. According to the doctor whom Mark sent for, this was the crisis, and the next few hours would decide Adam's fate. Sophie stayed by his bed all night, dipping cloths in cold water and wiping his face and upper body, talking softly to him. She was on the point of exhaustion herself, but would not rest. She prayed as she had never prayed before.

Towards dawn she could not keep her eyes open any longer and dozed, but she was instantly awake when she felt a movement in the bed. His eyes were open and he was smiling. 'Still here, Sophie?'

'Of course I am. Where else would I be?'

'Very improper.'

Pleased that he was alert and aware, she grinned happily. 'Who cares? I do not. Besides, if you had been well we would have been married by now.'

'Why? What day is it?'

'Sunday, September the twelfth. It would have been the first day of our married life.'

He smiled and shut his eyes again.

It was the beginning of his recovery. He was soon sitting up and beginning to eat proper meals and grumble about the time he had lost lying abed when there was work to be done. Mark had been managing very well with the aid of his estate manager and Mr Harcourt at the mill, but he was itching to see how everything was progressing. Most of all, he worried about Sophie. She was thin and pale and obviously exhausted.

He was also concerned about the proprietary of having her in and out of his bedchamber all the time, especially now he was sitting up and all he was wearing was a nightshirt.

'I am going to dress,' he told her one day about a week later.

'I'll help you.'

'You will not! Alfred will help me. It's what I pay him for. So go away and amuse yourself elsewhere.'

Hurt by his brusque manner, she left him and went to wander round the house. He had been right to describe it as half old and draughty and half an elegant modern home. Evidence of Anne's exquisite taste was in the wing that had been refurbished: the drawing room, formal dining room, the breakfast parlour, the library and some of the bedrooms. The furniture was in the French style, the curtains were made of the richest fabric, no doubt woven in what was then her father's mill. There were pictures and ornaments everywhere. One of the pictures in the drawing room was of a very beautiful young lady in a dress of amber silk. She had soft brown eyes and dark lustrous hair woven with a strand of jewels. A pearl drop hung on her forehead. Her gown was a rich pink brocade. She had small hands and dainty feet. This, Sophie surmised, was Anne. Beside her was a matching portrait of Adam dressed in a dark green coat and white breeches. He wore a sparkling pin in his cravat.

With a heavy heart, she turned away and went to explore the rest of the house. It was just as it had been more than two hundred years before. The stone floors were covered with rugs, the wall hangings were faded and the furniture dark and heavy. She imagined the friars going about these rooms centuries before. She went back to the lived-in part of the house to find Adam in the small parlour, sitting in an armchair before a good fire. He was dressed in superfine pantaloon trousers and a shirt of fine lawn. He wore no coat or cravat. The sight of him apparently well and cheerful and almost back to his old self sent her heart skittering as it always did.

'Oh, you are looking so much better,' she said, walking towards him and kneeling at his side.

'Yes, almost back to the man I was, thanks to you.'

'I did not do anything that someone else could not have done.'

He took her hand. 'Oh, yes, you did. I may not have shown it, but I knew you were there. All time I was aware of you. You gave me the strength to fight and exhausted yourself in doing it. But why did you come?'

'Mr Farley sent for me. He said you needed me.'

'I shall have to have words with that gentleman.'

'Why, did you not want me to come?'

'I did not want you to see me in that unmanly state.'

'You were never unmanly, Adam, and no one could have prevented me from coming as soon as I knew you were in mortal danger.'

'I thank God for it, but now I am better you can leave me in Alfred's capable hands. Go and rest. You look tired.'

'You don't want me anymore. I can understand that,' she said miserably. 'You are here, in your own home, surrounded by memories of Anne, and there is no place for me. I shall ask Mark if we can go home now.' She scrambled to her feet and ran up to the room next to his where she had been sleeping, ready to wake and go to him the minute he stirred. She sat on the bed, put her face in her hands and wept. How could she hope to make him forget his first wife? How could she live with him among all those memories? She got up and began throwing clothes into her portmanteau.

'Just what, in God's name, do you think you are about?' Adam stood in the doorway, breathing heavily from the exertion of climbing the stairs.

'Packing. My job is done. It is time to go home.'

He strode across to her, grabbed her by the shoulders and fell with her onto the small bed. 'Sophie, I would spank you if I thought it would do any good. Perhaps this will do instead.' And he kissed her long and hard.

She began to struggle, but he was stronger than he looked and held her firmly, and gradually she relaxed and sank into a kind of euphoria that soon became something else as his kisses roused her, something sublime yet fiery, sweet yet passionate. There was a new feeling in the core of her, an opening out and at the same time making her want to draw this man into her, make herself one with him.

He moved back at last and smiled at her. 'Still want to go home?'

'Adam, you make me so confused. I don't know what I want.'

'Then I shall have to try again.' And he did, until she was aching.

'Why are you confused?' he murmured.

'I was looking round the house—'

'I was going to have it made ready for you.'

'I saw all the evidence of Anne and that picture in the drawing room,' she went on, ignoring his interruption. 'She was so beautiful. I cannot compete with your memories, Adam.'

'You don't have to. Do you know what Mark said to me weeks ago, when we were in London? He was urging me to marry again and I was telling him I would not.' He put his finger on her lips to stop her speaking. 'He said we are all unique in our own way, loved for different reasons. And he was right. I loved Anne, I cannot pretend otherwise, but I love you very, very much, indeed.'

'Do you? You never said that before.'

'Didn't I? How remiss of me. I'll say it again, shall I? I love you, Sophie Cavenhurst. I also remember you telling me that you would not attempt to make me forget Anne, but would try to make me look forward to a new life with you. Did you not mean it?'

'Yes, I meant it, but…'

'Sophie, you can do what you like to the house, change things to suit yourself. I intended to have Anne's things moved before I brought you here, but circumstances intervened. I am sorry if you were upset by them. I want this to be our home, yours and mine, not a mausoleum to a dead wife.'

'Oh, Adam…'

'Of course, I will still have to send you home,' he said, grinning. 'There is still the little matter of a wedding.'

October was a lovely time of year for a wedding. The uncomfortable heat of summer had gone, but it was not yet cold. The trees in the park and bordering the lanes were a glorious explosion of russet and brown and deepest red.

Greystone Manor was humming with activity as all the arrangements for the wedding came to fruition. Thanks to Jane's expertise the gown was a triumph. The scent of flowers filled the house, and down in the kitchens the food preparation was nearing completion. Sophie's fear that Adam would be prevented from coming either because of a crisis at the mill, or worse, that he might have a relapse and been too ill, had been unfounded. He had arrived at Broadacres the day before and had been over to the manor to reassure her. Together they had gone to the church and rehearsed their responses and received a little homily from the Reverend Caulder about the duties required of each of them as a married couple. They had left hand in hand, laughing joyously.

Sophie wondered how she could ever have thought of Adam as austere, nor how she could have been so naive as to lay down rules about falling in love. Jane had been right: falling in love was not something you can order like a new bonnet or a new pair of shoes, it just happened. And it had happened to her. She could not believe her good fortune.

Tomorrow the rest of the guests would come to the church: Aunt Emmeline, Lord and Lady Martindale with Lucy and Sir Reginald Swayle, to whom she had recently become betrothed. Likewise the Malthouse family with Cassie and Mr Richard Fanshawe. They were to be married in the New Year. Cassie had declared she was grateful to Sophie for introducing her to him, and they were friends again. They would be joined by friends and relations from far and wide, including most of the village. She would miss Teddy, of course, and Issie and Drew, but that could not be helped.

Her last evening as a single woman was spent quietly at home with her parents, though perhaps *quietly* was not the right description as the servants were still busy with last-minute preparations and Sophie was so nervous she could not sit still. 'I shan't sleep,' she told her mother. 'I am far too excited.'

'Bessie will give you a potion.' Bessie had agreed to go to Blackfriars as her maid and companion and help her to settle in. 'We cannot have you yawning through the service.'

'Who is that?' Sophie wondered aloud as the sound of horses and carriage wheels sounded on the gravel outside. 'Are we expecting anyone as late as this?' She rose and went to draw aside the curtains to peep out at the drive. A travel-stained coach was disgorging its passengers in the light from the flambeaux on either side of the front door. Sophie squealed. 'It's Issie and Drew! Mama, it's Issie and Drew and Aunt Emmeline.' She ran from the room and tumbled into the hall just as her sister came in from outside, followed by her tall handsome husband and their aunt. 'Issie, you came. I am so glad. Now the day will be perfect.'

Issie laughed as she hugged her. 'We could not miss your big day, could we? Let me look at you.' She held her at arm's length and studied her face. 'You have changed, little Sophie.'

'I have grown up.'

'Indeed you have.' She turned as her parents came out to greet the travellers with hugs and kisses.

The remainder of the evening was spent catching up with everyone's news while the travellers were served with a meal. Issie and Drew had already started for home and had reached Calcutta when they'd received the news of Sophie's engagement. They had known nothing of the postponement of the wedding due to Adam's injury until they'd arrived at Lady Cartrose's house in Mount Street. 'We knew if we set out again straight away we could be here in time.'

'They offered to bring me,' Emmeline said. 'So I shan't miss it after all.'

'There is only one person missing,' Lady Cavenhurst said a little sadly.

'Teddy,' Issie said. 'We have seen him.'

'When? Where? Is he coming home?'

'We were on the docks in Calcutta waiting to go aboard *The Lady Isabel* after stopping off there on our way back to England,' Issie went on. 'There was a convict ship berthed nearby taking on water and supplies. Naturally no one on board was allowed off and the miserable sinners were crowding the decks. I heard someone shouting my name and looked up to see Teddy leaning over the rails, waving to me and shouting. I could not believe it was him.'

'There was so much noise going on, we could not hear what he was trying to say to us,' Drew said. 'I managed to go on board and speak to him.'

'How is he? Is he well? Did you fetch him off?'

'I offered to, but he would not come. He said to tell you he is well and learning to be a good seaman. When the captain realised he was an educated man and not the usual sort of pressed man, which happened about halfway round the Cape, he made him a clerk in charge of the ship's stores.'

'Did he not want to come home?'

'He said he would come home when he had redeemed himself. He is deeply sorry for all the pain he has caused you and for letting Sophie down. I told him we had heard of Sophie's betrothal and were on our way home and he laughed and said, "Good old Sophie. I told her that was her best bet. And mine, too." I don't know what he meant by that.'

'I do,' Sophie told them, and explained about

the wagers. 'They each owe him a thousand pounds.'

'In that case, it can go towards repaying Adam,' Sir Edward said.

'I doubt he will take it,' Sophie said, smiling. 'He said it was a small price to pay for me.'

'I think it is time we all went to bed,' Sir Edward added. 'Tomorrow is going to be a long day.'

The wedding was a happy affair, shared by the whole village. Sophie looked radiant and Adam proud and handsome. Everyone said they had never seen such a well-matched couple. The wedding breakfast and the music and dancing went on late into the night, but Adam and Sophie were oblivious to it. They retired to the bedchamber that had been prepared for them in a distant part of the house, eschewing the help of valet and maid.

'Well matched, I heard them say,' Sophie said, giggling as Adam set about removing the beautiful gown.

'So we are.' The gown was set aside and he started on the ties of her petticoat. 'I am dull and staid and you are young and exciting and unpredictable—two halves of a whole.'

'You are a long way from being dull, but perhaps you are the unpredictable one. Do you remember ever saying you would never marry again?'

'No, did I?' He chuckled. 'Do you remember ever saying you would not be a second wife?'

'If I did, I was very foolish.' She was almost naked now and was doing her best to redress the balance by unbuttoning his shirt and slipping her hands inside. She could feel the ridge of his scar, the result of his caring for others. It had healed well. She ran her hands down his torso and down inside his breeches.

'Sophie,' he said, 'do you know what you are doing to me?'

She smiled. 'I think I am about to find out.'

* * * * *

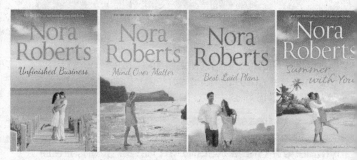

MILLS & BOON®

The Thirty List

* cover in development

At thirty, Rachel has slid down every ladder she has ever climbed. Jobless, broke and ditched by her husband, she has to move in with grumpy Patrick and his four-year-old son.

Patrick is also getting divorced, so to cheer themselves up the two decide to draw up bucket lists. Soon they are learning to tango, abseiling, trying stand-up comedy and more. But, as she gets closer to Patrick, Rachel wonders if their relationship is too good to be true…

**Order yours today at
www.millsandboon.co.uk/Thethirtylist**

HISTORICAL

AWAKEN THE ROMANCE OF THE PAST

A sneak peek at next month's titles...

In stores from 5th June 2015:

- **A Mistress for Major Bartlett** – Annie Burrows
- **The Chaperon's Seduction** – Sarah Mallory
- **Rake Most Likely To Rebel** – Bronwyn Scott
- **Whispers at Court** – Blythe Gifford
- **Summer of the Viking** – Michelle Styles
- **Wed to the Montana Cowboy** – Carol Arens

Available at WHSmith, Tesco, Asda, Eason, Amazon and Apple

Just can't wait?
Buy our books online a month before they hit the shops!
visit www.millsandboon.co.uk

These books are also available in eBook format!